The Kennedy Curse: Shattered

Les Williams

Published by Gayles Publishing 2016

Les Williams

ISBN 978-0-9956447-1-7

Photo Credits and Acknowledgements

The author would like to thank all those who have helped in researching, compiling and editing this book. Particular thanks go to Connor Anderson and Laurie Austin at the John F Kennedy Presidential Library, Boston, USA for their help and advice in sourcing photographs and other material from their archives.

All photographs used in this book are in the Public Domain or are of unknown copyright status, with those in the Public Domain being reproduced with kind permission of the John F Kennedy Presidential Library and the Whitehouse Photographic Library.

Les Williams

CONTENTS

"Somebody up there doesn't like us."
Robert F Kennedy

Les Williams

1   INTRODUCTION

We all know that John F Kennedy was assassinated in Dallas in November 1963 and that his brother, Bobby suffered the same fate and there are many who remember the incident at Chappaquiddick, where Ted Kennedy drove a car off a bridge killing young, Mary Jo Kopechne. But how many people know the story of how Joe Kennedy's eldest son, Joe Junior was killed flying a secret mission during World War II or that his eldest daughter, Rosemary was subjected to experimental brain surgery that left her completely incapacitated for life and led to her being hidden away from public view? How many know that Kathleen was killed in a plane crash and that many years later, JFK Junior would suffer the same fate, under what many believe to be suspicious circumstances? There have been hundreds of books written about the Kennedys and the tragedies that have befallen them, but few of them offer the reader a full and complete picture of each of these events, in chronological order and in context with one another in the way that we see here. This is not just another book about the assassination of John F Kennedy or the murder of his brother, Bobby. Those events are covered here in some detail, but only to give the reader a basic understanding of the way they happened and the controversy surrounding them.

This is the story of how the Kennedys rose from poverty and obscurity to become one of the richest and most powerful families in the United States and what it cost them in grief and in personal tragedy. In just three generations, the Kennedy family were able to achieve wealth and power beyond the dreams of most ordinary people and they became the closest America has ever had to royalty, but there was a heavy price to pay.

From the very beginning, Joseph Kennedy had determined that his family would achieve wealth and political power and he resolved that he would stop at nothing to get it. He had long harboured a desire to become President of the United States and when that dream began to fade, he turned his ruthless ambition onto his eldest son, Joe Junior. His intention was that Joe Junior would become the first Catholic President of the United States and that young Joe would be followed, in turn, by his other sons, Jack, Bobby and Ted. This may seem to us today a ludicrously idealistic prospect but to Joe Kennedy it was very real and wholly achievable. He devoted every day of his life to the accumulation of wealth and the acquisition of powerful, influential friends and he used both to his best advantage. He firmly believed that money could buy you just about anything and that every man had his price. For Joe Kennedy, money talked and wealth was the key to political power.

Joe and Rose Kennedy were very demanding of their children, but they were always made to feel special. They lived privileged and sheltered lives and were brought up to believe that they were better than anyone else and although they courted the press and welcomed publicity, they were always very private and insular. The Kennedys were, first and foremost, a strong and loyal family unit. They were a close-knit clan and very few were ever allowed to get even remotely close to them.

There have been ambitious men before, but few have shown the sheer grit and determination of Joseph Kennedy. Throughout his whole life, he had his mind set on a goal and he would stop at nothing to achieve it. He was an unstoppable force who cared nothing for other people or for the damage he caused in his wake; and God help anyone who got in his way. This approach made him a great deal of money and gained him a lot of influence in the world but it made him a lot of enemies, too. Friends would tell him he was too callous and too quick to cross all the wrong people, but Joe Kennedy would never listen. When the going was good he was untouchable, but the more he achieved, the more dangerous his enemies became. It was all bound to catch up with him in the end, and it would be his children who would pay the price.

It had taken three generations of hard work for the Kennedys to achieve what they had, but it all fell apart in just one. It had all started so well with Joe Kennedy's plans for young Joe Junior and in the early days, it must have seemed as though nothing could go wrong. But by the mid 1940's it had all begun to unravel. Young Joe would soon be gone and Rosemary would be as good as gone, too. And within a very short time of that, Joe's favourite daughter, Kathleen would cause a rift in the family and lose her life trying to mend it. And that was just the beginning. Jack would be murdered in 1963, followed by Bobby in 1968 and the downward spiral continued with Ted's fall from grace at Chappaquiddick and the death of JFK Junior in a plane crash.

Of the nine children of Joe and Rose Kennedy, two would be assassinated, two would die in aeroplanes, one would be hidden away in a home for the mentally ill and one would have his own political career ruined in a drunken night of merriment. Joe Kennedy suffered a debilitating stroke in later life, but not before he had witnessed almost all of these tragedies unfold before his very eyes. These and other tragic events have led to the idea of a family curse, but the intention of this book is to shatter that belief and to show that there was no curse at all. Almost all of the tragedies that have befallen the Kennedy family can be traced back to Joe Kennedy's ruthless and selfish ambition and are a direct result of the way he raised his children and the high expectations he had of them. He made them believe they were invincible and that they could always do just as they pleased and get away with it, but they would soon learn that it was never going to be quite that simple.

Joe Kennedy was, in many ways, the architect of his own terrible suffering and as he watched these tragedies unfold, one after another, he must have known deep down that that was true.

What price wealth and power!

2   THE FOUNDING OF A DYNASTY

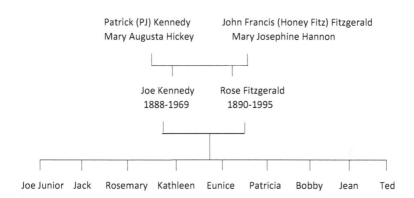

Patrick (PJ) Kennedy   John Francis (Honey Fitz) Fitzgerald
Mary Augusta Hickey   Mary Josephine Hannon

Joe Kennedy   Rose Fitzgerald
1888-1969   1890-1995

Joe Junior   Jack   Rosemary   Kathleen   Eunice   Patricia   Bobby   Jean   Ted

Family Origins

Patrick Kennedy was no stranger to hardship. The great grandfather of President John F Kennedy was the son of a hard-working Irish farm labourer who, when the great famine struck in 1845, had taken a boat to America in search of a better life. Like many Irish immigrants, Patrick settled in Boston where he worked as a cooper, making whiskey barrels and staves for cart-wheels. Life was hard and the days were long, but through sheer hard work and diligence, Patrick's business prospered.

Young Patrick was successfully building a new life for himself and within a short time of arriving in Boston, he was already thinking of marriage. He had fallen in love with Bridget Murphy, herself an Irish immigrant and the two were soon married. They would have five children together but in an age of high infant mortality, only four of these survived into adulthood. Of those that did, Patrick Joseph, born on January 14th 1858 and later to be known as PJ, was the youngest. PJ would never get to know his father as Patrick died from cholera on November 22nd 1858; exactly 105 years to the day before his great grandson was to be assassinated in Dallas.

PJ was a bright and intelligent boy who would go on to become the patriarch of the now famous Kennedy clan. He was the first of the Kennedys to receive a formal education, but his mother struggled to support the family on her own and he was forced to quit school when he was just 14, taking a job as a stevedore on Boston docks. But PJ was determined to succeed, despite the odds and by the 1880's he had saved enough money from his meagre earnings to launch his own business career. He bought a saloon in downtown Boston and used the profits from that to invest in other bars and a hotel in the area. He was already displaying a shrewd head for business and a determination to succeed.

With his red hair, blue eyes and handle-bar moustache, PJ became a well-known and much loved figure amongst the immigrant community in Boston. He was popular and well-liked by his neighbours and he quickly made up his mind to pursue a career in politics. He was elected to the House of Representatives no less than five times and served three terms in the Senate. He established himself as one of Boston's principle Democratic leaders and in so doing, laid the foundations for a successful political career that would eventually propel the Kennedys onto the world stage.

In November 1887, PJ married Mary Augusta Hickey, an attractive and vivacious young girl from a well-to-do Irish family and they would have three surviving children. The eldest of these was Joseph Patrick, and it would be he who would go on to make the Kennedy millions and to form the political dynasty we all know today.

PJ died on May 18th 1929 while his son, Joe was in Hollywood making a film with his then lover, Gloria Swanson. Joe Kennedy did not attend the funeral of his illustrious father but asked his own son, Joe Junior to attend in his place. It was not the first time that Joe Kennedy had put his business career and his own pursuit of pleasure above family ties and commitments, and it certainly would not be the last.

On the maternal side of the family the Fitzgeralds were, themselves refugees from the great potato famine. Thomas Fitzgerald took ship from Ireland in 1854 and settled in Acton, near Boston, living in the notorious Irish ghettos. Life there was short and brutal and the only real source of comfort to these poor and desperate people was the Catholic Church, to which most of them were entirely devoted. But Thomas was determined to break out of this arduous life of poverty and, saving every last cent, he was eventually able to buy a small grocery store. He worked hard to make it a success and as the business grew and prospered, Thomas was able to invest his money in other ventures. He began to invest heavily in real estate and he bought properties in the Acton area, renting out rooms to his fellow Irish immigrants at rates they could afford.

In 1857, Thomas Fitzgerald married Irish immigrant, Rosanna Cox and they were to have twelve children, although only three survived into adulthood. One of these was John Francis Fitzgerald, born on February 11th 1863 and later to be known as, "Honey Fitz." He was a bright, intelligent boy who showed great promise and his father wanted to give him a good education. Thomas was troubled by the misery and suffering experienced by the poor people of Boston and he wanted his son to become a doctor so he could help the sick and the needy. Fitz was educated at the Boston College and went on to study at Harvard Medical School, a great achievement for an Irish immigrant at that time, but he left after one year following the death of his father in 1885. Fitz never really wanted to study medicine anyway and only did so to please his father, so he was not too dismayed at having to give it up. He took a lowly clerical job in the Custom House in Boston and, showing a keen interest in politics, he soon became active in the local Democrat party.

Honey Fitz was a gregarious, larger than life character with a friendly, ruddy face, bright blue eyes and sandy hair. He was popular and well-liked and became famous around Boston for his Irish blarney and his silver-tongued story-telling and with his engaging personality, he was a natural politician. PJ Kennedy, his one-time rival for public office once said if him, "He didn't just kiss the blarney stone, he swallowed it."

In 1889 Honey Fitz married Mary Josephine Hannon and together they would have six children, the eldest being Rose Elizabeth. Fitz doted on young Rose and gave her everything she ever wanted.

"I sometimes thought I was the luckiest person in the world," Rose would later say, and it was from her father that Rose inherited her strong family ties and her passionate family loyalty. Honey Fitz valued family above all else and Rose was to be instrumental in instilling this same doctrine into her own large family later on.

Honey Fitz died on October 2nd 1950, aged 87; a great loss to Boston and an even greater one to the family. He was a true family patriarch and was adored by all who knew him. He was never far from their thoughts and when Jack became President in 1961, he named the Presidential yacht, the *Honey Fitz* in his memory.

Joe and Rose Kennedy

The union of the Kennedy and Fitzgerald clans came about through the marriage of Rose Fitzgerald to Joseph Patrick Kennedy on October 17th 1914. Honey Fitz had at first objected to the marriage as he thought Rose had rushed into marrying the first man she had met, but the two were obviously in love and seemed to be very well-matched. They had known each other since childhood and they began courting when Joe was still in college. Rose was a good catch for Joe. She was a bright, intelligent and attractive young woman from a wealthy and influential family, whose father just happened to be the first Irish Catholic Mayor of Boston. Joe seemed less of a prize for Rose but, as time would tell, he would prove his worth by making the Kennedy family one of the wealthiest and most powerful in the country.

Joe Kennedy enjoyed a very privileged upbringing but, being a fairly average scholar, he showed no real promise academically during his school days. He did, however, have a flair for maths and economics which would serve him well in later life. He was a good all-round sportsman and excelled at baseball and from a very early age he was obsessed with winning, every time and at all costs. He attended various Catholic schools and was eventually enrolled in the Boston Latin School before going on to study at Harvard in 1908, where he gained his B.A. in 1912.

Joe's first job after leaving college was in 1912, when he took a position as Assistant State Bank Examiner for

Massachusetts. But he was hungry for more and his big chance came when the Columbia Trust, a bank his father had helped establish, began suddenly to fail. Share-holders and investors started to panic and threatened to pull out completely and Joe saw in this the opportunity he had been waiting for. He was sure he could save the bank from ruin and after much cajoling, he was able to obtain backing to acquire a controlling share. He applied all his skill and knowledge and was soon able to turn the bank around and on the back of this success, he was elected to the Board of Trustees of the Massachusetts Electric Company. He was not yet 30 years of age, but he was already making his way in the world.

In April 1917, the United States entered into the conflict that was by then engulfing the whole world. Woodrow Wilson had tried to keep America out of the war but US involvement was inevitable, and the major manufacturing companies had seen it coming for months. They began to seek lucrative military contracts and were looking for bright, hard-working young men to manage their operations and maximise profits. Joe Kennedy had, by this time, made some very influential friends and in 1917 he became Assistant General Manager at the Fore River Shipyard in Quincy, Massachusetts. This was one of the largest shipyards in the country and was doing very well at the time, making boats for the Navy. It was all good experience for Joe and he would use it to good effect in the years ahead.

At the end of the war, Joe quit his job at Fore River and began a new and lucrative career on the stock markets. He again proved very successful in this venture and in 1923, he set himself up as a broker under the name of, "Joseph P. Kennedy; Banker," offering a wide range of financial services. He invested heavily in property, especially during the great depression when it could be bought cheaply. He bought homes for the family in Boston, New York and at Hyannis Port and he acquired the largest office building in the country, the Merchandise Mart in Chicago, thus establishing connections in that city that were to come in very useful, and would have tragic consequences later.

Joe Kennedy made a fortune on the US stock market but as with everything, he knew when to quit. He had always said that his pulling out of the stock market before the Wall Street crash was down to his uncanny ability to see what was coming and prepare for it. He had always been able to read the signs well ahead of most other people and he knew when to buy and when to sell.

"I have a compassion for facts, a complete lack of sentiment and a marvellous sense of timing," he once said, when asked to explain his fortuitous escape.

On the other hand, he liked to joke and make light of the way he had escaped financial ruin and he told close friend, Oleg Cassini a different story.

"I was having my shoes shined one day by a shoe-shine boy and he asked me for some advice on buying stocks and shares. I went back to my office and thought about this and I figured that if shoe-shine boys are getting into the stock market business, maybe it's time for me to get out?"

Joe's career on the stock market was over and he began to look for new ways to increase his already substantial fortune. He saw that the newly emerging movie business was going to be the next big thing and he began to invest heavily in this lucrative new enterprise. He could see that the movie business was poorly managed and very much decentralised and he thought he could bring better financial control. He already owned interests in movie theatres but he saw that the real money was in production rather than distribution, or even a combination of the two. In 1926 a production company called FBO (Film Booking Offices), which specialised in cheap western films approached Joe Kennedy to help them find a buyer and, seeing another opportunity, Joe bought controlling interests in the company for $1.5m.

Joe worked hard to change the fortunes of FBO and as he immersed himself ever deeper in the industry, he saw the huge potential in the new concept of talking pictures. He could see that this was the future and he wanted to be in at the beginning so he approached David Sarnoff, head of the Radio Corporation of America (RCA) about brokering a deal with him to use his new sound system, *Photophone* for his own movie productions. To help forge this connection he then acquired Keith–Able-Orpheum Theatre Company (KAO), in order to use its chain of 700 theatres across the country to show his films. His success was noted and he was asked to turn around other ailing studios, including Pathe De-Mille and First National. In 1928 he merged his new acquisitions, including FBO and KAO to form Radio-Keith-Orpheum, later known as RKO. But Joe Kennedy was always on the move. He did not want to get bogged down in any one area of business so by 1930, he had pulled out of most of his Hollywood commitments and was looking for new opportunities elsewhere.

An interesting incident around this time shows the astute business acumen and the cold, ruthless streak for which Joe Kennedy would become so well-known. Alexander Panteges owned a chain of 63 movie theatres across the US and Joe wanted to buy them to add them to his own network. He offered Panteges $8m for them but Panteges refused to sell. However, Panteges was tried for rape soon after and although he strongly protested his innocence, the affair had a shattering effect on his life and his business interests. Panteges was facing financial ruin and Joe saw this and took advantage of his misfortune. He made him a revised offer of just $4m, which Panteges was forced to accept. Panteges was found not guilty at a second trial, but the damage had already been done and he never really recovered financially. He later claimed that Joe Kennedy had set him up but he could produce no evidence to support the accusation.

In 1920, the United States Government introduced prohibition and this opened the doors for opportunists and racketeers to make vast fortunes from selling illegal liquor. There was easy money to be made and Joe Kennedy was not slow to see the potential. It has, for many years, been generally believed that Joe Kennedy made a vast amount of money by dealing with organised crime figures in the supply of illegal liquor to the thousands of drinking clubs and speak-easies that sprang up all over America at this time, but this has never really been proven. The accusations are that when men like Frank Costello and Lucky Luciano were looking for respectable businessmen to work with them in supplying illegal liquor, Joe Kennedy was only too happy to oblige. Frank Costello was known to have associated with the likes of Myer Lansky in Cuba and with Carlos Marcello in New Orleans but he was also well-connected politically. Costello was almost unique in having influential friends on both sides of the legal and political fence and he was known as the "Politician of the Underworld." He was the ideal conduit between organised crime and people in Government and there can be little doubt that Joe Kennedy would have known him well. Whether Joe had dealings with him or not is another matter, but Joe did make a lot of money around this time and it is hard to see how he could have resisted the temptation to cash-in on this lucrative and highly profitable market.

Joe Kennedy was never a big drinker himself but he did see the enormous business potential in selling it to those who were. He founded a liquor importing company, Somerset Importers, with James Roosevelt, son of Franklin D Roosevelt, and they shrewdly acquired sole import rites for Haig Whisky, Gordon's Dry Gin and Dewar's Scotch. This enterprise no doubt made them both a lot of money but Kennedy eventually sold off his interests in the business to Longy Zwillman, a well-known mobster, better known as "The Al Capone of New Jersey." When criticised for doing this he simply replied, "What do you expect, I'm a capitalist."

In his recent book, *The Patriarch; The Remarkable Life and Turbulent Times of Joseph P Kennedy*, David Nasaw states that throughout his extensive research for the book he found no credible evidence that Joe Kennedy had actually dealt in bootlegging during the prohibition. He says he had complete and unrestricted access to all the Kennedy records and papers, including those not available to other researchers and that he was tasked by the Kennedy family to find and publish the full facts, good and bad, on all aspects of Joe Kennedy's life. On the subject of prohibition, he claims that in four years of extensive research he found nothing to prove Joe's direct involvement in bootlegging. He also adds that when one looks at the kind of people that have come forward as witnesses over the years, they are generally somewhat less than credible. These include the wives and associates of known mobsters, third hand accounts of dubious deals and even, in one case, Al Capone's piano tuner. He says that the accusation that Joe Kennedy was a bootlegger never really came to light until the early 1970's when the tenth anniversary of President Kennedy's assassination sparked off renewed interest in conspiracy theories. He also said that Richard Nixon did all he could to find damning evidence against the Kennedy family in general and that, although Nixon accused Joe Kennedy of just about every form of vice and corruption he could think of, he never called him a bootlegger. It might be noted, however that shortly before his death in 1973, mobster Frank Costello claimed that he had, indeed engaged in bootlegging activity with Joseph Kennedy during the prohibition and that they had both made a lot of money from it. The simple truth is that if Joe Kennedy really was a bootlegger, he covered his tracks very well. But then, he always did.

Joe Kennedy had always craved political office and by the late 1930's he was working very closely with the Roosevelt administration. He was a staunch supporter of the President and in return for his loyalty, Roosevelt rewarded him with a job as Chairman of the newly formed Securities and Exchange Commission (SEC). Joe had by then gained a wealth of experience in stocks and finance and was an ideal choice for the role and this was his first real brush with politics. He was beginning to map out a career for himself and he lobbied Roosevelt for a cabinet post, but the President was not prepared to go quite that far. He was grateful for Joe's support and for the work he had done with the SEC, but he knew he could be a dangerous loose cannon and he was reluctant to include him in his cabinet. But good and loyal service deserves its just rewards and in 1938,

Roosevelt appointed Joe Kennedy US Ambassador to the Court of St James and sent him off to the American Embassy in London. It was a decision he would soon live to regret.

Europe at this time was in turmoil as Germany, under Adolf Hitler, began to re-arm on a massive scale and to demand the return of territories lost through the Treaty of Versailles. Joe Kennedy had some very strong views on how Britain and the rest of Europe should deal with Hitler and he openly and forcefully expressed them at every opportunity. He admired Hitler's achievements in rebuilding Germany and his frank and open praise for the Nazi dictator won him few friends in London. To make matters worse, he had long been suspected of anti-Jewish sentiment and has been quoted as saying that, "Some Jews are alright, but as a race they stink. They spoil everything they touch."

When US diplomat, Harvey Klemmer returned from a fact-finding trip to Germany he told Joe Kennedy what had been happening to the Jews there and Joe's response was simply that they had brought it on themselves. Joe made no secret of his disdain for the Jews and was completely unmoved by events in Germany. He seemed less concerned about what was happening to the Jews in that country than he was about the bad publicity this was creating for Hitler and his regime; a point he communicated quite openly in a letter to his close friend and fellow Nazi supporter, Charles Lindbergh.

Roosevelt had said that although he did not wish to engage directly in a war in Europe, he would do all he could to support Britain if it came to it but Joe Kennedy in London disagreed with, and ignored, Roosevelt's strategy. Joe Kennedy was clearly out-of-step with his own Government on this and other issues and he took every opportunity to say so. He strongly believed that there would be nothing to gain from going to war with Hitler and that if Britain and Germany were to engage in a war, Britain stood no chance whatsoever of winning.

"Democracy is dead in England," he boldly claimed, "and may be in the United States as well?"

Ambassador Kennedy's views on the futility and hopelessness of opposing Hitler pushed him ever more onto the side-lines and he became very unpopular in Britain. He was seen as a defeatist and a coward and one minister even commented in an interview, "I thought my bananas were yellow until I met Joe Kennedy."

But Joe Kennedy was only saying what he firmly believed to be true. He did not want to see American lives wasted on what he believed to be a hopeless cause but, perhaps more to the point, he did not want to lose his fortune or his future money-making potential in a devastating and destructive all-out war. He did all he could to try and persuade the people of England that they should do business with Nazi Germany and he fully supported Chamberlain in his bid to appease Hitler in Munich. But when that failed he, like everyone else, had to face the inevitable truth. On September 3rd 1939, he sat with some of his older children in the public gallery in the House of Commons to witness the historic debate that would result in Britain declaring war on Germany.

Once war had been declared, Joe faced up to the truth and threw himself into the fray with his usual, unbounded energy. He had failed in his attempt to dissuade Britain from opposing Hitler but now that they had, he supported their cause as openly as he had previously opposed it; at least in public. He looked on in admiration as the sandbags were stacked up at the windows and the anti-aircraft guns were set-up in Hyde Park and he was impressed by the way the people of London faced up to the coming ordeal. He publicly endured the bombing with them and once tried to make light of it by saying that, "Bombing, as far as it interrupts a night's rest, is nothing new to men who, like myself, have many children."

But the British people were in no mood for the Ambassador's jokes. He had, by now, begun to support the provision of arms and other aid to Britain but for many it was too little too late. Joe Kennedy had clearly lost face in Britain and in late 1940, he resigned from his post as Ambassador and returned to the United States.

The whole episode had been very damaging for Joe Kennedy and his controversial views and outspoken political beliefs had effectively put an end to his own political ambitions. He had tried to convince the American people that it would serve no useful purpose for the United States to become embroiled in another petty war in Europe, but he had failed and his political career was in tatters. He openly blamed Roosevelt for ruining him politically and he swore he would not support him in his bid to run for a record third term as President, but Rose stepped in to calm him down. She quite rightly pointed out that a refusal to support Roosevelt would be seen as sour grapes and would do even more damage to his reputation and that of the family. She also reminded him that their hopes were now pinned on young Joe and that any further rift with Roosevelt would reflect badly on him and may ruin his chance of running for office when the time came. Joe was nothing if not a pragmatist and he knew that she was right so with his family's best interests at heart, he reluctantly threw his weight behind Roosevelt's successful campaign.

Joe Kennedy was a man of many vices and of all of these, he is perhaps best known for his shameless and relentless pursuit of women. He was a notorious womaniser and had countless affairs and one-night-stands, many of them under the noses of the whole family. He has been described as vulgar and uncouth and many women, and men for that matter, found him lewd and repulsive. He would force himself on women he had only just met and felt he could treat them in any way he pleased. One Hollywood actress said that when she first met Joe Kennedy he took her into a room, supposedly to discuss a possible film role then, in her own words, "He immediately flung himself at me and stuck his tongue down my throat. I threw him out then went into the bathroom to be sick. When I re-joined the group outside, he acted as if nothing had happened."

Joe Kennedy was blatantly open about his sexual liaisons and he saw no wrong in carrying on in this way. His doctrine was that Kennedy men could use and abuse women as often and as much as they liked, and the women just had to put up with it. He would make no secret of any of his dalliances and would often bring women home with him, occasionally even having them join the family at dinner. He cared nothing for the feelings or opinions of others, not even Rose, and he would sometimes be in the bedroom with his latest conquest while Rose was in the lounge watching TV. Rose knew all of this, of course, but she accepted her lot and said nothing; at least not in public, and Joe continued to chase women until illness and a stroke finally curbed his ardour.

There can be no doubt that Joe Kennedy loved his family very much and that he put a great deal of effort into providing for them, but he openly lived two very separate lives. He would be at home with his family one weekend, then the next he would be shacked up in some hotel somewhere with a string of starlets and call-girls. In Joe Kennedy's world, women were put on this earth for the enjoyment of men and he cared nothing for their thoughts or feelings. This was a particularly ugly and unattractive side to his character and it was one which he would pass on, in varying degrees, to his sons.

Most of Joe Kennedy's sexual encounters were brief and short-lived but he did have some longer-lasting and at times more meaningful relationships. Perhaps the most famous of these was his 3 year affair with Hollywood actress, Gloria Swanson. He helped make her a star and at one-time the biggest earner in Hollywood and they seemed to be very close. Swanson spoke a great deal about Joe Kennedy in her autobiography and claimed he had wanted to marry her and have children together. She even said that he had approached the Catholic Archbishop to ask if he might help him get a divorce from Rose. But the affair was doomed to fail and as Joe tired of her, they drifted apart and began to argue. Their relationship gradually worsened and Swanson began to notice that Joe was being less and less attentive towards her as time went on. She finally saw her true worth when Joe bought her an expensive present which she then discovered had been charged to her own account. She later said she felt bitter that Joe Kennedy had made a huge profit from their relationship while she had faced financial ruin; a sentiment that was entirely lost on Joe.

Another long-term relationship, and perhaps a more meaningful one for Joe, was with playwright, Congresswoman and former Ambassador to Italy, Clare Booth Luce. Luce was a bright, intelligent woman whom Joe felt he could really relate to and he grew to love her very much. He would, of course, still pursue other women but Luce was very special to him. He became very close with her and would often turn to her in times of trouble. She was a great comfort to him when young Jack went missing when PT109 was lost, or when Joe Junior died in the skies over England.

Clare Booth Luce was a close friend of all the family and would often travel openly with them on their various trips abroad, all with the full approval of Rose. She helped promote young Jack when he published his exploits in the war and again when he first entered politics and Joe depended on her enormously. But he was still Rose's ever-loving husband and would write her very affectionate letters whilst away. Rose never confronted him on his wayward behaviour and Ted would later say that he never saw his parents argue. Rose knew the measure of Joe Kennedy when she married him and despite his many failings, she was content to accept him for what he was most of the time.

It takes a special kind of woman to stick by a man like Joe Kennedy and Rose was a remarkable woman in her own right. She has often been overlooked and overshadowed by her illustrious husband and famous sons, but the recent publication of her personal diaries paints a detailed and compelling picture of a fascinating and highly intelligent woman. Born in Boston on July 22nd 1890, Rose was the eldest daughter of John (Honey Fitz) and Josie Fitzgerald. Honey Fitz doted on his bright young daughter and it was at his side that she learned the art of politics and public office. She was a natural with people and was always able to combine wealth and privilege with the common touch.

Rose has often been credited with being the real driving force behind the Kennedy family and she was a formidable woman, as much feared by her children as she was loved. That's not to say she was not a good mother; she was. But she drove her children very hard and expected nothing less than the best from them, all of the time. She had very strong views on how a family should act and behave and how they should be perceived by the public. Everything had to be just so and there was nothing more important to her than how her children should be raised and what kind of people they would grow up to be. She would even have their teeth straightened to ensure they would always appear perfect and blemish-free. Rose saw motherhood as a privilege and a calling and she took her role and responsibilities very seriously. She would give the children lessons on Geography and American history and she would take them to visit historical places and battle sites. She even had a filing system in which she kept records on details such as birthdays, illnesses, schooling and other key events in their lives. Rose ran the family like a business, planning everything down to the tiniest detail, and she left nothing to chance.

But Rose Kennedy's diaries have also revealed a deeper, more thoughtful side to her nature that has up to now been hidden from public view. She accepted her lot in life and considered herself fortunate to be the mother of the Kennedy children, but she was still a strong, independent woman inside and she had a bright and inquiring mind that she loved to feed and nurture. She was a very well educated woman and she loved to read and to learn all she could about the world and the people in it. One example of this was when she read James Joyce's, *Ulysses* when the Catholic Church had strongly urged people to boycott the book. Rose was a strong and devout Catholic but her natural curiosity and her need to explore and to learn proved stronger than her formidable religious convictions. She was extremely intelligent and a deep thinker and she once commented in her diary that, "I would sometimes wonder why I had spent so much time reading Goethe and Voltaire if I have to spend my time telling the children why they should drink their milk. But then I would think, raising a family is a new challenge, and I am going to meet it."

Family Life and Values

Life as a Kennedy child was a bizarre combination of pampered privilege and ruthless oppression. The family was wealthy beyond belief but it was a harsh environment in which to grow up. Joe and Rose had nine children and they were all raised according to the strict Kennedy doctrine of winner takes all and only the best will do. Joe was a hard task-master and expected nothing but perfection from his children at all times. He was a strict disciplinarian and would always teach his children that in the game of life, there is no second place. Life is about winners and losers; and the Kennedys were expected to be winners. Joe was quite attentive towards his children when he was at home but as he was often away, Rose was usually the one in charge. And she would be just as demanding as their father.

There can be no question that Joe and Rose Kennedy loved their children very much, but there can be no denying either that they made life very difficult and challenging for them. Family and friends would say that there was no joviality or laughter in the Kennedy household and although this seems a rather extreme statement to make, one can't help feeling that there may be some truth in it. Life for them was hard, but pictures and home movies of the Kennedy family at play show a happy, normal family and all of them would later comment on how happy their childhood had been and how they all got along well together. In his autobiography, *True Compass*, Ted recalls these times with affection.

"I recall the way my parents made the household and the dinner table places of inclusion and learning and the dolls and the soldiers that Dad brought home from his travels; the endless larking competitions on the lawn and by the shore and out in the waters of Nantucket Sound. And I recall the way we would joke as children that none of us would marry because we were having such a good time with one another."

This clearly shows that there were many happy times but that harsh, regimented regime was always there in everything they did. Mealtimes were a case in point. The children were expected to be at the table five minutes before dinner every day and there could be no excuses for lateness or absenteeism. Once seated, Joe or Rose, or sometimes one of the children, would open a debate about some current affairs issue or a newspaper story that had been cut out of the paper and pinned to a notice-board earlier in the day. As the meal progressed, the family would debate and discuss the topic at hand, each encouraged to express a view or to offer a reasoned argument. Despite Ted's rosy-eyed recollections, some of them would feel pressured by this ritual and would dread the very thought of it. The boys were especially encouraged to express their opinions and of the girls, Kathleen was always the most outspoken. It was a gruelling ritual but there would be no avoiding it and the practice was later adopted by Bobby for his own family.

The children were taught to be grateful for what they had and for the privileged lives they all led. On one occasion the family were engaging in one of their meal-time discussions when young Joe, just back from Russia, began to describe his experiences there and to express opinions on the Russian political system and way of life. He commented that he saw some good in the way that in Russia, everyone was treated as equal and good work repaid by good reward. Joe's father slammed his knife and fork down on the table and rose to his feet.

"When you have given up your car and your yacht and your horse," he said, "then you can sit there and tell me what a good system that is." He then stormed angrily out of the room.

The Kennedys were expected to excel at everything, especially sports like football and sailing and there was no room at their table for second best. They would play touch football on the lawn almost every day and friends who joined in said that these games were anything but friendly and that the Kennedy kids would knock the stuffing out of one another. Even the girlfriends and wives were expected to take part and Ethel in particular played with sheer grit and determination, even during her frequent pregnancies. These games often resulted in cuts and bruises, but Joe and Rose would have no whining. Any injured party would be expected to get up, dust themselves down and get back into the fray, and heaven help those too weak to take it. The family were keen sailors, too and would sail at every available opportunity. They would enter races and regattas around Cape Cod and fight tooth and nail to win.

The Kennedys were a very insular, isolated family with a clan-like culture common in Irish-American families at that time. Joe Kennedy would never integrate in any way with the local community and he would shun any contact with their neighbours, which made him unpopular around Hyannis Port and Palm Beach. Another curious family trait was that, although one of the richest families in America, they were incredibly thrifty when it came to spending their hard-earned cash. On one occasion the Kennedy house in Palm Springs became so shabby and run-down that Joe eventually conceded that he would have to do something about it, so he had it painted. However, when he called in the painters he told them to paint only the front and the side that could be seen from the road. The back and the other side, invisible to onlookers, he left untouched. After all, why spend money on something nobody would see? And they were often less than generous with friends and house guests. One sunny afternoon, Joe Junior had friends over to play football in the garden and when they all became thirsty Joe brought out a jug of water, arguing that lemonade was too expensive when water would do just as well.

Rose was even more careful with the family coffers and became well-known amongst family and friends for giving presents, only to ask for them back later. She would also buy expensive clothes and gowns, wear them once then take them back to the shop for a refund. This was a habit that Rose maintained all through her life and in his autobiography, *True Compass*, Ted candidly recalls with some amusement an exchange he had with his mother not long before she died. She called him up one day and said.

"Teddy dear, do you recall the blue sweater I gave you at Christmas?"

"Yes, mother," replied Ted.

"Have you worn it yet? Because I have just got the bill and it was $220. Will you check it out and if you haven't worn it will you send it back because I've got another blue one which I think is just as nice but it is not nearly as expensive."

Rose would even refuse to heat the family swimming pool and one neighbour recalls how Rose would come over to her house, costume on and towel in hand, to swim in her pool rather than heat their own. Bobby's wife, Ethel also adopted Rose's frugal habits, to the point that many stores refused to do business with either of them.

Joe Kennedy's money had been hard won. It had been a tough road and nothing came easy for an Irish immigrant family fighting for power and recognition, and this only strengthened Joe's resolve. His own dream of becoming President had been dashed in 1940 but he determined that young Joe would one day achieve that goal, and he had no doubt that his other sons would follow. This would become his driving ambition and he would stop at nothing to make sure that it happened. He knew it would not be easy in the tough, dog eat dog world of politics and power and he knew he would have to push his boys hard if they were to have any chance of success.

Joe Kennedy expected nothing less than perfection from his children and they certainly had a lot to live up to. They had to be the best swimmers, the best ball players, the best sailors and, in fact, the best at just about everything. This was hard enough for the fit and able-bodied among them but for some, it was impossible. This was especially true of the eldest daughter, Rosemary. She would be the first victim of the destructive force that was Joe Kennedy and the first to pay, if not with her life, then certainly with her right to have one.

3   ROSEMARY

Rosemary Kennedy (affectionately known as Rosie) was born at her parents' home in Brookline, Massachusetts on September 13th 1918, the third child and eldest daughter of Joe and Rose Kennedy. There was a flu epidemic raging at the time and when the doctor was called, he was delayed elsewhere. Rose had to hang on until he arrived and it has been suggested that this delay may have been the cause of the mental impairment that became evident in Rosemary later on. It was a difficult birth but in the end, all seemed well and they had no reason to suppose that young Rosemary would not grow up to be a happy, normal little girl. Joe and Rose Kennedy already had two boys and the birth of a daughter was a welcome addition to the family. In those early days Rose described her as a, "Sweet and peaceable child who cried less than the first two."

Rose was proud of her new arrival and would take her for long walks in the sunshine, with Young Joe and Jack hanging on to the pram as they tagged along. Rosemary seemed happy and contented and was a joy to have around and she would play quite happily on her own in her nursery. But as the months passed to years, it became clear that there were issues with her development, and her parents were becoming concerned.

Young Rosemary had been slower to crawl and to walk than most other children and she was having difficulty learning to speak. She was clumsy and awkward and as she grew older, she struggled with reading and writing. She would often write from right to left and she found it hard to form words and sentences and although this may now be attributed to dyslexia, that did not account for Rosie's other developmental problems. Joe and Rose both hoped she would improve with time and Joe even paid for specialist help, but they eventually had to accept that their daughter was mentally disabled and that no amount of money could make that better.

While Joe engaged experts from across the country in an effort to find a cure for young Rosie, her mother gave her all the love and affection she could. Rose Kennedy was always very hard on her children, but she was especially kind and caring towards Rosie. She would spend hours with her on an intimate, one to one basis and she would encourage her to swim and to play tennis. Joe was often away but Rose would write him almost every day, telling him how Rosie and the other children were getting on and how Rosie was doing. The experts advised Joe and Rose to send Rosie to a special school but in those early days, they chose to keep her at home with the family, where they felt she could be cared for. "What can these people do that we can't do better ourselves?" Joe would ask, and he refused to take their advice.

Joe and Rose did all they could for Rosie at home but in the end they had to admit defeat and at aged eleven, Rosie was sent to the Devereux School in Pennsylvania. Devereux was a good choice for Rosie as it offered help and support for people with mental impairment and had "specialised" lesson plans for intellectually challenged students. Rosie was popular with the teachers, who praised her for her social poise and described her as, "quite charming." But she still struggled with her studies. She would often lash out at people around her and she felt frustrated with her own lack of progress, especially as she knew that her father so wanted her to do well. Like all the Kennedy children, Rosemary tried very hard to please her father and would write to tell him how she was doing at the school in a desperate effort to get some praise from him.

Rosemary missed home, too. She longed to be back with her brothers and sisters and she often wrote to her mother asking to be allowed home for the holidays. She enjoyed playing and dressing up with her sisters and she loved to watch the boys play football on the lawn. The other Kennedy children were all very good to Rosemary and they tried hard to include her in everything they did and to make her feel normal and part of the family. She was especially close to her younger sister, Eunice and would write long and loving letters to her, begging for a long letter in reply. Eunice took Rosie very much under her wing and she would go on to care for her until the day she died. Close family friend, Lem Billings once said.

"Somehow, Eunice seemed to develop, very early on, a sense of special responsibility for Rosemary, as if she were her mother and not her sister."

On seeing little progress in her development, Joe moved young Rosie to Elmhurst School in Providence, Rhode Island. He had concluded that the regime at Devereux was not right for Rosie and he sent her to Elmhurst as he thought they could get more out of her. But this proved not to be the case and she stayed only two years at Elmhurst before moving on again, this time to Brookline. Joe asked Joe Junior and Jack to see Rosie as often as they could and young Joe, being just a short distance away at Harvard would visit her often and take her for long walks. Rosie was very proud of both Joe and Jack and she always looked forward to their visits.

Despite her obvious mental difficulties, Rosemary was by no means a lost cause. In her early teens she was a bright and happy child with a vivacious, outgoing personality and a disarming naivety that people found both charming and irresistible. She was described as sweet and friendly, with glowing red cheeks and a beautiful smile and she was often said to have been the prettiest of the Kennedy girls. She was an incredibly sensitive young girl and for many years she kept a diary that, although sometimes quite simple and naïve in style, reveals the thoughts and feelings of a normal, adolescent young woman. Rosemary was always different in temperament from any of her siblings. She was more sensitive and caring and she lacked the competitive edge of the other Kennedy children. She did enjoy playing sports and games but for her the thrill was in taking part rather than winning and she was the only one of the nine children to be allowed to adopt this non-competitive approach to life.

When Joe Kennedy was appointed Ambassador to Great Britain in 1938, he moved all of his family to London, where they took up residence in the Ambassador's house in Grosvenor Square. At first, the Kennedys were much admired in Britain for their rich and affluent lifestyle and they were very popular with the press and with the people. They were courted by the rich and famous, too and they soon began to immerse themselves into London's high society. Rose Kennedy had always craved acceptance and social status and in London she thought she had found it, although the snobbish British press disapproved of her garish dress sense and her "New Money" look.

Nevertheless, within weeks of arriving in London the Ambassador and his family were presented to the King and Queen at a ball at Buckingham Palace and Rose seized the opportunity with both hands. Joe and Rose would be accompanied by Kathleen and young Rosie and there was some concern that young Rosie might embarrass them in some way, but their fears proved to be unfounded. Rosie stumbled a little when curtseying to the Queen, but she quickly recovered and very few people even noticed. Rosie was every bit the perfect lady and everyone loved her. She danced gracefully with all the big names in London and she made Joe proud to be her father. Rose and her two daughters were the belles of the ball and their pictures were in all the papers the next day, but it was young Rosie who shone out the most. Rose even complained that the press had lavished too much attention on Rosie and not enough on Kathleen, but her protestations fell on deaf ears.

Whilst in England, Rosemary was sent to a Sacred Heart School in the London Borough of Wandsworth, but she found it hard to keep up there and was later transferred to the Convent of the Assumption School in Kensington Square, just across from Hyde Park. She fared very well at the Convent of the Assumption, where she worked towards a Diploma that she thought would qualify her to be a kindergarten school teacher. It was the happiest Rosie had been for a long time. The nuns were very kind to her and the regime suited her very well and she made it quite clear that she would like to stay there, telling her father this as often as she could.

When Britain declared war on Germany in September 1939, Joe Kennedy knew that his days in London were numbered.

He had warned that Britain could never win a war with Germany and he firmly believed that the Germans would successfully invade Britain within a very short time and that America should not intervene. He had seen what the Germans had done in Poland and in Spain and he knew that it would not be long before the bombs would rain down on London, so he decided to send his family home to the United States. He at first agreed that Rosie could stay on at the school but as the threat of bombing increased, he felt he had to send her home, too.

"We will be in for a terrible bombing soon," he wrote home to Rose, "and I will do better if I just had myself to look after."

Rosemary collected her Diploma in June 1940, then she returned to the United States. She was bitterly disappointed at having to leave her friends in England and this disappointment manifested itself in her behaviour. She became cantankerous and belligerent and she would often lash out at the people around her. She was now a fully-grown woman and was difficult to handle and Joe felt she should not return to the family home with the others and that it would be better for all concerned if she went to another special school. Furthermore, she had the body of an attractive, mature woman but the brain of a small child, and he worried that her new-found interest in the opposite sex might one day cause embarrassment. She had become interested in boys and would flirt openly and quite innocently with them. She seemed happy in their company and that worried Joe a great deal as he feared that, being of a low mental capacity, an opportunistic young man could easily take advantage of her. After all, he knew better than anyone how easily that could happen in a world full of predatory men, ready and eager to prey on vulnerable young women.

Joe Kennedy could see that his daughter's condition was worsening. She was making very little progress in her lessons and she was becoming increasingly moody and disruptive, and in the end his patience ran out. He firmly believed that if he looked hard enough and paid enough money, he could find a cure for Rosemary and one day, he thought he had found the ideal solution. In 1941, Joe was advised that a Lobotomy, a new and revolutionary form of brain surgery, would help cure young Rosie and would calm her mood swings and violent outbursts. The originator of the procedure, Antonio Egas Moniz was awarded the Nobel Prize for his development of the technique in 1949 and at the time, it was hailed as a new "miracle cure" for people with certain mental or psychotic conditions. However, in more recent years the operation has been seriously called into question and the whole issue is embroiled in controversy. So much so that there have been calls to have Moniz stripped of his Nobel Prize, although this has not yet happened.

The operation, performed while the patient was awake, involved cutting through the scalp and scraping away the white, fibrous tissue linking the frontal lobes to the rest of the brain. This was a new and risky treatment and was very much un-proven. Less than 100 people had had the operation and there was almost nothing on which to base a judgement on the chances of it being a success. In fact, it had already received a great deal of bad press. Washington reporter, John White, who had studied the procedure, told Kathleen that the results were not good. He said it did leave patients calmer and less anxious but that they are usually, "Just gone as a person; just gone!"

In August 1941 the Journal of the American Medical Association warned against using the procedure until more research could be done, but Joe would not be swayed. He agreed to the proposition and the operation was performed by Dr James W Watts at the George Washington University Hospital in Washington DC (the prestigious St Elizabeth's having refused Watts permission to conduct the operations there). Joe did not even consult Rose before committing Rosemary to the operation and he never told any of the children; he just went ahead and did it. This caused a rift between Joe and Rose that would never heal and Rose never did forgive Joe for what he did to young Rosie.

It was apparent almost immediately that the operation had been a complete disaster. Rosemary went from a beautiful, vibrant (if somewhat slow) young lady to a bad-tempered five year old trapped in a grown woman's body. Her facial features had changed and she was completely incapacitated and unable to take care of herself in any way. She could not walk or talk and she could not even recognise her own parents. Joe may well have thought he was doing his best for his daughter, but the consequences of his actions were catastrophic and irreversible and Rosemary would never be the same again. She had never been the perfect child he had always wanted her to be and through his own actions, however well-intended, Joe had rendered her mentally incapacitated for life.

The response was cruel and swift. Although deeply traumatised by what had happened to Rosemary, Joe vowed that the world should never know the truth, and she was sent away. From that point on, no one was allowed to even mention Rosemary's name and she was no longer mentioned in Rose's many letters. The Kennedys had always been a very close-knit family and these events had a devastating and traumatic effect on the other children. Ted, who was only nine years old at the time, was especially affected by this, writing in his memoir that he thought he had, "Better do as Daddy wanted, or the same would happen to me."

The hospital in Washington could do no more for Rosemary so Joe asked close family friend, Eddie Moore to look after her interests and to look for a place where she could live and be cared for. She was sent for a time to Craig House, 50 miles north of New York City, where she learned to speak once more and to regain some of her movement, but that was only ever going to be a temporary solution. Rosemary was happy at Craig House and fared well there but Joe soon came to realise she would need something more permanent and in 1947, on the recommendation of Archbishop Cushing, she was sent to the St Collotta School for Exceptional Children in Jefferson, Wisconsin, where she would live out the rest of her ruined life. Joe donated $100,000 which was used to build a swimming pool and other amenities and he continued to support the school financially. Meanwhile, a small, single-storey cottage was built in the grounds for Rosemary's personal use, and this would remain her home for the next 60 years. Joe would never see his daughter again.

Joe Kennedy feared embarrassment and humiliation over the situation with Rosemary and the whole affair was covered up. The official line from Joe was that Rosemary, being a devout and ardent Catholic, had gone to a convent to teach.

There was just no way that Joe Kennedy could admit to the world that the Kennedy family had produced an anything less than a perfect child. Rose was very bitter towards Joe for destroying their daughter's life in this way and claimed she did not know the full story of what happened to Rosemary until 1961. She did, however, gradually come to terms with the situation and following the death of Joe Kennedy in 1969, Rosemary was allowed to make occasional visits to the family home under the supervision of her younger sister, Eunice.

In later years, the family finally admitted the truth and openly declared Rosemary mentally handicapped. Her sister, Eunice continued to care for her and she set up an organisation to help people with special needs. This evolved into the Special Olympics, an international organisation designed to help children and adults with intellectual and learning disabilities. It now helps train and promote around 4 million athletes from 170 countries worldwide. Joe, although he could still not face seeing Rosemary, also donated huge sums of money to mental illness charities and funded trusts for people with learning difficulties. It is also thought that what happened to Rosemary had a deep and profound effect on the political beliefs and social conscience of her three bothers. Both in the Senate and as President, Jack campaigned tirelessly for improvements in the care of the mentally disabled, as did both Bobby and Ted later.

Rosie died on January 7th 2005, at the Memorial Hospital in Fort Worth, Wisconsin and is buried alongside her parents in Holyhood Cemetery in Brookline, Massachusetts. She was 86 years old.

Rosemary was the first unwitting casualty of Joe Kennedy's desire to raise a perfect family in a perfect, Kennedy-controlled world. He could not be held responsible for her condition or her impaired development but he was certainly the architect of her tragic demise, however well-meant. Joe Kennedy was a ruthless, ambitious tyrant who would accept nothing but the best from all of his children, whatever the cost, and what happened to Rosie was just the beginning.

4 JOE JUNIOR

Joseph Patrick Kennedy Junior (or Young Joe, as he was known to the family) was born at his parents' rented summer home in Hull, Massachusetts on July 25th 1915 and from the day he arrived, his life was already mapped out. Joe Kennedy had determined that his eldest son would one day be the first Irish-Catholic to be elected President of the United States and that he would stop at nothing to make it happen. Joe Kennedy would tell anyone who would listen about his ambitious plans for young Joe, and no-one ever doubted that he meant it. He wanted more than anything to make his son President, and Joe Kennedy always got what he wanted.

Young Joe was a strong, healthy child and was everything Joe Kennedy ever wanted in a son. He was bright and intelligent and from a very early age he had a winning way that made people adore him. Joe senior was often away on business but when at home he would spend as much time with young Joe as he could, playing with him in his nursery and making sure he had everything he could ever need or want. He had all the best toys and was looked after by the best nurses money could buy and, through Rose's letters, Joe followed the boy's progress in minute detail.

Joe and Rose Kennedy would go on to have eight more children, but it was always young Joe who came first, and he ruled the roost. The Kennedys were a large family but Joe always knew how to get his own way in a strict and somewhat harsh environment. He would use his overbearing physical presence in his battles with his siblings and his winning smile with the grown-ups, and this useful mix of brute force and an engaging personality would serve him well in later life. Everyone who knew Joe as a boy said he could turn on the charm at the drop of a hat and he would flash his famous, disarming smile whenever he wanted to get his own way, which he almost always did.

As he grew older, Joe began to develop the strong, hard-nosed persona that would later mark him out from others. He was special, and he knew it. But in the confines of his own family, that was never quite enough and he would have to prove himself every day. The Kennedys were a fiercely competitive family and all of Joe Kennedy's children, with the exception of Rosemary, were expected to look after themselves and to hold their own in a tough, dog eat dog world. Joe Kennedy pushed his children to compete against one another in everything they did and to give nothing but their best effort every time. They were expected to be winners and to never accept second place, even amongst themselves, and this was especially true of Joe and his younger brother, Jack.

Jack was two years younger than Joe and was a sickly, weak child, but this did not matter to young Joe. To Joe, Jack was a competitor, a challenge to his own position with his father and with the world and he had to be beaten in everything, every time and at all costs. This was hard for Jack at first but he soon learned to rise to the challenge. The family often played touch football on the lawn and Joe would slam the ball into Jack's chest as hard as he could and just grin as he gasped for breath. Their father would sometimes tell Joe to go easy on Jack but their mother was every bit as demanding as Joe and would prefer to let it go. They all had to learn to take knocks in life and Jack had no choice but to toughen up. On one occasion, Joe and Jack raced around the block in opposite directions on their bicycles and when they came back around and were rushing head-on towards each other, both refused to give way. They collided and Jack ended up with 28 stitches in his head. Joe was unhurt.

Jack soon learned to hit Joe where it hurt. Joe had a real weakness for the cook's home-made chocolate cake and on the days they were to have it, Joe would ask the cook to cut his slice early so he could pop in and out of the house to just look at it, savouring every moment in the lead-up to the final act of devouring. On one such occasion, Jack took Joe's precious piece of cake and stuffed it into his mouth, right before Joe's eyes. Joe chased him into the sea and waited until Jack, shivering from the cold, was forced to come out then he laid into him for all he was worth. But Jack didn't mind that at all. He had put one over on Joe and that was good enough for him. But this fierce in-fighting was only skin deep. Outside the confines of the family unit Joe was quite protective towards Jack, as he was to all of his siblings. When Jack was in college, Joe would visit him often and he was always sensitive towards Jack during his many bouts of illness.

When he turned five, young Joe was sent off to school and his father chose for him the much acclaimed Devotion School in Brookline. Young Joe had a rocky, emotional start at Devotion as he had, to that point, spent very little time away from the security of his family. But he soon settled in and began to make new friends. He seemed happy at Devotion and Joe senior was pleased with his progress but during his third year there, the school dropped a bombshell when they declared that they were selling up and closing. Joe Kennedy was furious. He quickly got together a consortium of investors and bought the school, renaming it Dexter after one of its founders and keeping on the much-loved headmistress, Miss Fiske, who Joe Kennedy thought was so good for his son. They re-opened the following term without even a break.

From Devotion, Joe moved on to Noble and Greenough, another prestigious institution that had a good name at Harvard, and that would be useful later on. He was not a particularly good student at Noble but he did show a real aptitude for sport, especially swimming and baseball, but he would often argue with umpires and was considered by some to be a poor loser.

Joe moved from Noble to Choate where he continued to live a confined, cocooned life, somewhat isolated from the rest of the world. He lived in a vacuum created by his father's wealth and, although by now a teenager, he knew almost nothing of the world outside. When some of his friends had to leave the school following the Wall Street crash in 1929, Joe found it hard to comprehend what was happening and why they had to go. He later said he knew nothing of the crash until he read about it in *Liberty Digest* some time afterwards and when one considers his isolated, privileged existence, this is not hard to believe. Joe was too busy trying to look after himself in a world where he was on his own. He was very much in a minority at Choate due to his being a Catholic and he learned to take jibes and mockery well, even mocking himself much of the time. He had a terrific sense of humour and became quite a practical joker and he thoroughly enjoyed his time there.

Young Joe was growing from the boy to the man and his father was pleased with how his eldest son had turned out. He was smart, intelligent and well-bred and was ideal material from which to mould a good and successful politician. As Joe grew older, his father began to treat him more like an adult than a child and if he wanted him to do something or to act in a particular way, he would ask and suggest rather than tell. Joe Kennedy nurtured his son into maturity in a gradual, structured way and Joe loved and respected him for it. He knew why his father had pushed him so hard and he appreciated the way he had driven him on to be a winner. He realised that losers usually work just as hard as winners but get none of the rewards, and the world was no place for losers.

When home from school, young Joe would step in for his father as master of the house when he was away and he would try to act as Joe senior would in any given situation. On one occasion, Kathleen pleaded with her mother that she needed a new school bag as her old one was tattered and worn. Young Joe stepped in and said that she did not need a new bag and that they would not waste money on something they did not need. He made Kathleen go up to her room and write 100 times, "I must learn to mind my own business."

Kathleen was Joe's favourite amongst the girls, but he was good and kind to all of them. They liked to hear from him when he was away at school but he would seldom write to them, claiming he was always too busy. They once nagged him so much that he addressed a postcard to all of them that simply read; "Hi girls, don't say I never write to you!"

Joe was always very good to his brothers and sisters, and they all adored him in return. He was strict and firm but, at the same time very caring and attentive. He was especially kind to Rosemary and he loved her soft, caring nature, so in contrast to the rest of the Kennedy children. But it was Ted, the youngest, that Joe took to the most. Joe adored young Ted and he was the one to whom he would remain the closest for the rest of his life, the eldest and the youngest in a deep and special bond. When Joe came home from school he would go straight up to the nursery to play with young Teddy and the boy idolised his attentive big brother, especially when he had joined the military and would come home in his uniform. Joe was Ted's hero and he cherished every moment they ever spent together. Ted was not singled out for preferential treatment, however. Bobby recalled that young Joe once threw the very young Ted into the pool to make him learn to swim the hard way.

"He'll be OK", said Joe. "He'll have to be."

On another occasion, while sailing with Joe in a race, Ted messed up a tack and Joe threw him out of the boat. Ted was special to Joe, but he still had to learn to be tough.

Joe was generally less popular than Jack, as many found him to be quite serious but he often tried hard to win people over. The Kennedys had a private movie theatre in the basement of their house and Joe would invite friends around to watch his father's latest westerns and other big films and he liked to mix with people his own age. He liked animals, too, especially dogs. He had a pet dog named Satyr who he once threw off a pier into the sea to break up a fight between him and another dog. He then worried for the poor animal and jumped in after him, which was more than he ever did for his brothers and sisters.

Young Joe discovered girls at a very young age and was always very popular with women. As a Kennedy boy he was brought up to believe that women were there for the enjoyment of man and that the role of a wife was to have children and raise a family, but Joe never fully bought into that creed. He loved to be around women and he had many girlfriends, but he was always more sensitive and caring towards women than his father or any of his brothers. Many women who knew Joe said he was very sweet and considerate and that he was wonderful to be with but on the other hand, some said they found him quite aggressive. He enjoyed life and liked being around people and, although he would sometimes use women in the same way his father had, he preferred a more meaningful relationship and always liked to make a woman feel special. He had a number of serious girlfriends, the first of which was when he was just thirteen. In that summer he met and fell in love with a young girl named, Eleanor Leavens and he remained close to her for many years, writing to her long after he left school.

By the time he was sixteen, young Joe began to realise that he would have to work harder at his studies if he was going to fulfil his potential and meet his father's expectations. He enrolled at Harvard with a new determination to apply himself and to do well. He took his studies there very seriously and would even keep copies of his own school reports to plot his progress and identify areas where he needed to improve. He was very popular with his teachers and fellow-students and he served for a time on the Student Council, although his habit of preaching his Catholic faith to anyone who would listen did not endear him to some of the more Protestant-minded pupils. But he worked hard, going to bed early and rising at dawn and he won the Harvard Trophy for the sixth-former who best combined academic and athletic achievement.

Joe Kennedy always believed that people should experience as wide and varied an education as possible and he chose the controversial Harold Laski to provide this for his son. Professor Laski was a brilliant economist and was extremely left-wing in his political views. He once taught at Harvard but was dismissed for his support of the Boston Police strike in 1919. He moved to London in 1926 and became a teaching professor at the London School of Economics. He was a Marxist sympathiser and seemed an odd choice for a Kennedy, but Joe senior believed that exposure to left-wing politics would strengthen Joe's commitment to a career in US politics.

Young Joe enrolled at the London School of Economics in 1938 and he and Laski soon became firm friends. Joe would go to the Laski's flat for tea and would talk for hours with Laski and his wife, Frida about politics, social divide and the growing threat of war in Europe. Frida said that Joe was always charming and delightful and had a smile that was, "pure magic," but he always struggled to see someone else's point of view. His way was the right way and she sometimes found his arguments and beliefs quite naïve. Joe visited Russia with Laski and the trip had a lasting impression on him. He learned a lot about left-wing politics but he never wavered from his own political beliefs and he remained a firm and committed Catholic.

Joe took a flat in London's Earls Court district which he shared with Aubrey Whitelaw, a fellow student of the LSE who, not having the wealth and power of the Kennedys, struggled to pay his way through school. The two became close friends and were to remain so for the rest of Joe's life. Aubrey visited the Kennedy home often and became almost one of the family. He said that Joe missed home very much while living in England and that he would call his mother every day, at a set time. He said Joe had a family photograph on the sideboard and would point to each of his siblings in turn and tell him what they were going to do with their lives.

"He had it all mapped out for them," he said. "It was like he was talking to the photograph."

Joe and Aubrey had a great time in London. They met all the right people and dated famous movie stars and they did all the things a wealthy, single man might do in the city at that time. They bought an old car and went to Rome, where Joe said he intended to see the Pope. Aubrey, of course, did not take him seriously so was dumbfounded when Joe actually did get to secure an audience with the Pontiff. They took in all the sites of Rome and Joe wrote to his mother telling her he had climbed the Holy Stairs on his knees. But there was still time for high- jinx. On one occasion, Joe almost got them arrested by standing in the back of their open-top car and, mocking Mussolini, giving the Fascist salute whilst driving through the city.

They eventually left Rome and travelled back via Austria and Germany, where Joe was keen to observe the political and social climate at the time. In Berlin, they stood to watch a Nazi parade and when everyone thrust out their right arm in salute, Joe and Aubrey were the only ones who didn't. A man in the crowd shoved Joe in the shoulder and gestured to him to salute, but Joe stood firm. The man shoved him again and Joe drew back his fist to whack him, but Aubrey stopped him just in time. Joe had once admired the German people for their drive and determination but he saw that the mood had turned violent and ugly. He had now come to hate the Nazis, and Germany had become a dangerous place to be.

On returning to London, young Joe took a keen interest in his father's activities as US Ambassador. Joe Kennedy had been making enemies with his isolationist views and his firm conviction that Britain should not go to war with Germany and young Joe told him how Germany had changed since his last visit and how evil and sinister the atmosphere had become. He felt that Hitler was hell-bent on war and conquest and, although he still hoped that America could avoid direct involvement, he felt that war in Europe was almost inevitable. He did, however, support his father in any way he could and he would often carry out some of the ambassadorial duties on his behalf.

The other great benefit of being back in London was that young Joe could again spend time with his family. He was able to see more of his sisters and would ride in Hyde Park with his father in the mornings before joining his mother and her friends for afternoon tea. He especially enjoyed his time with young Teddy and would take him to the lake in Hyde Park to sail his model boats. It was an idyllic life, but he knew it could not last.

War Clouds over Europe

Europe was on the verge of war and Joe, being now more politically astute and inquisitive, had a burning desire to see the gathering war clouds up-close. He had written a thesis at Harvard entitled, *Intervention in Spain* and he was keen to see for himself what was really happening there. The Republican forces were defending the country against the Fascist, General Franco and fighting was raging all around in a bloody civil war. Young Joe was desperate to get close to the action and he exchanged his diplomatic passport for that of an ordinary citizen and set off for Spain, listing his occupation as a Journalist, but his father's actions would again work against him. Joe Kennedy had made yet more enemies with his avocation of a non-intervention policy in Spain, and young Joe would feel the brunt of this during his travels there. Joseph Kennedy had persuaded Roosevelt to refrain from selling arms to either side in the conflict but Franco got his from Germany anyway, and this angered many Americans. Ernest Hemmingway, who was in Europe at the time, wrote that the Fascists in the State Department had done their, "Level, crooked, Roman, British-appeasing, disgusting, efficient best to defeat the Republic by denying the Spanish Government the right to buy arms and defend itself against German and Italian aggression."

There were many who echoed Hemmingway's impassioned words and tempers were running high. Joe Kennedy was not popular in Spain and it was into this hornet's nest that young Joe was about to step.

Joe set off for Spain just as most Americans were leaving. The civil war was raging with growing intensity and Franco, with German and Italian support, was pounding the country into submission. Joe travelled the country alone and in considerable danger, eating when he could and often sleeping out in the open and he spoke to people on both sides of the divide. He rarely witnessed any fighting first-hand but he was often close to it, arriving in Barcelona the day the city fell to Franco's forces and seeing for himself the devastation the bombing had caused. He then moved on to Madrid to witness the carnage there. He favoured neither side in the war as he disliked equally the policies and philosophies of both the right-wing Fascists and the left-wing Republicans. To him, it was the ordinary, common folk who were bearing the brunt and paying the price. He felt such pity as he saw them bombed out of their homes by German and Italian bombers and he wrote to his father that to be on the receiving end of a bombing raid was the most horrible and terrifying experience and that he was shocked at the feeling of complete helplessness as the bombs fell all around him.

There were now very few Americans left in Spain and Joe's reports from the front made him a well-known and well-respected reporter. His articles appeared in newspapers in England and in the US and he was much-acclaimed for his willingness to get close to the action and to give a clear, honest and unbiased account of what he saw. What let young Joe down here was his poor spelling and grammar. Joe Kennedy gathered up young Joe's despatches from Spain and he had intended to publish them under the title, *Dear Dad*, but the grammar was so poor they would need a considerable amount of editing, so the idea was quietly shelved.

On leaving Spain, Joe returned to London where his father was arranging transport for thousands of Americans wishing to escape back to the United States as war was declared in Britain. Joseph Kennedy had failed in his efforts to avoid a war in Europe and, conceding defeat, he now began to send his own family home. He arranged for them to travel in small groups in order to limit the loss should any of the ships be attacked by German U-Boats and he was greatly relieved when they all arrived safely back in the US. Joe Junior was the last to go and sailed for the US on the SS Mauritania.

Once back in the United States, Joe resumed his studies by enrolling at Harvard Law School. He was clearly a changed man following his experiences in Spain and in Europe and he appeared far more confident and self-assured. He had put away childish things and had grown up to be a mature, politically astute man with a real empathy for other people and a genuine desire to help make the world a better place.

Young Joe had hoped that war in Europe could have been avoided but in the end, he had to accept the inevitable. Adolf Hitler was hell-bent on conquest and appeasement had failed to stop him.

In other ways, however, Joe was unchanged by all these experiences. He still had that charming smile and a great sense of humour and he was, if anything, even more popular than he had been before. Jack said that Joe had a keen wit and that he saw the funny side of things quicker than anyone else. But he also felt that Joe had a slight detachment from things and people around him; a wall of reserve that few people succeeded in penetrating.

"I suppose I knew Joe as well as anyone," Jack said, "but I sometimes wonder if I ever really knew him at all."

But, Joe was Joe, and he soon resumed his habit of acquiring speeding tickets and he still loved to play practical jokes. He had a pet alligator named Snooky, which he kept in his rooms at Harvard. On one occasion when his room-mate was taking a bath, he crept in and threw the animal into the bath with him then roared with laughter as his friend leapt out of the bath and ran naked down the hall at break-neck speed. He repeated this trick three times before the alligator escaped one day, and they never saw it again. On another occasion, a friend was starting a new job the day after a party at Joe's and was keen not to be late for his first day. He fell asleep at Joe's and Joe put all the clocks (and his friend's watch) forward by three hours then woke him to tell him he should hurry or he would be late. The friend then rushed around to get ready, thinking he was already late then arrived at his new job in a blind panic, only to find he was actually a couple of hours too early.

Joe had always been self-opinionated, but when he returned from Europe he was even more so. Friends would tell how he always liked to lead the discussion and he would argue his point much stronger than anyone else. He hated to lose a debate and would go on for hours about how he was right and everyone else was wrong. He would, however, always listen to other people's point of view before enforcing his own on everyone, and he liked to absorb knowledge and information like a sponge. A college friend once said that Joe had an annoying habit of scanning newspapers whilst having a conversation at the same time, but he never missed a word of either. He said he had a photographic memory.

Joe spent Christmas of 1940 in the bosom of his family and he enjoyed the precious time they had together, but he was still working hard to keep America out of the war. He never actually joined the America First Committee but he agreed wholeheartedly with their fervent view that America should not become directly involved in the war. He even went so far as to say that if Britain failed to stop Hitler, the United States should recognise and do business with Nazi Germany rather than step in and join the fight. He was no Nazi-lover and he firmly believed that the US should help Britain as much as possible, short of direct intervention, but there were limits. Like his father, he wanted to protect American interests and safeguard its international trade and he felt that to intervene directly in the war in Europe would ruin the country and its standing in the world. He was no naïve pacifist or campaigner for disarmament, but he truly believed that the country was not yet ready for war and that its military was too weak and disorganised to be very effective at that time.

But Joe's was becoming a lone voice, and he knew it. There was mounting public pressure in favour of direct support for

Britain and this only increased with the RAF's defeat of the Luftwaffe in the summer of 1940. There had already been a fierce debate about whether the United States should escort supply convoys to Britain and Joe argued strongly against this too, but with the signing of the Lend-Lease agreement (whereby the US would supply Britain with weapons and other supplies on a casual "lend-lease" basis, whilst technically still remaining neutral), the course was set. Joe could see the writing on the wall and soon both he and his father had to accept the inevitable. The United States would enter the war eventually; it was just a question of when?

This period at Harvard proved to be quite a challenging time for Joe. He was heavily involved in the America First campaign and this proved to be quite a distraction from his studies. His father appointed a private tutor for him and he did his best to succeed, but his mind was always elsewhere. In December 1941, America finally entered the war following the Japanese attack on Pearl Harbour and Joe, like many other Americans, felt he had to do his bit. He had always opposed American involvement in the war but, once committed, he threw himself behind the cause with as much drive and determination as he had always shown in everything. By early 1941 he had already quit his studies and had enlisted as a volunteer pilot in the United States Navy Reserve. Joe's war was about to begin.

Navy Training

What a come-down! Joe arrived at his first basic training camp in a car driven by Boston Police Commissioner, Joe Timilty, but his high-born connections would cut no ice here. Joe was now just an ordinary seaman second class on $21 per month and in Navy terms that meant he was nothing. He was the lowest of the low and he knew he had a long way to go before he could even make it to Naval Air Cadet. The success rate for this first stage of training was just 50% and even fewer made it to full flight status after that. Joe had a huge hill to climb but he was up for the challenge and, picking up his bags and waving goodbye to Timilty, he walked boldly up to the gate.

The regime at the camp was tough, but Joe responded well. Reveille was at 5am, closely followed by an hour of physical exercise then breakfast. There would then be 8 hours of ground school before another 3 more hours of physical exercise. Fridays were field days; endless treks into the countryside for fitness and survival training and lessons on how to evade capture if shot-down over enemy territory. Joe was very fit and had no problem with this gruelling regime but others did and they began to fall by the wayside in no time. Joe loved the physical training, but he struggled with the theory and he had to work harder at that than most. He also resented being ordered around by what he called, Little Hitlers and he found it hard to accept authority. He was well-liked at the camp and made a lot of friends and his card-playing skills became legendary. His room-mate was Billy Ash and he, like all of Joe's room-mates before, soon learned from experience just how good Joe was at Black Jack. He cleaned up every time.

But Joe had joined the Navy to fly and he was ecstatic when his chance finally came. He had drilled and marched and studied and slogged and now, at last, he had made it through to flight training. He was shown around the small plane and, having had the controls explained to him, he took to the air with his instructor at the stick. Joe so wanted to fly this thing, but he found it hard at first. He had a tendency to ignore his instructor's commands and to do what his instincts were telling him instead, a common failing in students new to flying. When learning to fly you have to do as you're told quickly and without question and it took Joe a long time to suppress his instinctive impulses and follow instruction. His instructor wrote.

"This student does not absorb instruction readily. He does not remember things from one day to the next and he does not look where he is going. His judgement is poor and he can only do one thing at a time."

Joe did prove to be very good at night flying which, curiously enough, was considered even more difficult and required a very special kind of skill.

Young Joe persevered and was eventually passed out as an aviation cadet, finally earning the tiny gold anchors that his own father pinned onto his uniform at the passing out parade. Young Joe had joined the most elite group in the US military and he could not have been more proud. But his old nemesis, Jack had once again loomed large. Despite his ill-health and weak constitution, Jack had managed (with his father's help) to pass the Navy physical and had already won the golden bars of an Ensign, a fully-fledged naval officer. Young Joe was proud of his younger brother but at the same time he felt beaten by Jack and he genuinely worried for Jack's health in the harsh, tough world of the US Navy. Here he was, a lowly naval cadet while his little brother, Jack was a fully-fledged commissioned officer. Joe's only consolation was that, for the time being at least, Jack was safely behind a desk in Washington. It was not the first time Jack had beaten him at his own game, and it would not be the last.

Joe arrived at Jacksonville Naval Air station with just 10 hours flying in his log book. He had made the grade (just) and was about to embark on his new career as a Navy pilot. Most new pilots wanted to fly fast, single-seater fighters but Joe chose multi-engined aircraft, which at that time meant flying boats. His reasons were simple. In a multi-engined plane you had a crew and Joe wanted to command a crew. He wanted to be a Patrol Plane Commander (PPC), which was known to be a difficult rank to achieve and the pass rate for applicants was low. It was an ambitious target for a rookie pilot, but Joe would settle for nothing less.

Life at Jacksonville was a strange combination of intense hard work and training, mixed with a curious and somewhat disarming sense of ease and relaxation. Joe went swimming in the sea and played golf and he would hang-out in local bars with friends. And, of course, there was the praying. Joe was, first and foremost, a devout Catholic and he still found time to pray several times each day. He befriended the camp chaplain, Father Sheehy and he became his right-hand man in doing God's work on the base. He would get up early every day and go around waking up all the Catholic students, urging them to attend Mass before breakfast and making sure they never missed. He was also appointed station reporter in recognition of his obvious abilities as a writer and his frequent articles in the camp newspaper were eagerly read by all.

Joe worked hard to master essential skills like formation flying, aerobatics, navigation and engineering but he was beginning to get bored with this routine and craved to be close to the fighting in Europe. Joe was keen to get into action before Jack could beat him to it and after a short leave, he graduated from flight training with 192 hours in his log and immediately volunteered to fly PBY Catalina flying boats from Banana River, Florida (then just a small town, but later to become the Kennedy Space Centre). This was a step in the right direction but Joe knew that to get onto active service he would need more flying hours, so he took a gamble and volunteered as a flight trainer. He was able to clock-up over 1,000 flying hours in this role and in January 1943, his gamble paid off when he was assigned to his first operational squadron.

But Jack still lurked in the shadows. Despite his poor health and weak constitution Jack had somehow managed to get himself passed fit for active service and in early 1943 he was posted to a PT boat squadron in Tulgai, in the Solomon Islands. This was deep in the heart of the Japanese theatre of war and dangerously close to the action, and Joe envied Jack the opportunity. Joe was certainly moving in the right direction, but he followed Jack's progress very closely. It would be a race to see who could get into action first, and Joe could see that Jack was winning.

Joe's unit was a squadron of PBM flying boats operating out of Miami and Key West, hunting for submarines out in the Atlantic. These planes were very slow and cumbersome and were a far cry from the fast fighters that most pilots wanted to fly. But they had a crew and they needed a skipper, and that was what appealed to Joe. He honed and perfected his flying skills on these low-level patrols, but he also made sure that he knew the job of every other crew member as well as his own. It was not enough that he could fly the plane, he wanted to know how to navigate and to work the tracking equipment and how to manage the in-flight mechanics and electronics of the flight engineer. Joe was a stickler for perfection and the other men in the squadron found him rather distant and thought him reluctant to mix with anyone not of his class. But Joe was just focussed on his own agenda and determined to make his mark and play his part in the war.

In the summer of 1943 Joe heard that the Navy had acquired some army B24 Liberator bombers and had adapted these much faster aircraft for ant-submarine work in the Bay of Biscay, operating out of bases in England. Joe's squadron was one of the first to be selected for training for this task and Joe grabbed the opportunity with both hands. The Liberator was a far more advanced plane than the PBY. The cockpit was a vast array of dials and switches that Joe had to learn and master and its four, wing-mounted engines had far more clout than anything he had flown before. Joe trained on this new aircraft whilst still in Norfolk, Virginia but he was soon assigned to VP-203, a newly formed Liberator squadron under the leadership of Jimmy Reed, a tough but talented commander.

These anti-submarine patrols were hard and tedious work and were very wearing on the crew. The planes would take-off from their bases in England and fly out over the Bay of Biscay for anti-submarine patrols of up to 12 hours at a time. The weather was almost always atrocious, the aircraft were cold and draughty and they saw very little action.
"Hours and hours of endless, dull monotony sprinkled with a few moments of sheer terror," was how one close friend of Joe's described these missions. "We looked out more for fighters than we did for subs."

The cumbersome aircraft were easy targets for enemy fighters and pilots often complained that they had no fighter cover of their own to combat the threat. Joe even commented once or twice that he might transfer to fighters out of sheer frustration, but he never made any formal request to do so.

Meanwhile, on the other side of the world, Jack was faring much better. He was now a PT boat commander and was close to the action in the Coral Sea and he was often called out to chase and harass Japanese shipping in the area. His was a far more glamorous life than Joe's and he was fighting the enemy up-close while Joe was flying aimlessly over the choppy, grey sea, looking for submarines that never showed. It was still a question of who would go into action first, and that question was about to be answered.

In August 1943, Jack's boat, PT-109 was rammed and sliced in half by a Japanese destroyer and sank almost immediately, bursting into flames and killing two of Jack's men. Jack took control of the situation and urged the surviving crew members to swim to a nearby island, actually dragging one of them in his teeth all the way. The surviving crew members were eventually rescued and suddenly, Jack's heroic exploits were splashed all over the papers in the US and in England.

Joe was proud of his brother's exploits and he was pleased to see him alive and well when he returned home on leave that summer. Jack had done amazingly well to get into active service in the first place, and to have achieved what he did was nothing short of miraculous. But there was a downside, too. Joe Kennedy was bursting with pride over Jack's achievements and the house was filled with visitors and well-wishers, all keen to pat Jack on the back and tell him what a swell, all-American boy he was, and young Joe found that hard to bear. He was the chosen one, he was the one who would be groomed for President; so why all the fuss about Jack? After all, would he not give his all, too when the time came? Joe's father urged him to cast-off his jealousy and to let Jack have his moment, and Joe was forced once more into the background. He would nod and smile as friends congratulated Jack on his heroics but a family friend who was there at the time said he would often hear Joe crying in his bedroom late into the night. His time would come, his father told him, and he would still be President one day; he just had to be patient. But young Joe was not a patient man. Jack was already a decorated war hero, and he had a lot of catching up to do.

Return to England

Joe returned to active service in England with a renewed sense of vigour and determination. He arrived with his squadron in September of 1943, just in time to witness the wettest British autumn on record. The rain was relentless and the field was thick with mud and Joe was billeted in an area they called *Mudville Heights*, a motley collection of draughty old huts set aside for the officers on the base. The enlisted men fared even worse. Here they sat-out the winter, flying anti-submarine patrols in atrocious weather and trekking down to the local pub for some welcome light relief later. Joe was not a big drinker but he usually went along anyway, just to escape the boredom of his daily routine.

But the Royal Oak pub was not the only distraction for Joe. His sister, Kathleen was still in England and she would often visit Joe in the officer's mess at the base. Joe and Kathleen were busy most of the time but whenever they could they would retreat to Crastock Farm, a quiet and secluded place outside of London that they affectionately christened, *Crash-Bang*. It was a place where they could relax with friends and feel free, and they would while away the hours playing cards and listening to music. For just a few short days at a time they could escape the rigours of daily life, away from public gaze under the protective wing of the influential Lady

Astor and it was here that Kathleen would meet her new lover, Billy Cavendish. It was here, too that Joe would meet the new love of his life and as the winter turned to spring, Joe began to see more and more of her. He would call her every day from a call-box on the base, pumping in coins as they chatted for hours at a time. He would see her as often as he possibly could and, as the weeks dragged into months, Joe became ever-more drawn to Pat Wilson.

Joe had had a lot of affairs over the years, some of them quite serious, but when he did finally fall head over heels in love it was not quite what his parents would have expected. Pat Wilson was a beautiful, lively young woman with deep blue eyes and an engaging smile. She lived life to the full and was good for Joe, but they both knew it would not be easy. Pat was an Australian divorcee, twice married and had three children. Her estranged husband was an officer in the British army and was away fighting and Pat and her children were living with friends. Joe would write to his parents every week, but he never told them about Pat. Everyone at the base knew about her and so, of course, did Kathleen but he would never acknowledge her in his letters home. He must have known that his mother would reject her outright and that a twice married divorcee would not fit well into his father's plans for the Presidency, so it is hard to see where Joe thought their relationship could go? Nevertheless, he saw her as often as he could and his close friends at the time said he even spoke of marriage after the war, whatever his parents might think. He did write to Jack just a week before he died telling him that any rumours of marriage were simply untrue and saying, "I am not, repeat not contemplating marriage, nor intending to risk my fine neck in any crazy adventure."

However, given that he was about to embark on one of the most daring and dangerous missions of the war, a mission that would ultimately cost him his life, one might question the sincerity of these remarks.

Joe was by now one of the best pilots in the unit and was respected, if not exactly liked, by his men. He was a strict commander in the air and he did his job well. On one occasion, his plane became lost in a storm and crashed into the sea, forcing Joe and his crew to bail out. He held them all together in the freezing cold water until rescue arrived and eventually they all returned safely to base. Not a bad effort, but it was still a far cry from Jack's heroic deeds in PT109. Jack's exploits were commended in every newspaper in the land and his book, *Why England Slept*, had become a best seller back home (thanks largely to the thousands of copies bought by his father to give out as presents). Young Joe was slipping ever-further behind Jack, and he just had to do something about it.

Joe and his crew had successfully flown the required 35 missions to complete their tour of active duty and, in the face of all adversity and against all the odds, had earned their ticket home. But Joe's ambitions were still not met. He became more and more aggressive and determined and was bitterly disappointed that he had not yet been decorated as Jack had. The weather was improving, the ground was drying out and the long-awaited invasion of Europe was just weeks away. This was not the time to pack up and go home. He was worried that the war might be over before he could get into action and he looked anxiously around for an opportunity; then he saw it. He heard talk on the base that a risky operation was being planned and that they would want good pilots, so he opted to stay on and see what happened.

Meanwhile, on May 6th 1944 Joe gave away his sister, Kathleen, at her controversial marriage to Billy Cavendish. Her parents had been against the marriage from the start and had refused to accept Cavendish into the fold, so Joe was the only family member to attend. Young Joe had always supported Kathleen in her fight for her parents' approval and he must have thought as he looked on at the happy couple that he, too might have such a fight on his hands sometime soon. But that day was still a long way off. There was a war to be won, and he just wanted to get back into it.

The Mission Conceived

On June 12th, 1944 the Germans launched the first of their new terror weapons against Britain. The rocket was fired from a launch site close to the French coast and landed without warning in Grove Road in Hackney, killing six people. The V1 flying bomb was a new kind of weapon. Codenamed "V" for Vengeance, it was a rocket-powered pilotless aircraft that was launched at high speed and guided to its targets by an advanced giro guidance system. It was faster than any British or American fighter and, as such, proved very difficult to shoot down and by the 17th of June 1944, 73 of these new and deadly bombs had already landed on London. Nicknamed the *Doodlebug*, they would roar overhead before the engine cut out, causing the bomb to drop like a stone onto the streets and houses below. Their choice of target was random and indiscriminate and the people of London were, once again, under severe strain. The allies then learned that as well as the V1 and the V2, another rocket-powered missile, the Germans had developed a supergun, christened the V3. This was a gigantic, 25 barrel gun that had the potential to fire shells from Northern France onto targets in London at a rate of up to 600 shells per hour, 24 hours a day. Something had to be done to stop it before it became fully operational.

The supergun launch site was in Mimoyecques in Northern France and was hidden away under massive concrete bunkers, deep in the forest and buried deep under-ground. The allies had been trying for 8 months to destroy the site by conventional bombing but the raids had caused very little damage, so an alternative solution had to be found. For their part, the British called in Barnes Wallace, the inventor of the bouncing bomb of dam-buster fame. He studied the problem and concluded that the only way to break the 6 meters of concrete protecting the gun installations was to destroy their very foundations. He then designed what he called an, "Earthquake Bomb" that could penetrate deep into the earth and explode underground, this destroying the buildings from underneath. The bomb was considered ideal for attacking the V3 sites and a plan was hatched to try it.

Meanwhile, the Americans had come up with a novel solution of their own, and it was this risky project that would claim young Joe's life. The idea was the brainchild of Major General James H Doolittle and both the US Army and the US Navy would be involved in the project. The Army's effort was assigned to the 562nd Bomber Group, whilst that of the Navy fell to the US Navy Special Attack Unit (SAU-1) under the command of James A. Smith. The Army operation was codenamed Aphrodite (after the butterfly, not the Greek goddess) whilst the Navy took the codename Anvil, and the competition between the two would be fierce.

In both cases, the idea was to fill an old bomber up to the gunnels with powerful high explosives and fly it by remote control directly onto the chosen target. This would be the first time that attack drones had been used in this way and the very idea was, at that time, revolutionary. These were both high-profile, high risk operations and the call went out for volunteer pilots to get the drone planes into the air before the remote control could take over once airborne. They were not told that the targets would be the V3 launch sites but they knew this was a very high-profile project and that it would have a significant impact on the course and outcome of the war. It would be a risky and dangerous job, and Joe was the first to sign up.

The plan was to take a number of old, clapped-out B17 bombers, strip them of all unnecessary equipment and pack them to the gunnels with high explosives. They would then install two TV cameras and a radio-controlled piloting mechanism made up of rods and levers attached to the control stick and the pedals. With one camera pointing at the controls and the other looking out ahead, the plane could then be flown by remote control by a controller watching the screens in a follow-up plane and crashed directly onto its target. The only draw-back with this was that they needed a pilot and a co-pilot to get the drone plane off the ground and with a full load of volatile high explosives on board, that would be a very risky and dangerous undertaking. This pilot was expected to get the heavy plane into the air and test the controls before handing over control to the operator in the follow-up plane. He and his co-pilot would then arm the explosives and bail out, leaving the controller to fly the rest of the mission remotely. The concept was trialled off the Florida coast and, having refined the plan, Joe's unit was eventually sent to Dunkeswell in England for further development and training.

The Navy's effort was gathering pace and a bright young engineer named Thomas Martin was called in to design and build the required control and detonation devices. It was also decided that the Navy would change from the B17 to the bigger PB4-Y Liberator as it could carry more explosives and so PB4-Y 32271 (lettered T–11) was assigned to the project and flown to Dunkeswell for fitting. It was at Dunkeswell, too that Joe met the rest of the team for the first time. Commander James Smith and Wilford (Bud) Willy explained the concept to Joe and outlined how it would work then they took him to meet Thomas Martin, who explained all the electronics. Joe was hooked and on July 30th 1944 the unit was transferred to Farsfield in East Anglia, where the real work was about to begin.

Joe had completed his tour of missions and had done another 10 before he volunteered for Anvil. He had lost a good many friends in the squadron and had come close to death himself but he had still not been decorated as Jack had, and that bothered him a great deal. He had volunteered for Navy flying as he thought it the least dangerous option but once Jack had begun to have success in the Indian Ocean, he knew he would have to stick his neck out to catch up. When he arrived at Farsfield in July 1944, Joe was a very different man from the one who had signed-up just a few years before. The war had aged him and he had become far more serious and thoughtful. He was sullen and broody and his quiet demeanour was often taken for arrogance and snobbery. But it was none of that. Joe was a man on a mission in more ways than one, and he was determined to see it through.

He began to see more of Pat Wilson, too. She was staying with Lady Virginia Sykes, an old friend of Kathleen's and he would visit her there at every available opportunity. His friends thought he might be planning to marry her but he denied this in letters to his family, who were expecting him home any day. Joe Kennedy thought his son would be coming home to Hyannis Port following his extended tour of duty but in August he received a letter from young Joe telling him he had volunteered to stay on for one more mission. He wrote back saying, "I can quite understand how you feel about staying, but don't push your luck too much."

By early August, the plane had been stripped of all unwanted equipment and the engineers were busy installing the TV cameras and control mechanisms. TV was still a very new technology in those days and, having seen only a very small version at a trade fare, Joe was fascinated by it. He wanted to know everything about how the whole thing worked. It was not enough to be just the pilot, he wanted to know about the TV system, the remote controls, the explosive charges and the detonation method. He took a trip in a PV-1 Ventura that was to act as the mother-ship and squeezed into the controller's seat behind the pilot, watching the small TV screen, just as his controller would on the day. Joe wanted to see and experience every part of the mission and he was flushed with excitement at the prospect. He watched closely as the plane was modified and all the electronics installed and, as had been his wish all along, he began to pick his own crew.

On August 2nd the Liberator was test-flown under full load (25,000lbs of sandbags) and the radio control gear and remote flying mechanisms all check-out OK, although the aircraft was found to be very sluggish and difficult to get airborne. This exercise was repeated several times over the next few days as Joe familiarised himself with the controls and rehearsed his role. Pressure continued to grow as the Navy battled to beat the Army in being the first to launch a successful mission, but it was the Army that would win the race. On August 4th they took four Army B-17s (nicknamed "Snowbirds" as they were painted white for better visibility) and crammed them with high explosives before launching them at targets in France. The Army were confident of success as their remote control and detonating systems were much simpler than those used by the Navy, but all four aircraft were lost before reaching the target, killing four crew members. On returning to base, one of the surviving crew members turned to Joe and said.

"You know, if my old man was the Ambassador, I would get myself transferred out of this outfit."

Joe just smiled back at him, but he was beginning to have his doubts.

By now Joe's plane was almost ready, but there were still some serious concerns. Joe had been very involved at every stage of the build and had requested various modifications to the flight controls and TV equipment, but it was the arming device that troubled him the most. The Army had been using a simple mechanical trigger device, but the Navy had opted for a more complex electronic system activated by a radio signal from the mother plane, and this was proving troublesome. It was unstable and unreliable and during tests in the US and again in England it had sometimes gone off accidentally. Something clearly had to be done and Wilford Willy came up with a simple fix that he was sure would solve the problem. He devised a simple safety pin that had to be withdrawn from its socket manually (by pulling a string) before the system could be fully armed. This way, the arming device could not move and so the detonators could not possibly go off until the pilot and his assistant pulled the pin prior to bailing out. Joe was not entirely happy with the device, but he accepted this solution and agreed to use it. As it turned out, this fix may well have been the cause of the premature explosion that would kill him and his co-pilot in a few days' time.

Mission Day

Farsfield, East Anglia, Saturday August 12th 1944. The plan had been to fly the day before but fog had delayed the mission 24 hours so, weather permitting, they would go today. The sun rises early in England in the summertime and as it rose today, its golden glow twinkled through the heavy morning dew-drops on the Perspex of the aircraft cockpit. The plane had been loaded with 374 cases of Torpex high explosives and the detonators had been installed and as it stood silent in the morning mist, its bulging tyres sinking deep into the wet grass, Joe lay on his bunk a short distance away and thought hard about the task ahead. He got up and looked out of the window and saw clear skies at last, and he knew this would be it. This was the day he had been waiting for; the day he would show the world, and his father, just what he could do to help win this war. He knelt down beside his bed and prayed, asking God to bless his mission and to bring him safely back home, then he went out to check his aircraft once again.

Joe was unusually irritable and on edge as he emerged from his hut and he seemed thoughtful and deeply troubled. The day before, his electronics officer, Earl Olsen had told him there had been some problem with the electronics on the plane and that he was concerned. He had advised Joe to postpone the flight until repairs could be made and witnesses later said that Olsen left Joe in no doubt that to ignore the problem and fly anyway would almost certainly end in disaster. The final decision on whether to go ahead rested squarely with the pilot and Joe wanted no more delays; they would go regardless. To make matters worse, they were having trouble with one of the aircraft's four Pratt and Whitney engines and the mechanics had pointed this out to Joe, too. The magnetos on number 3 engine were playing up again but still, Joe insisted on going ahead with the mission.

In the early afternoon, Joe began to prepare for the flight that was to take place later that day. Some said he seemed gloomy and depressed and not at all optimistic about the prospects for success. He had handed out some of his personnel possessions to friends in the event of his not returning, but that was not unusual for pilots going out on combat missions. He wrote a last letter to his father then called close friend, Lorrelle Hurst and asked him to give his father a message.

"I'm about to go into my act," he said. "If I don't come back, tell my dad that, despite our difficulties, I love him very much."

At 2pm it was announced that the mission was definitely on and Joe's mood changed dramatically. He became happier and upbeat and he went back to the plane for one last check. The engines had been run and number 3 engine was now performing well and all systems checked out OK.

"This is it," he said, flashing his famous Joe Kennedy smile. "We're going to get a 48 hour pass after this."

Joe had arranged to go to *Crash-Bang* the following day to see Pat Wilson and late in the afternoon, he called her for what would be the last time.

Joe's co-pilot for the mission was supposed to have been Ensign Simpson but his electronics engineer, Wilford Willy pulled rank on Simpson and insisted on going himself. Willy was a qualified pilot and as he had built much of the aircraft's electronics, he wanted to fly the mission with Joe. At 3pm Joe and Willy went over to the Op's room to be briefed on the mission and to find out, at last, what the target would be. It had been thought that the target would be one of the known V1 launch sites but at the meeting Joe learned it would be the V3 Supergun battery at Mimoyecques, 5 miles from the French coast. He was told how conventional bombing had proved ineffective and that the flying drone would be an ideal weapon for such a target and Joe was delighted at the prospect. What he was not told was that the RAF had attacked the site with Barnes Wallace's Earthquake Bombs just a few days before, and the damage was still being assessed.

Joe took his seat in the crowded briefing room as, through a haze of cigarette smoke, Commander Smith outlined the plan in detail. The objective would be to get Joe's plane into the air and guide it onto its target in France, but there would be an armada of other aircraft involved. As well as the drone aircraft (Joe's Liberator) there would be two mother planes, two navigation planes, a film crew aircraft, fifteen fighter escorts and a few observers. The mother ships would be flown by rookies, Rosy Lyon and Harry Wherry and would control the drone once Joe and Willy had bailed out. There would be a B-17 navigation plane to guide them over the Channel and another one to scout the target, all closely watched by Col. Elliot Roosevelt (the son of the US President) who would fly alongside in a Mosquito to film the bail-out. Joe's commander would follow in a P-51 Mustang, as would station commander, Col. Roy Forrest and the whole operation would be supported by fifteen P-51 Mustang fighters.

The plan was simple. All of the support aircraft would take off before the drone and once Joe had got this off the ground and up to 2,000 feet, he would turn north to test the controls and equipment. If all this checked out OK, he would turn south towards the coast and, giving the code signal, "Spade Flush," he would arm the explosives and hand over control to the mother plane. He and Willy would then bail out near the south coast, leaving the mother plane to guide the drone onto its target in France. The whole flight would take less than an hour and only 15 minutes of that would be over enemy territory. Estimated time for impact on target was 7pm.

Joe bounded out of the briefing room and looked over at the behemoth that awaited him near the runway. Gone was the brooding, spoilt brat that some of his comrades sometimes saw in him and gone, too was the man with the messiest room on the base. Joe was sloppy and untidy when not on duty but once in the air, he was a meticulous and professional pilot. He flew every mission by the book and always gave his best, and he would expect nothing less from his men. The aircraft were fuelled-up and ready to go, and so too was Joe.

At 5.30pm everyone from cooks and clerks to officers and mechanics all gathered on the grass to watch the show. The base echoed to the sound of aircraft engines coughing into action and the air was filled with the familiar smell of burning fuel. Joe gathered his things and headed out to the jeep that would take him out to his aircraft.

"Good luck," said Jimmy Simpson as he shook Joe by the hand. "I wish I was going with you."

"Don't worry," said Joe, smiling back. "You'll make the next one."

Joe and Willy then took the short Jeep ride to the plane and, taking one last look back and waving to friends, they climbed aboard and Joe strapped himself into the worn leather seat to begin his pre-flight checks. Joe's mechanics had told him that they were still less than happy with No3 engine, but Joe was convinced it would be OK. He switched on the magnetos and fired up the engines in a 3, 4, 2, 1 sequence and with a cough and a splutter, all four Pratt and Whitneys burst effortlessly into life.

The two Ventura mother-planes took off first and circled the base to check communications with the drone plane, then the rest of the armada got airborne. As the fighters climbed to 8,000 feet and the other aircraft formed up below them, Joe revved up his engines and slowly guided the lumbering bomber to the end of the runway. He cranked up the engines to full throttle and was about to release the brake when he saw his mechanic, Red Bradfield, signalling to him from the side of the runway. Joe eased back the throttles and motioned him over to the cockpit. He was still concerned about No3 engine and said it just didn't sound right, but Joe told him not to worry and sent him on his way. He revved up the engines again and ran them on full power for 7 minutes before finally releasing the brake to move off.

The plane moved sluggishly forward, slowly gaining speed as the four powerful engines forced the heavy bomber on and as it gradually picked up speed, Joe saw the end of the runway looming ever-closer. It would be a close-run thing and Joe was beginning to wonder whether he would clear the trees but it was already too late, he was committed and there could be no turning back. The plane lunged forward, slowly gaining more speed until, at the last possible moment, the cumbersome flying bomb finally took to the air. Joe continued to rev the engines on full power and grappled desperately with the controls to gain some height. He just cleared the trees on the edge of the airfield and he breathed a sigh of relief as the aircraft slowly gained altitude and soared safely over the green fields below. He climbed to the cruising altitude and flew north for 18 minutes before radioing to the mother plane to take over on remote for a while to test the equipment. All checked out OK, so the operator handed control back to Joe.

Joe flew the aircraft up to Framlingham and then on to Beccles, somewhat further north than had been planned and they were now 12 miles off course. But all systems appeared to be working well so Joe radioed, "Spade Flush," the code-word for the mother plane to take full control. One mile south of the river Blythe on the edge of the Westwood Marshes, the accompanying aircraft could clearly see Joe in the pilot's seat and Willy in the nose. All seemed normal and there was no cause for concern so at 6.20pm, the controller initiated a gentle turn to the left to guide the aircraft back towards the coast and on towards France. It was time for Joe and Willy to prime the detonators and bail out.

Suddenly and without warning, there was a massive explosion. Joe's plane was engulfed in a huge ball of fire as 12 tons of Torpex high explosives ignited over the peaceful English countryside. The support planes were rocked by the force of the blast as their pilots struggled with the controls to keep them airborne. Roosevelt's Mosquito banked away as it flew through the debris, breaking its windows and damaging the airframe. John Demlin in the number 2 mother plane said he saw two huge orange columns, one heading skyward and the other, down. Roosevelt's plane tipped almost onto its back and he later said that it was the biggest explosion he had ever seen until the pictures of the Atom Bomb the following year.

Miss Ada Weitgate lived in a cottage nearby and she was out chatting to a neighbour when the explosion happened. She said she saw a bright flash and heard a terrific "crack" as her windows were blown out and her ceiling fell in. Wreckage was scattered for miles and one man, Dick Collit, found a bomb-bay door on his land a mile away a full 6 months after the event. He took it home and kept it as a souvenir. We also have accounts of other wreckage falling in the area. A local landlord said that three engines fell close to his pub and another by a water tower nearby. This one apparently lay there for years.

Local resident, Mick Muttitt remembers the explosion and gave the following account to the Suffolk Coast, "Open Skies Open Minds" website.
"I watched in horror as the lead aircraft exploded in a huge fireball. I vividly remember seeing burning wreckage falling earthwards while engines with propellers still turning, and leaving comet-like trails of smoke, continued along the direction of the flight before plummeting down. A Ventura broke high to starboard and a Lightening spun away to port, eventually to regain control at tree-top height over Blythburgh Hospital. While I watched spellbound, a terrific explosion reached Dresser's Cottage in the form of a loud double thunderclap. Then all was quiet, except for the drone

of the circling Venturas' engines as they remained for a few more minutes in the vicinity. The fireball changed to an enormous black pall of smoke resembling a huge octopus, the tentacles below indicating the earthward path of burning fragments."

Joe and Willy were dead and no bodies were ever found, which is hardly surprising. Commander Smith stated that there was no point in searching because nothing bigger than a button could be found and the focus now was on what might have gone wrong. On landing back at the base, Smith gathered his men together and, looking down at the floor, he said.

"This accident was very unfortunate. In Mr Kennedy and Mr Willy we have lost two valiant gentlemen. But we are not going to give up."

With that, he walked slowly into his office and closed the door behind him. He was not seen again for the rest of the day.

The mission had been shrouded in secrecy and remained so for many years to come. Some of the records remained classified until 1994 and even then, it was thought that not everything had been released. Operation Anvil did fly more missions but with little success and the project was scrapped by the end of the year. The real irony in Joe's case, and one reason why it may have remained a secret, was that it all seemed rather pointless anyway. It later emerged that the target had been bombed by the RAF just days before but the US Navy were never told. This raid had been a total success and if Joe's plane had reached its target, it would have landed on an already destroyed installation.

The cause of the explosion was not known and could not be fully explained. Any rogue signal from any of the accompanying aircraft, or even from the ground, could have activated the detonators and this was considered to be a strong possibility at the time. Torpex is a volatile explosive and, although more powerful than TNT, it is also less stable. One theory suggested that a lack of electrical shielding caused electromagnetic emissions to open up a relay solenoid that should have been closed. When the solenoid opened it set off one of the MK9 detonators which, in turn, set off the load of Torpex. However, British engineer, Hugh Hunt recently acquired the original circuit diagram for the control panel and on reconstructing the device, he discovered an obvious flaw in its design.

The safety pin did its job in preventing the arming mechanism from moving prematurely but in doing so, it sent a constant live current to the solenoids. These solenoids then overheated and on reaching a certain temperature, they failed. They then activated the detonators which, in turn, set off the explosives. The tragic irony was that the pin that was supposed to prevent the explosives from going off too soon, was probably the very reason that they did.

Aftermath

The day after the explosion, Pat Wilson waited for a visitor that would never come. She was staying with her children at Lady Sykes' house when she heard the news that Joe had been killed and she was still reeling from the shock when, just 2 days later, she heard that her own husband, now estranged, had been killed in action in Italy. Dee Vilan delivered Joe's personal effects to his friends at *Mudville Heights* and they, in turn, sent them on to the family.

Meanwhile, back in Boston, Rose Kennedy and the younger children were at home when Father O'Leary and another chaplain came to the door and asked for Joe senior. He had retired for a nap and Rose asked them to wait but when they told her that Joe had been killed, she went upstairs to tell him herself. "Be brave," she whispered as she told him the news, then she left him alone. He stayed in his room all day listening to sombre music while Jack, Ted and the others thought up their own way of dealing with their grief.

"Joe wouldn't want us to sit and mope," said Jack. "He would want us to go sailing and be happy," which was exactly what they did.

Joe Kennedy senior had made the ultimate sacrifice, and he was shattered by it. He never recovered from the loss of young Joe and he would brood on it for the rest of his life. He would often sit alone on the porch at Hyannis Port, looking out over the sea, crying, until he eventually fell asleep. Not only had he given his eldest and dearest son in the service of his country, he had lost his dream of making him President. This honour, or burden, would now fall on Jack. Jack never really wanted a career in politics and had a passion to become a writer, but his father called him into his study one day and told him straight.

"You know my father," Jack later told a reporter, "It was like being drafted. My father wanted his eldest son in politics. Wanted is not really the right word; he demanded it."

Joe Kennedy and the family slowly began to come to terms with their loss. Joe set up a trust for the family of Wilford Willy and he financed Mrs Willy's two sons through college. Jack wrote a book entitled, *As We Remember Joe,* but Joe senior could never bring himself to even look at it. The book is now very rare as only 500 copies were ever printed and these were given as presents to family and close friends.

Joe was remembered by the Navy, too. He was posthumously awarded the Air Medal and the Navy Cross for heroism and in 1946, US Navy destroyer 850 was launched and named the *USS Joseph P Kennedy Jr* in his honour. Young Joe's remains were never recovered but his name is inscribed in the *Tablets of the Missing* in the American Cemetery in Cambridge, England and he has a memorial marker in section 45 of the Arlington National Cemetery. Joe and Rose Kennedy also founded the Joseph P Kennedy Jr Foundation in remembrance, an organisation aimed at helping those with mental impairment disabilities, no doubt, with Rosemary in mind too.

After the war, Kathleen found herself back in London. She had moved into a house in Smith Square and was dating Peter Fitzwilliam when her home was broken into. Among the items stolen was a gold set of Navy Flier's wings that Joe had given her and this was her most treasured possession. She campaigned to get it back, even offering a substantial reward, but to no avail. It may be languishing unnoticed and ignored in a drawer somewhere to this day, the new owner having no idea what it is.

But it was time to move on. Jack would step into Joe's shoes and the rest of the family would resume their own lives and respective roles. They had suffered a shattering blow with the loss of Joe, as had millions of other families the world over, but Joe senior must have thought the worst was behind them. Kathleen, too, was moving on and was ready to marry again following the death of Billy Cavendish.

"Luckily, I'm a Kennedy," Kathleen told Lem Billings. "I have a very strong feeling that makes a big difference about how to take things. I saw Daddy and Mother about Joe and I know that we've all got the ability to not get down. There are lots of years ahead and lots of happiness left in the world though sometimes nowadays, that's hard to believe."

If only she knew!

5 KATHLEEN (KICK)

Kathleen was the fourth of Joe and Rose Kennedy's children and in her, they got more than they had bargained for. Affectionately known as Kick, Kathleen was a lively, energetic young girl who would grow up to be a strong and independent woman and her actions later in life would have a profound effect on the entire family. Born on 20th February 1920, Kick was the second of the Kennedy daughters, but she would eventually take the senior role due to Rosemary's mental impairment. Kick was always Joe Kennedy's favourite and she was the only one of his daughters allowed to argue her point at the dinner table. Described as pretty rather than beautiful, she was considered by many to be the nicest of the Kennedy children and her engaging charm and sheer force of personality would be both a blessing and a curse in the years ahead.

Joe and Rose Kennedy's children were a mixed bag intellectually, but Kick was certainly one of the brightest. The family custom was for Joe to manage the education of the boys while Rose took care of the girls' and for this reason, the girls were all educated by nuns. Kick performed well at school and attended the Noroton Convent of the Sacred Heart before spending a year at the Holy Child Convent in Neuilly, just outside Paris. In Rose Kennedy's eyes, nothing mattered more than her Catholic faith and she instilled this firmly in her children. Their whole lives revolved around the church and Catholic ritual and this had a huge effect on them all, especially Bobby and Kick. They were always the most pious and devout of the Kennedy children and in those happy, care-free days no-one would ever have believed that Kick would one day forsake her strong religious conviction for love.

In her teenage years Kick loved to mix with girls her own age and to buy all the latest swing records. She wore fashionable clothes and was meticulous about her appearance and she soon caught the attention of the boys. Kick had a number of casual relationships around this time but she eventually settled on Peter Grace, the son of a wealthy shipping merchant and one of the country's most eligible bachelors. The two became very close and there was even talk of an engagement, but that was never going to be. Joseph Kennedy had been appointed US Ambassador to Great Britain and Kick was about to begin a love affair with England and the English that would last the rest of her life.

The Kennedys were already minor celebrities by the time they arrived in London and the people of Britain just could not wait to meet them. The minute they landed, they were mobbed by reporters and newsmen wanting to know everything there was to know about them, and this was especially so of Kick. The press affectionately dubbed her KK and they followed her every move. They reported everything she did and what she wore whilst doing it and she became, in many ways, the Princess Diana of her day.

Joe Kennedy's appointment to the Court of St James offered the family an ideal opportunity to mix with the real upper crust in a society obsessed with class and status. The English social calendar was centred on what was known as "The Season" and that started in the spring, just as the Kennedys had arrived. There would be the Derby and Royal Ascot and exciting hunts on horseback over the rolling hills of the lush English countryside; and Kick just couldn't wait to take part.

Kick immersed herself wholeheartedly into the social scene in London and she was invited to just about every party in town. She was popular and well-liked and she made a lot of new friends and in July, she met the man who was to completely change her life. Billy Cavendish, Marquis of Hartington and heir to the Devonshire fortune, was the most eligible bachelor in England and was even rumoured to have been a possible match for the young Princess Elizabeth. He was handsome and charming with a quiet, unassuming disposition and Kick was attracted to him from the start. She had planned to spend some time with Peter Grace, who had sailed over to England to see her but when he arrived, he was told that Kick was at the races with Cavendish and she was not even there to meet him. Knowing Kick as he did and seeing the writing on the wall, Grace immediately took the next boat back to the States.

Kick had first met Billy Cavendish at a garden party in the spring and by early summer they were already an item. Cavendish was as quiet and reserved as Kick was vivacious and outgoing and the two extremes in temperament seemed to complement one another perfectly. But at the end of the day, she was a devout Catholic and he a staunch Protestant and a match between the two of them was an unsavoury prospect for both families. The Duke and Duchess of Devonshire expected their son to marry into the English aristocracy and to the Kennedys, the thought of their daughter marrying a non-Catholic was unthinkable. It was not going to be easy, but Kick and Billy Cavendish were already in love and their course was firmly set.

Kick's War

By the summer of 1939, the social scene in London was feeling the strain as war in Europe loomed ever-closer. Joe

Kennedy's isolationist views had caused bad feeling among Kick's aristocratic friends, but Kick was firmly on their side and she openly opposed her father on the matter. Billy Cavendish was commissioned into the Coldstream Guards and Kick knew that one day soon he may be going off to war, but she felt it was right for Britain to make a stand against Hitler and she supported his decision to enlist. On September 1st Hitler's forces invaded Poland and on the 3rd of September Kick, along with young Joe and Jack, watched from the public gallery of the House of Commons as Prime Minister Chamberlain declared war on Germany. The people of Britain braced themselves for what was to come and Kick wanted desperately to stay and support her new friends in their hour of need, but her father refused to allow it. He knew that London would soon be bombed and he was convinced that Britain would be overrun by the Germans, so he shipped his family back home. Only he and Rosemary stayed behind.

Once back in the United States, Kick resumed her education but it was clear to everyone that her time in London had changed her. She tried hard to adapt but she longed to be back in England, especially when she learned that Billy Cavendish had been sent to the front in France. She just had to do something, so she took a job working for Frank Waldrop on the Washington Post newspaper. Kick was quick to learn her new trade and went on to run the paper's *Did You Happen to See?* Column with great success. She was a good reporter and was popular with the readers and she did all she could to drum up US support for her beleaguered friends in war-torn London.

It was during her time on the Washington Post that Kick met gritty, hard-nosed reporter, John White and they became close friends. White found Kick insufferable and the two of them argued all the time, but their friendship soon turned into love. But they were two very different people from very diverse backgrounds and they both knew that it could never work. And besides, Kick still loved Billy Cavendish, and they both knew that, too. Kick and White enjoyed a brief, stormy relationship but in the spring of 1942, White joined the Marines and they just drifted apart. Kick stayed on for a time at the Washington Post but she could think of nothing but her friends in London and she longed for a chance to go back.

That chance came when in the spring of 1944, Kick learned that the Red Cross were looking for volunteers to work in England and she immediately put her name forward. Red Cross volunteers could be sent anywhere in the UK but Joe Kennedy pulled strings to get Kick posted to London, where she was assigned to an officers-only club in Hans Crescent, Knightsbridge. On 25th June Kick boarded the *Queen Mary*, bound once more for England and she told none of her friends she was coming. They all welcomed her back with open arms and within days, Kick and Billy Cavendish were together again.

This was a very different London from the one Kick had known before, with blackouts and rationing and the streets were filled with the rubble of bombed-out buildings. But it was still the place Kick loved the most and she was still the darling of the English press. She was photographed by the Daily Mail, cheerfully riding her bicycle through the rubble of the bomb-damaged streets and the picture was splashed all over the papers on both sides of the Atlantic. Kick and her bike became a familiar site on the streets of London and people would wave as she rode by, smiling and waving back at them.

Kick returned home to spend Christmas with the family but was back in London with her friends after the holiday. Joe Junior was in England at this time and he and Kick became very close. They talked frequently on the phone and saw each other almost every weekend at the cottage they called, *Crash-Bang*. It was a place where she could meet with friends and wind down, away from the strains of war-torn London and away from the prying eyes of the press.

Marriage

With the Allied invasion of Europe growing ever-closer, Kick and Billy Cavendish were talking more of marriage, but it was never going to be easy. Kick genuinely believed that she would be damned to hell if she married a non-Catholic and she desperately feared for her soul. Her father begged her not to go through with the marriage and her mother, Rose made it quite clear that if she did, she would be cut off and disowned by the family. She would lose her stake in the family fortune and she would never see her siblings again, and Kick was forced into making a choice. She was mortified at the prospect of forsaking her religion and of upsetting her parents so badly, but she was in love, so she chose to follow her heart. Rose remained defiant, but her father eventually softened and sent Kick a telegram saying.
"With your faith in God you can't make a mistake. Remember, you are still, and always will be, tops with me."

On Saturday, May 6th Kick and Billy were married in a civil ceremony at the Chelsea Registry Office in London. Kick wore a pale pink dress and a hat with blue and pink ostrich feathers and Billy wore his Coldstream Guards uniform. The

Duke and Duchess of Devonshire were there to wish them well, but young Joe was the only one of Kick's family to attend. The reception was held at a town house in Eaton Square before the happy couple boarded a train to Eastbourne for their honeymoon. Kick had finally got what she had wanted all along and she was proud to have had young Joe give her away. They had both chosen non-Catholic partners and they both knew that if Joe were to even think of marrying Pat Wilson, he would face the wrath of the family, just as Kick had over marrying Billy. It was a daunting prospect.

Kick was now an army wife and on returning from Eastbourne, the couple took rooms at the Swan Hotel in Alton. But their happiness would be short-lived. On 6th June 1944, the Allies invaded Normandy and within weeks of their wedding, Billy Cavendish was posted to the front. The separation was hard and Kick moved in with Billy's parents to help ease the pain of being apart. Billy was on the front line in Belgium and was close to the fighting and Kick prayed every day for his safe return. Like many army wives, she dreaded that awful knock on the door but when it finally did come, it was not quite what she had expected. On August 13th Kick received the shattering news that her dear brother, Joe had been killed whilst flying a secret mission. The family were of course devastated by this shocking news and despite the rift between them, Kick flew home to Hyannis Port to be with them. They had all suffered the most grievous loss and Kick could think of only one thing worse; and she prayed that would never happen.

Billy Cavendish was a good commander, well-liked by his men and within a few weeks of his posting he had been promoted to the rank of Major. On September 8th his battalion set out in the pouring rain to attack the village of Beverlo in Belgium and after a short but bitter struggle, the German garrison there surrendered. By the following day the rain had stopped and Cavendish stepped out from his tent to survey the ground in preparation for his next assault. The area was still swarming with Germans and, against the advice of fellow-officers, Cavendish wore a light coloured raincoat which made him an easy and conspicuous target against the dark greens and browns of the wood. He stood up and adjusted his belt and was about to walk over to the command tent when a German sniper picked him out in his sights and shot him straight through the heart, killing him instantly.

Kick was shopping in New York when she heard that her husband had been killed and the news shocked her to the core. She felt bitter and cheated and was, of course, completely heartbroken but she unselfishly rushed back to England to be with Billy's mother and father in their hour of need. The Duke and Duchess had always been kind to Kick and she wanted to support and comfort them in any way she could. She also felt that to be close to them was to be close to her dear Billy, and that somehow made her feel better. Kick had lost her brother and her husband in just a few short weeks and she must have wondered whether God was, indeed punishing her in some way for turning her back on her Catholic faith. Billy's body was buried where he fell and a memorial service was held at the little church in Edensor, close to Chatsworth House. Kick's world had fallen apart. She had lost the love of her life almost as quickly as she had found him and she could see no way forward for her now.

In May 1945, Kick celebrated the end of the war in Europe along with everyone else in London, but to her it was a hollow victory. In a letter to Frank Waldrop she wrote, "I'm glad and thankful but I don't think anyone here feels all that joyful, do you?"

Kick spent the summer in London with Jack and a few close friends but following VJ Day in August, she resigned from the Red Cross and returned to the United States. She was desperate to get back to a normal life with her family, but she soon realised that would be quite impossible. Everything had changed and she was no longer the Kick they had all known and loved. She had grown into a strong and independent woman and she refused to be ruled by her father in the way that she had before. Despite the pain of her loss and the need for family comfort she still hankered to be back in England, so she returned to London and took up residence in a town house she had bought in Smith Square.

London was slowly recovering from the austerity of six years of war and was beginning to come alive and to breathe again. Food and clothing were still rationed and life's luxuries were hard to find, but it was still swinging London, and Kick still loved every brick of it. Many of her old friends were now gone but some, like Virginia Sykes and Pat Wilson still remained. Kick was slowly emerging from the agony of her grief and was learning to live life to the full again. Then along came Peter Fitzwilliam.

Peter Fitzwilliam was the son of the 7th Earl of Fitzwilliam and was a well-known British aristocrat and war hero. He was handsome and charming but he was also reputed to be an irresponsible womaniser with a passion for horses and gambling. He could not have been more different from the quiet, unassuming Billy Cavendish and that may well have been the attraction for Kick. Either way, the two soon fell deeply in love and Fitzwilliam, who was already separated from his first wife, agreed to marry Kick once his divorce came through.

It was all happening again and Kick knew that her parents would be horrified when she told them about Fitzwilliam. An English Protestant and a divorcee to boot, she knew this was going to be a hard sell. But her mind was made up, so she returned home to face the music. Kick flitted between Palm Springs and Washington, seeking support from wherever she could as she prepared herself for the big moment and when that moment finally came, it was just as she had expected. Kick knew that her mother's opposition would be stronger than her father's but she had no idea just to what extent. Joe objected to the match but Kick's mother, Rose was positively seething. She again swore that she would cut Kick off from the family completely if she married Fitzwilliam but this time she put pressure on Joe, too. Rose insisted that Joe support her wholeheartedly in opposing the match and threatened to leave him if he refused. She even went so far as to say that if she did not get his full and complete support on the matter she would reveal things about him that only she knew, and that would ruin his name and reputation.

Kick was shocked by the severity of her mother's scathing response and she knew there was no point in staying any longer. Jack and Eunice had done all they could to help smooth the waters but it was clear that Rose would not budge. Distressed and distraught at the prospect of losing her family again, Kick felt compelled to follow her heart and to return to her friends in England. They were the only people who really knew and understood her and she was only ever really happy when she was with them. At a farewell dinner with some old friends in Washington Frank

Waldrop, who was sitting next to Kick, asked her when she would be coming back to see them again.

"Frank," she replied, "I am never coming home."

Within weeks of Kick's return to London, her mother visited her at her house in Smith Square. She was alone and had not told Kick she was coming and the sole purpose of her visit was to try one last time to dissuade her from marrying Fitzwilliam. They argued and the scene turned ugly as Rose told Kick she would be damned if she went ahead with the marriage and Kick tried to make Rose see that she had no choice. Kick had always respected her mother a great deal and the thought of upsetting her broke her heart. She wanted desperately to heal the rift between them, but they parted on bad terms and they would never see one another again. Kick's maid, Ilona Solymossy, who was present at the time, said she found Rose Kennedy cold and detached. She said that in all her life she had never seen an adult cower before a parent the way Kathleen had done with her mother that day. "It was just awful to watch," she said.

Kick's only hope now was her father. He had been sympathetic and supportive of her conviction to marry Billy Cavendish and she very much hoped that she could talk him around again. She felt sure that if only he would agree to meet with Fitzwilliam, he would see why she loved him so much and that he was the one man on earth who could make her happy again. Kick and Fitzwilliam were planning a trip to Cannes and Kick learned that her father would be in Paris that same weekend. It would be a perfect opportunity to get her father and Fitzwilliam together, away from the family and from the prying eyes of the press. She approached her father with the suggestion and was delighted when he agreed. They would meet for lunch at the Paris Ritz on Saturday, May 15th.

Kick and Fitzwilliam left London for Cannes on Thursday, May 12th. Kick was excited and happy to be going on her first trip away with her new lover and at the prospect of the meeting with her father. They would fly to Cannes that morning, stopping briefly in Paris on the way, then on the Saturday they would make the short hop back to Paris for the meeting with her father. Kick was nothing if not an optimist and she was sure that everything would be alright in the end. They were due to fly from Croydon at 10.30 that morning but they were already running late.

"Shall I cross my fingers?" shouted Ilona as Kick hurried out of the door with Fitzwilliam.

"Yes," replied Kick smiling, "both hands."

The happy couple took a taxi to Croydon where the privately chartered De-Havilland Dove, piloted by former RAF pilot, Peter Townshend was waiting for them. There had been reports of bad weather over southern France but Townshend thought he could avoid it if they left right away. He was not happy at being already behind schedule but if there were no more delays, he was confident they would be alright. The passengers boarded the plane and they finally took off, heading for their short stop-over in Paris.

On arriving in Paris, Fitzwilliam informed Townshend that they had arranged to meet up briefly with some friends in town but that they would be back in less than an hour. The stop had been built into the flight plan so Townshend saw no cause for concern but when they failed to show up on time, Townshend became anxious. He had been getting regular updates on the worsening weather and it did not look good. There were storms forecast over the Rhone Valley at exactly the time they would be flying through there and he had already changed his flight plan four times due to their lateness. When they finally did arrive, with their Parisian friends in tow, Townshend was livid. He told them that their delay had put them all at risk and, having told them of the storm brewing directly in their path, he refused to continue the journey.

There followed a bitter argument between Townshend and Fitzwilliam as Kick and the others stood by and watched. Townshend was a skilled and experienced pilot and he insisted on playing it safe. The tower had advised them not to fly and all commercial traffic had been grounded, but Fitzwilliam just would not listen. He relentlessly badgered Townshend into submission and he eventually agreed to go on. They boarded the plane and with great trepidation, Townshend started his engines and taxied out onto the runway and by 3.20pm they were airborne.

At 4.50pm co-pilot, Arthur Freeman radioed in for a weather report and was told that the storm was expected to hit Cannes around 6.30pm, their expected landing time, but they requested no further updates after that. They lost contact with the tower as the bad weather closed in and, seeing the murky squall ahead, Townshend tried to climb to avoid it. The little plane was battered by strong winds and driving rain and as the pilot struggled to maintain control, he became disoriented and confused. It was hard to tell up from down and as Townshend tried to make some sense of what his instruments were telling him, the plane went into a dive. Townshend grappled with the controls and tried to pull up out of the dive but he lost control and as it finally submitted to the force of the wind, the aircraft began to break up. They lost one of the wings, then the other and what was left of the stricken machine plummeted down into the side of a mountain. All of the occupants were alive and conscious the whole time and they must have known they were going to die. Local farmer, Paul Petit heard the noise and saw the plane come down and he was able to quickly lead the rescue teams to the scene of the crash. There were no survivors.

Joe Kennedy was informed of Kick's death whilst staying at the Ritz in Paris and he travelled down to Privas to identify Kick's body. He called the family to confirm what they already knew to be true but he spared them the anguish of knowing the extent of Kick's injuries, saying she looked calm and peaceful, as if in sleep. Jack, who had been the closest to Kick, was at home with Billy Sutton listening to a recording of Ella Logan singing, *How Are Things in Glocca Morra?* when his father called him to confirm the news that Kick had died. "She has such a sweet voice," Jack said. Then he turned away and cried.

On May 20th 1948, Catholics and Protestants alike gathered for the funeral of Kathleen Kennedy. As the unmarried widow of Billy Cavendish the Duke and Duchess of Devonshire requested she be buried as a Devonshire family member and, to their surprise, Joe Kennedy agreed. He knew that when all was said and done, that was just what Kick would have wanted and that was good enough for him. He had only ever wanted for her to be happy and it was the least he could do for her now. So, with her father's blessing, Kick was buried in the small graveyard behind the little church in Edensor, close to Chatsworth House; she was just 28 years old. Her father, Joe was the only member of the Kennedy family to attend.

Kathleen quickly faded from memory and within a short time of her death her name was hardly ever mentioned in the Kennedy household. Bobby later named his eldest daughter, Kathleen Hartington but he insisted that she never be called Kick. But Kick would never really be forgotten by those who knew and loved her the most and her presence is still felt to this day in the Cavendish family home at Chatsworth. There is a stone marking her grave at Edensor and in the summer of 1963, the now President John F Kennedy visited the site to remember the sister he once loved and still missed so much.

6 JACK (JFK)

At the end of the Second World War, Joseph Kennedy once again turned his attention to the acquisition of power for the family. The loss of Joe Junior had hit him very hard but he was as determined as ever that a Kennedy would one day sit in the Whitehouse, so he now set his sights on Jack. Jack had not expected this, of course and he had no real political ambitions of his own at that time. He had always been interested in world affairs and political history but he had no desire to enter a career in politics and his father even wondered whether his weak constitution could bear it. Jack was always more bookish than Joe Junior and he had wanted to be a teacher or a writer, but his father had other ideas and Jack soon came to realise that he would have no choice but to comply.

Born in Brookline, Massachusetts on May 29th, 1917 Jack Kennedy was a most unlikely hero. He was a bright and happy child and although very thin, he inherited the Kennedy good looks that would serve him well in later life. He had a mop of thick brown hair and his skin had the smooth, golden glow of a charmed and privileged life in the sun. He had large, protruding teeth, causing his friends to name him *Ratface* but his dad's money soon took care of that and his teeth were straightened by the then famous Doctor Cloney.

Jack spent his early years in Brookline before the family moved to Riverdale and then on to Bronxville, New York. They would spend their summers at their big house in Hyannis Port and their Easter and Christmas holidays at their home in Palm Beach. Like many of the Kennedy children, Jack attended a number of different schools, but he was a good mixer and was popular with other pupils so this never really bothered him very much. He had a gregarious and energetic personality and despite his privileged upbringing, he had the common touch and could relate to people from all walks of life.

If there was one overriding factor that would dominate Jack's early life the most, it was his constant bouts of illness. He had always been a sickly boy and this weak and fragile constitution would stay with him all of his life. When he was just three years old he fell ill with scarlet fever and from then on he was constantly plagued by coughs, colds and other illnesses such as throat infections, measles and chicken pox. At the age of 13 he began to suffer from a mysterious, undiagnosed illness which left him feeling weak and tired and he lost over six pounds in weight in just a few weeks. He then suffered a bout of appendicitis and this cut short his stay at Canterbury School as, on recovering from his illness, he asked to be sent to Choate in Wallingford, where his brother Joe was already a star pupil. On moving to Choate he continued to complain of weakness and fatigue and his growth and physical development appeared to be severely impaired. He complained of constant pain in his knees and had trouble with his eyes, ears and teeth and he had fallen arches in his feet. In 1934 he was rushed into New Haven hospital with suspected leukaemia and he was kept under close observation there for several weeks. He was also admitted to the Mayo Clinic in Rochester, Minnesota, diagnosed with colitis.

Joseph Kennedy found it hard to accept that a son of his could be so weak and frail. He had little patience with Jack's pain and suffering and he resented his constant bouts of illness and hospitalisation. Joe Kennedy had no time for complainers and he was hard on his children. A family friend once said, "Jack was sick all the time and the old man could be an asshole around the kids."

But for all that, Jack was still a Kennedy and he was nothing if not a fighter. As his sister, Eunice once said, Jack hated to lose at anything and despite his obvious disadvantages he would always strive to be at least as good as anyone else; if not better. He would accept any challenge and was always ready to take on his big brother, Joe in anything, and he would take pain and injury in his stride. He felt privileged to be a Kennedy and he believed that the family had a special place in the world and that gave him an almost unreal sense of invincibility.

Jack's performance at school was generally quite poor, except in subjects he liked. He developed a passion for English and History and his marks in these subjects were well above average. But he was very much in Joe Junior's shadow at Choate and his mother once wrote to the headmaster to point out that Jack was not Joe and that they should not expect the same high standards from him as they had seen in his older brother. Young Jack also felt the strain of his father's unyielding demands in a family where only winning counts. One biographer wrote of Joe Kennedy that, "As his own heroes were not poets or artists but men of action, he took it for granted that his children too wanted public success. All too often, his understanding about their desires were fruits of his experience and his dreams; not necessarily theirs."

Once at Choate, Jack developed a rebellious streak that his teachers found hard to control. He soon came to realise that being the son of a Kennedy, he could get away with a lot more than most other boys and he became famous as a practical joker. He would play tricks on fellow students and teachers alike and on one occasion, he threw fire-crackers into their study so he could watch them come running out in terror. He formed what he called the *Muckers Club*; a group of rich, spoilt kids hell-bent on causing mischief and mayhem in any way they could and he loved every minute of it. His life-long friend, Lem Billings said that Jack was one of most fun-guys he had ever met and was a joy to be around. He played baseball and golf and enjoyed sailing, but he was unable to make the football team due to his small stature and weak constitution. Despite all of this, Jack eventually fared quite well at Choate and his teachers said he showed great promise once he matured.

But that day was still a long way off. Jack had no intention of growing up too quickly and he would continue to do exactly as he liked, with no thought or consideration for anyone else. The Kennedy children would go around buying goods and saying that dad would pick up the tab, and local traders grew tired of chasing the family for payment. The Kennedys were notorious for not paying their bills and this instilled in Jack a very casual attitude towards money. He hardly ever carried cash and would expect friends to pick up the tabs; not because he was too mean to pay but because he had no real experience of actually having to pay for anything.

If Joe Kennedy was frustrated by Jack's endless bouts of illness and poor performance at school, there was one aspect of his character of which he could be immensely proud, and that was in his attitude towards women. Jack was, from the very beginning, obsessed with sex and he pursued this vice with a vigour and determination that he applied to almost nothing else. Jack was generally less sensitive than his older brother and would boast openly to his friends of his conquests and his sexual exploits. Jack loved the idea that his father was a notorious philanderer and he was more than willing to follow in his footsteps. Lem Billings said that one of the reasons for Jack's promiscuity was that he liked to be successful and he knew he was very successful with women. "He didn't even have to try," said Billing. "They just flocked around him and he was always more than happy to oblige."

Old Joe encouraged this behaviour in all of his sons and Jack was proud to be able to measure up to his father's expectations. Jack would tell stories of his father's exploits and found the whole thing rather amusing. He even told how his father had tried to sneak into bed with a friend of one of his sisters and he once told another of them, "Be sure to lock your bedroom door, the Ambassador has a tendency to prowl at night."

Jack graduated from Choate in 1935 and in September of that year he travelled to London to study under the great Harold Laski at the London School of Economics, just as Joe had done before him. But again he was more interested in girls than books and he wasted much of his time there chasing women. In October he enrolled at Princeton, but another bout of illness saw him hospitalised again and he spent several months convalescing. By the spring of 1936, Jack was much recovered and ready to go back to college but he changed his mind and dropped Princeton in favour of Harvard, again following in young Joe's footsteps. Jack's time with Laski had had little effect and he continued at Harvard as he had at Choate, lacking in commitment and struggling to live in young Joe's shadow.

Joseph Kennedy wanted his sons to experience the world at first hand, so in 1937 Jack took a trip to Europe with Lem Billings, travelling around in a beat-up old convertible. Jack then returned to Harvard but he sailed to Europe again when his father was made Ambassador to the Court of St James in London, and he at last began to take life more seriously. Jack was finally growing up and his experiences in pre-war Europe began to influence him a great deal. He took a keen interest in European affairs and he watched closely as the build-up to war intensified.

Jack's second tour of Europe took place in 1939, just as war was about to break and in Munich his car was mobbed by a group of storm troopers when they saw his English number plates. He then travelled through German-occupied Czechoslovakia and he drove through Poland just days before the Germans launched their Blitzkrieg. On returning to London he joined other family members in the public gallery at the House of Commons to watch the debate on why England had felt compelled to go to war with Germany, and he was enthralled by the discussion. He was especially impressed by Winston Churchill and remained an avid admirer of his writing all his life. Jack and his sister, Kathleen did not share their father's isolationist views and Jack felt that the fate of the United States was closely linked with that of England and that it was naive to think they could avoid entering the war.

Despite his growing political enlightenment, Jack could be very right-wing in his views of other nations and cultures and he would often express his thoughts openly and with no sense restraint. He was extremely anti-communist and once called Russia, "A slave state of the worst sort, embarked on a program of world aggression." The French fared no better either. He felt that they exploited American tourists and wrote in his diary that, "The distinguishing mark of the

Frenchman is his cabbage breath and the fact that there are no bath tubs."

In 1940 Jack completed his thesis, *Appeasement in Munich* and it was at once hailed as a masterful piece of writing. The thesis was made into a book and published under the title, *Why England Slept* and with a little help from dad's ample financial resources, it became a best-seller. Jack graduated from Harvard in 1940 and in 1941 he helped his father write a memoir of his years as an American ambassador. He then packed his bags again for a fact-finding tour of South America. Jack absorbed knowledge and information like a sponge on these trips and the experience would serve him well in later life.

In September 1941, after being rejected by the Army due to back problems resulting from a football injury, Jack enlisted in the US Navy. His poor health became an issue there, too but his father pulled strings and was able to get him accepted and he was given a desk job in Washington as a Naval Ensign. Jack was in Washington when the Japanese attacked Pearl Harbour and when the US entered the war, he was keen to get into active service and join in the fight. He applied for a front-line posting and against all the odds and to everyone's surprise, he was accepted and was sent to the Motor Torpedo Boat Squadron Training Centre at Melville, Rhode Island. He was assigned to active service in Panama before going on to serve in the Pacific, where he earned the rank of Lieutenant, commanding Motor Torpedo Boats.

PT Boats were small, fast vessels made from plywood that were used for carrying out lightning attacks on enemy shipping before slipping away at high speed. They were equipped with three fast engines that were unreliable due to water ingression and they were fitted with old, recycled radios from scrapped aircraft. They enjoyed some success, but their light construction made them very unstable and vulnerable to attack from even the lightest weaponry. They would bounce around violently as they skimmed the waves at high speed and this further aggravated Jack's already ailing back.

On the night of August 2nd 1943 Jack's boat, PT109 was on a mission in the Solomon Islands with two other PT boats when they sighted four Japanese destroyers. They gave chase and lost them in the darkness but the destroyer, *Amagari* suddenly appeared from nowhere and began to bear down on the unsuspecting PT109. The other PT boats tried to warn them of the danger but the destroyer slammed into the tiny boat, slicing it clean in half. There should have been plenty of time to get out of the way but Jack took no evasive action and he was much criticised for this later. The boat burst into flames, killing two of Jack's crew outright and throwing the rest of them into the burning, black sea.

The men clung desperately to the wreckage and called out for help but the other boats could not find them in the dark and by morning they had drifted many miles from the spot where the boat had gone down. PT boats were well-equipped with life rafts but Jack had had his boat's raft removed to make room for an extra 37mm gun; a decision he now bitterly regretted.

The exhausted survivors swam to a nearby atoll and Jack, being a very strong swimmer, dragged one of his wounded crew all the way, thereby saving his life. He urged them all on with every gruelling stroke until eventually, and quite miraculously, all the surviving crew members made it to shore. The island was very small but it did offer some food and shelter and Jack swam out to sea every day to try to catch the attention of any rescue party that might be looking for them. The men hid in the undergrowth and prayed they would soon be found, but the area was teeming with Japanese patrols and they knew they could not evade capture for long.

On the fourth day they were discovered by some local natives who were no friends of the Japanese and who were only too keen to help them. Jack wrote a message on a coconut shell and asked them to take it to the nearest US Naval base and two days later, a rescue boat piloted by the natives arrived to pick them up. The men were weak and malnourished but Jack had done an excellent job of keeping up their morale and they all survived their ordeal and made a full recovery.

Jack was not entirely without blame in this episode but his father made sure that the American public heard only his side of the story and Jack came back a hero. His exploits were splashed all over the papers and were shown on cinema newsreels everywhere and he was awarded the Navy and Marine Corp Medal, with a citation for valour. Jack enjoyed all the attention but in his usual, nonchalant way he tried to play down his heroism, once telling a reporter, "It was entirely involuntary, they sank my boat."

Lieutenant John F Kennedy went on to have a distinguished, if short, career in the Navy before his back problems flared up again and he was admitted to Boston's Chelsea Naval Hospital for treatment. They could do very little for him and he was honourably discharged from the Navy in March, 1945. He then received the shocking news that his brother, Joe had been killed while on a secret bombing mission in England and his world was suddenly, and quite unexpectedly turned upside-down.

The death of Joe Junior changed everything for Jack and he knew from that moment on that his own hopes and dreams would have to give way to those of his father. The loss of young Joe had been a shattering blow for the whole family and one that Jack felt more than most. They had all lost someone very dear, but Jack knew in an instant that he had lost even more. He knew that with Joe gone, he would now become the focus of his father's obsessive pursuit of power and he knew that his life was no longer his own. He had to face up to the fact that his career and his future were now in the hands of his domineering father and, although he resisted at first, he was no match for Joe Kennedy and he was forced to accept the inevitable. He picked up the baton left by young Joe and after a short but aggressive campaign, he was successfully elected to Congress in June 1946. There were claims that Jack had bought his way into Congress and that his father had spent an unprecedented $300,000 to put him there. The East Boston Leader wryly wrote, "Congress seat for sale – no experience necessary – only millionaires need apply."

However he got there, once in Congress Jack took a keen interest in politics and in domestic affairs and he began to work hard to learn the tools of what would become his trade. He served on a number of sub-committees and was successfully re-elected for a further two terms in Congress. Jack's career was gaining momentum and he was beginning to get noticed. The 1950's saw the beginning of the McCarthy era in America and Jack gained further notoriety by supporting McCarthy in his relentless crusade against the far left. But in 1948, Jack suffered another shattering blow when he was diagnosed with Adison's disease during a trip to

England. The diagnosis was kept secret from the public but the disease would plague Jack for the rest of his life.

Jack performed well in Congress and in 1952 he made his bid for a seat in the Senate. He had, by this time, gained a wealth of valuable experience and had grown in stature from a weak and ineffective politician to a canny, clever statesman with a wide-ranging knowledge and a good understanding of domestic and foreign affairs. Jack's opponent in his battle for the Senate was the well-known and influential Henry Cabot Lodge Junior, and he knew the fight would be a tough one. He would need a strong and effective campaign manager and for this his father chose his younger brother, Bobby.

Bobby had at first been reluctant to accept this challenge as he wanted to pursue his own career in law but once again, their controlling father insisted and Bobby had no choice but to concede. Once committed, however, Bobby threw himself into his task with the gritty, hard-nosed determination that would become his trademark and that would prove invaluable to Jack. Bobby was young and relatively inexperienced but he was tough and hard-working and was ruthless in his determination to put Jack in the Senate. He managed Jack's campaign like a holy crusade and he worked tirelessly, day and night to ensure Jack's election, and there can be no doubt that it was Bobby who put Jack Kennedy in the Senate in 1952. It was the start of a long and successful partnership that would continue until the day Jack died.

Jack was enjoying the bachelor life and was in no rush to marry, but he knew that to get to the top in politics he would eventually have to take a wife. Jack had, of course, had countless affairs with countless women, but around this time he began to focus his attention on one young lady in particular. Jacqueline Bouvier was a bright and sophisticated young socialite from a wealthy Boston family and was becoming a prominent figure on the Washington social circuit. She was a writer for the Washington Post and as an independent, enlightened young woman she was very much a product of the modern age. Witty, intelligent and with a striking beauty and impeccable taste, Jackie was quite a catch for Jack and he knew she would make a perfect First Lady once his Presidential aspirations had been realised. Their romance blossomed and on September 12th 1953, the happy couple were married in a dazzling society wedding at Newport, Rhode Island. They looked the perfect, happy couple and in many respects they were, but the pressures of public life and Jack's persistent womanising would make theirs a difficult and stormy relationship.

Over the coming years, Jack suffered even more from his bad back and was eventually admitted to hospital for surgery. He was very ill following the operation and was often close to death, at one point even receiving the last rites. But he had that Kennedy fighting spirit and although the road to recovery was a long and hard one, he eventually pulled through.

The long convalescence kept Jack out of the Senate for several months and he used this time to write his now famous book, *Profiles in Courage*. The book was about US Senators who had overcome adversity in one way or another and, although credited solely to Jack, it is widely believed to have been mostly ghost-written by his speech-writer, Theodore Sorensen. In any event, the book was a huge success and was awarded the Pulitzer Prize for biography in 1957. This was a great consolation to Jack, who had always wanted to be a writer and he was immensely proud of his achievement. The book was well-received and old Joe made sure that the Kennedy machine squeezed every last drop of PR value out of it.

But these were difficult times for Jack and Jackie. Jack's poor health often left him tired and frustrated and for a while it looked as if Joe's concerns over Jack's ability to cope with public life may have been well-founded. Jackie desperately wanted to have children and on August 23rd 1956, she gave birth to their first daughter, Arabella; but the child turned out to be still-born. They were both shattered and grief-stricken by this but their prayers were soon answered when a bright and healthy Caroline Bouvier Kennedy was born on November 27th 1957. Things were finally on the up and it was time to put Jack's political career back on track. In 1958, he beat Vincent J Celeste for a second term in the Senate before at last setting his sights on the Presidency.

In 1956, Jack ran for the Vice Presidency slot in the upcoming election but he was beaten by Estes Kefauvener as running mate to Adli Stevenson. Both Bobby and Joe Kennedy had advised him against running in favour of a run for the Presidential nomination in 1960 and, as it turned out, they were right to do so. Stevenson was beaten in the election by Dwight Eisenhower and if Jack had been Stevenson's running mate for his failed attempt in 1956, he may well have failed to win the Presidential nomination in 1960.

The Presidential election of 1960 was to prove the hardest fought and the closest run in American history and Jack beat off Herbert Humphrey and Wayne Morse to become the Democratic nominee against Republican, Richard Nixon. Bobby had run a brilliant campaign for Jack's election to the Senate and Jack called on him again now. Bobby was again reluctant to accept the challenge, but his father convinced him that Jack needed him now more than ever and in the end, Bobby gave in and agreed to manage the campaign.

Richard Nixon would prove to be a tough adversary for Jack. Nixon was an experienced and ruthless politician with friends in very high places, and he was prepared to do whatever it would take to win. But the Kennedys could play rough, too. They had an almost limitless amount of money and it has been claimed that old Joe even called in some favours from the mob to help get Jack elected. It is alleged that Joe Kennedy used his connections with mob leaders like Sam Giancana and Carlos Marcello to help put Jack in the Whitehouse and that in doing so, he cut a deal with the devil. Joe had had dealings with mob figures in the past and he would have been well-placed to call in help from them now, so it is highly likely that he did just that. Frank Sinatra's daughter, Tina later said that her father had been approached by Joe Kennedy to be the go-between for himself and Sam Giancana in "buying" the union vote for Jack. The meetings are said to have taken place at the Cal-Neva Hotel in Las Vegas, owned by a consortium including Sinatra and Giancana, and there is no doubt that both Joe and Jack Kennedy were regular visitors there around this time.

The 1960 election was always going to be a hard-fought battle for Jack Kennedy, and this was especially so in the south. Many people in the right-wing southern states considered Jack Kennedy soft on communism and opposed his stance on Civil Rights. They wanted their own man, Texas-born Lyndon Baines Johnson in the Whitehouse and for that reason, Jack was forced to consider Johnson as his running mate in the election. This infuriated Bobby, who despised and mistrusted Lyndon Johnson, but he knew that political expediency and plain common sense would leave him no choice but to agree. Bobby had gained a high public profile from his fierce attacks on Jimmy Hoffa and on organised crime and Johnson felt he was nothing but a spoilt brat. The two harboured a strong dislike for one another that would develop into pure hatred in the years ahead. But Jack knew that he would need Johnson's support to win votes in the south so, against the advice of Bobby and other close aides, he reluctantly put Johnson's name on the ticket. Johnson never really wanted to be Vice President but he accepted the offer as he thought it might improve his chances of one day becoming President. As he once said to Clare Boothe Luce, "I looked it up and one in four Presidents has died in office. I'm a gamblin' man darlin' and this is the only chance I got."

Jack hit the campaign trail hard and began touring the towns and cities of America, shaking hands and flashing that famous Kennedy smile until his face ached. He would stagger back to his hotel rooms exhausted and in pain from his back, but he would sit down with Bobby and the team long into the night to plan the next day's gruelling schedule. They planned every move and left nothing to chance in their determination to achieve Joe's dream of putting a Kennedy in the Whitehouse.

The polls showed Kennedy and Nixon to be neck and neck and in an effort to boost his standing, Jack challenged Nixon to a live TV debate; the first of its kind and the start of a new era in the use of the media in politics. The debate took place on September 26th 1960 and it was a resounding triumph for Jack. He was cool and controlled and answered every question with an ease and confidence that won him many new friends. The camera loved Jack Kennedy and he knew exactly how to work it. He looked directly into the lens when speaking and his casual, confident manner made the viewers feel he was talking directly to them. By contrast, Nixon struggled with this new way of campaigning. He was clumsy and awkward in front of the camera and despite the make-up, it was clear he was sweating profusely. Jack won the debate outright and his performance won him a great deal of support across the whole of the United States.

The voting took place on November 8th and Jack won by the narrowest margin in history (less than 1%) to become the 35th President of the United States. He was the youngest person ever elected to that office and the first Catholic. He had made his father proud and he had achieved what Joe Kennedy had been working for all his life and as the family celebrated their unbelievable good fortune, they must have thought about those who could not be there to see it.

"It should have been Joe," Jack said to a close friend when reflecting on his victory, and that thought never really left him.

Jack had even more to celebrate when his son, John Junior was born on November the 25th and as 1960 drew to a close and '61 beckoned, it seemed all of his troubles were behind him. It had been a hard and expensive campaign but whatever deals had or had not been made, it had all paid off. Every last vote had been crucial and Jack had made it to the Whitehouse by the skin of his pearly-white teeth.

A Kennedy in the Whitehouse

President John F Kennedy was sworn in on a freezing cold day in January, 1961. The streets of the capital had been cleared of snow and as his father looked proudly on, the

35th President of the United States delivered his inaugural speech to the shivering crowd. He promised to sweep away the old, stuffy Eisenhower epoch and he spoke of a new hope for a new generation. It was time to leave behind the austerity of the post-war years and to move forward into a brave new frontier. He spoke of a world in harmony and of peace and prosperity, and he asked everyone to play their part.

"My fellow Americans," he said as he faced the sea of red faces. "Ask not what your country can do for you, ask what you can do for your country."

And that simple statement summed-up Jack's view of how the country should be run. The Kennedy family had worked hard to achieve what they had in life and the new President wanted to encourage that same ethos in the country as a whole. He believed that if they all pulled together, the United States could achieve just about anything and that the people of America were privileged to live in a land of real hope and opportunity. The United States had emerged from the war a superpower and it was time for them to take a leading role on the new world stage, and Jack was just the man to lead them.

The Kennedys moved into the Whitehouse and as he settled into his coveted new chair in the Oval Office, the new President began to build his team. He chose close friends and advisors that he knew he could trust and some of those choices were contentious, none more so than the choice of his brother as Attorney General. Bobby was nowhere near qualified or experienced enough for the job and he certainly didn't want it, and even Jack had his doubts. But old Joe was still pulling the strings and he insisted that Jack select Bobby so, despite the cries of nepotism and abuse of power, Robert Kennedy was duly appointed Attorney General.

As it turned out, the appointment was a master stroke. Jack came to rely heavily on Bobby and they formed what would prove to be a very strong and powerful political partnership. Bobby attended all the important cabinet meetings and he became the President's closest and most trusted advisor. He held more power and influence than any other Attorney General before or since and he soon became known as the second most powerful man in Washington. Jack's Vice President in the administration was, of course, Lyndon Johnson and he would always be a thorn in Jack's side. Johnson bitterly resented having to accept the role of Vice President and hated playing second fiddle to Bobby. His goal was to become President himself and as we shall see later, he may well have played a key role in making that happen.

The Kennedy Whitehouse was very different from that of his predecessor. Jackie had it completely modernised and refurbished and she replaced some of the stuffy old furniture with new, more tasteful décor, which she proudly showed off to the public on TV. The once empty rooms now echoed with the sound of parties and of children playing and the air was filled with glamour and excitement. Jackie was an educated, cultured woman and she would invite poets and writers to her lavish dinner parties while Jack entertained ambassadors and leaders from around the world, all eager to get a glimpse of this vibrant and glamorous new administration they had christened "Camelot."

But it was not all champagne and roses. There was a lot to be done and Jack knew from the very beginning that he would have his work cut out. He was keen to begin work on the economy and on the social and domestic issues he cared so much about, but it was in the area of foreign policy that he would face his toughest challenges in the early days of his administration. He had inherited from Eisenhower a number of major headaches in foreign affairs, and these would soon test him to the limit. There was, of course, the on-going struggle with the Soviet Union and Eisenhower had already sent US military advisors into Vietnam, but it was Cuba that would dominate these early months, as it would do for the rest of Jack's Presidency.

Relations with Cuba had been strained since Fidel Castro had seized power in a military coup in 1959. Castro immediately aligned himself to the Soviet Union and the US suddenly found it had a communist state just 90 miles off the Florida coast. This posed a real threat to national security and was a major concern for the US Government and the issue was to dominate the Kennedy administration from the very beginning, eventually playing a major part in its downfall.

Kennedy had inherited a plan devised by the CIA, with approval from Eisenhower and Nixon, to support Cuban exiles in an invasion of their homeland with a view to seizing control back from Castro. The plan was well advanced by the time Kennedy took office and he was briefed by the military and the CIA on the details and its chances of success. He was misled into believing that the rebels would meet with little resistance and that once ashore in Cuba, the Cuban people would rise up to support them. Kennedy accepted the advice of his military experts and, although wary, he agreed to go ahead with the plan.

The invasion was launched on April 16th 1961 as Cuban rebels, trained by the CIA and elements of the US military in Florida, landed at the Bay of Pigs in Cuba. They were well-armed and well-organised but despite assurances to the contrary, they met fierce resistance from Castro's forces. They were pinned down on the beach and their backers in the US urged President Kennedy to send in air strikes to support them, but he refused to commit the US military to any direct intervention and the invasion turned into a complete disaster. Many of the rebels were killed and the rest taken prisoner. They had been promised US air support and they didn't get it; and this sowed the seeds of anger and betrayal that would grow and fester into bitter hatred in the months and years ahead.

President Kennedy was furious. He felt cheated and betrayed and he realised that his so-called expert advisors had been less than honest about the chances of success and that they had pinned their hopes on being able to pressure him into sending in air support once the invasion had begun. He was forced to admit the fiasco to the world and he took full responsibility for the disaster, but he never forgave the CIA and the advisors that had led him into the trap. He came out of the affair trusting no one but Bobby and his closest aids and he railed at Allen Dulles, firing him from his job as Director of the CIA. In Jack's opinion the agency was out of control and he swore he would, "Splinter the CIA into a thousand pieces and scatter them into the wind."

President Kennedy had made some very dangerous enemies in the CIA and in military intelligence and the whole Bay of Pigs fiasco would foster a bitter resentment that would never go away. Jack's mistrust of the CIA and other Government agencies opened a rift that would become a chasm and his actions against them would one day come back to haunt him. Jack did gain some credit for taking full responsibility for the Bay of Pigs disaster but the Russians took his failure to act as a sign of weakness, and they would soon test his resolve in their own showdown in Cuba.

President Kennedy's first year in office had not been the resounding success he had hoped it would be. He had failed to get many of his health and social welfare policies through Congress and although he had made a pledge to act on the issue of Civil Rights, to date he had done next to nothing. By early 1962, his popularity was at its lowest ever and many began to believe he was just not up to the job. But all that was about to change, and he would soon have the opportunity to show just how strong and decisive a leader he could be.

At 8.45am on Tuesday, October 16th 1962 the President's National Security Advisor, McGeorge Bundy informed him that a U-2 spy plane had taken photographs showing clear evidence that the Soviets were building a missile base in Cuba. This was startling and very worrying news and Jack immediately called a meeting of his National Security Council (NSC). They examined the photographs and agreed that the United States could not, and would not, tolerate such a threat so close to the US mainland and, having learned his lesson from the Bay of Pigs debacle, the President took immediate and decisive action. He decreed that the NSC would meet every day during the crisis and that he would confront the Soviet Union on the issue without delay. The NSC was made up of a mix of political and military advisors as well as representatives from the intelligence services and, unusually, the Attorney General. Bobby was Jack's closest advisor and Jack wanted him there by his side, every minute of the day throughout the crisis. Jack had come to rely heavily on his younger brother and he knew he would need him now more than ever. Bobby was the grafter in the outfit and was Jack's fixer and Jack once described him as, "The most impressive man I have ever seen."

On October 18th President Kennedy spoke to Andrei Gromyko, the Russian Foreign Minister and, not letting on that he knew about the missiles, he gave him every opportunity to inform him of developments in Cuba, but Gromyko denied any such action. He stated categorically that the Soviet Union posed no threat to the US in Cuba and this signalled to Jack that the Russians were lying and were, in fact, covertly trying to gain some strategic advantage.

The Council met again on the 18th October and identified two possible courses of action. They could either invade Cuba and take out the bases that way, or they could impose a quarantine and set-up a naval blockade of the island. The Council became divided into two distinct camps that would come to be known as the *Hawks* and the *Doves*; those who wanted war and those who argued for a peaceful solution. The President was under enormous pressure to invade Cuba and take out the bases before the missiles could be activated but after deliberating at length with Bobby, he chose the quarantine option as a first step. At 7pm on October 22nd Jack appeared on TV to tell the people of America (and the world) about the presence of the missiles and calling on the Russians to remove them immediately. He told the Soviets that the US would not tolerate such an act of aggression and he announced the imposition of an exclusion zone around Cuba that would be enforced by a US naval blockade.

In the meantime, Adli Stevenson, the US Ambassador to the United Nations was raising the matter there. He did an excellent job in rallying support for the US in condemning the Russians for their actions and this put enormous pressure on Khrushchev. But still he refused to back down, saying he needed more time to consider his actions.

"I'll wait 'til hell freezes over if I have to," said Stevenson, to rousing applause from the floor. Stevenson resumed his seat and defiantly folded his arms across his chest as he stared across at the Russian delegation. They were at a stand-off, and there seemed nowhere to go.

On October 25th President Kennedy learned that some of the missiles were already fully operational and he drafted a letter to Khrushchev urging him to reconsider. Khrushchev, in response, wrote to the President accusing him of inflaming the crisis by using threatening behaviour in a deliberate effort to provoke a response. The UN proposed a cooling off period, but Kennedy refused. He pulled no punches and insisted that the missiles be removed immediately and he refused point-blank to enter into any negotiations or cooling-off period until they were. But Khrushchev still would not budge. Tension continued to mount and surveillance photographs taken on the October 26th showed a number of missiles ready for launch. They also showed a great number of long and short range Soviet bombers on various airfields around Cuba.

The world held its breath. Kennedy and Khrushchev were eyeball to eyeball and were on the brink of nuclear war. It was the closest the world had (or has) ever been to an all-out nuclear war and around the world, people were going to their beds at night not knowing if they would wake up in the morning. Jack and Bobby worked late into the night, walking together in the Whitehouse gardens as they discussed every minute detail of the crisis and considered every possible outcome, supporting each other in their conviction that they must stand firm. The President was under increasing pressure to strike out at Cuba as the *Hawks* held their finger on the button, just waiting for the order to fire, but Jack held his nerve. He knew that a nuclear war could destroy the entire civilised world and he was not going to be the one to start it. He would wait a little longer.

Then on October 26th Kennedy got the break he was waiting for. A Soviet diplomat had contacted an ABC News reporter suggesting that Khrushchev might be willing to negotiate if he could do so without losing face. Kennedy's aids investigated this claim and found it was a genuine approach from the Russians and that they were, at last, willing to back down. Khrushchev's proposal was that he would remove his missiles from Cuba if the US would remove their own missiles from bases in Turkey. There was still much to discuss but it was a start, and as they all breathed a heavy sigh of relief, Ken O'Donnell turned to Jack and said, "I think the other guy just blinked."

The NSC discussed this option and, as the US Jupiter missiles in Turkey were due to be phased out soon anyway, they agreed, on condition that the removal of the US missiles be kept secret. An agreement was reached and on October 28th, Radio Moscow finally announced the removal of the missiles from Cuba.

It was President Kennedy's finest hour. No doubt inspired by Churchill's stand against Hitler, Jack had squared up to Khrushchev's bullying threats and had won. He took an enormous risk in acting as he did, but he was driven by a firm belief that right would prevail. He also acknowledged the vital role Bobby had played in keeping the *Hawks* at bay whilst he and Bobby (and a few very close aids) carefully navigated their way through the crisis. Robert Kennedy was a tough, hard-nosed realist and he would not be pushed around by anyone, and there can be no doubt that Jack's success in dealing with the crisis was very much a joint effort between the two of them.

The Cuban missile crisis and the fight against communism were not the only issues facing the Kennedy administration at this time. The early 1960's was a time of extreme political and social unrest in the United States and Jack faced many challenges on the domestic front, too. There were issues with housing, social welfare and the unions, but the real thorn in Jack's side would be the contentious and emotive issue of Civil Rights. Although he had voted against Eisenhower's Civil Rights bill in 1957, Kennedy had spoken in favour of Civil Rights legislation whilst in the Senate and he had pledged to act on this issue during his Presidential election campaign, but to date he had done very little. He had applied pressure on agencies like the FBI to recruit more black Americans but he was very much stuck between a rock and a hard place on the issue. On the one hand, he had secured a large part of the black vote by promising to act on their behalf, but on the other hand he would lose a lot of support in the south if he did. In 1961, the issue of Civil Rights was low on the political agenda as the President tried to address problems in social reform and health care and the Government was very much distracted by events in Cuba. Jack did ask Bobby to apply pressure where he could and Bobby brought a number of law suits for violation of already existing laws, but that was never going to be enough.

On May 4th 1961, a group of African Americans took matters into their own hands by beginning what would become known as the Freedom Rides. They boarded "whites only" inter-state buses and rode through the southern states, meeting violent resistance on the way. This sparked off riots as the police and National Guard used water-cannon and tear gas to disperse the crowds and restore order. President Kennedy was strongly opposed to the actions of the Freedom Riders, calling them "trouble-making SOB's" and Robert Kennedy, too tried to dissuade them from their actions. But the torch had been lit and there would be no stopping it. There were riots in Alabama as angry Ku-Klux-Klan members clashed with black activists and the nation watched in horror as TV news footage showed black people being attacked with night sticks, rubber bullets and dogs. But still, President Kennedy did nothing.

Jack was finally forced to act when a young black student named James Meredith applied to enter the "all white" University of Mississippi in September 1962. Meredith was refused entry, but he took his case to the Supreme Court and they ruled that he had a right to enter and should not be barred. However, when he went to enrol, riots again broke out and Robert Kennedy sent in 500 extra marshals to try to restore order, but they failed to do so and the President once again ordered in the National Guard. Hundreds were injured and the riots spread to other towns and cities, especially Birmingham, Alabama where the rioting and the violence shocked the nation as they again watched events unfold on TV.

Civil Rights was now a major issue in the United States and in August 1963, Martin Luther King Junior organised a mass rally in Washington to promote and defend the rights of coloured people in America. King had become a leading light in the Civil Rights movement and he spoke out openly for the rights of the millions of black Americans, gaining growing support from both blacks and whites alike. Both Jack and Bobby had opposed the rally and had strongly advised against it, fearing it would provoke more riots and civil unrest, but King would not be dissuaded. The event went ahead and was attended by over 250,000 people and to the surprise of many, it passed off peacefully as King addressed the crowd with his, *"I have a dream"* speech. He spoke of a world where everyone is judged not by the colour of their skin but by the strength of their character; a world where all men are equal and where people can live in peace and harmony. The speech was a resounding triumph for King and ended with these words;

"And when this happens, when we allow freedom to ring from every village and every hamlet, from every state and every city, we will be able to speed up that day when all God's children, black men and white men, Jews and Gentiles, Protestants and Catholics, will be able to join hands and sing in the words of the old negro song; Free at last, thank God almighty we are free at last."

President Kennedy was moved and impressed by King's rousing speech and felt compelled, at last, to act. In 1963 he proposed a bill prohibiting discrimination for reasons of race, religion or country of birth and ending segregation in schools, restaurants, theatres and public transport and in any other place of public accommodation. It was a daring and radical bill for its time and although his actions won him many friends, they won him some dangerous and resentful enemies too; especially in the south. In the end, the bill proposed by President Kennedy would not be passed until signed by the new President, Lyndon Johnson shortly after Jack's death.

In the meantime, Jack had been working hard to ease the tensions of the Cold War without appearing too soft on the Russians. He wanted desperately to improve relations between the United States and Russia while at the same time placating the *Hawks* and the war-mongers in his own administration, and this was a delicate balance to achieve. There were many in Government and in the military who wanted all-out war with the Russians and they continually pressured Jack to attack them before they had a chance to attack the US. Jack considered these people mad and reckless and on one occasion, when being briefed by his military advisors, he walked out of the meeting saying, "My God, and we call ourselves the human race?"

Jack's handling of the Cuban missile crisis had established his reputation as a strong and decisive leader and even Khrushchev came to respect and admire him. Jack had met with Khrushchev in 1961, where they failed to agree on anything, but they met again in August 1963 and this time they were more successful. Jack's firm stance on Cuba had strengthened his position with Khrushchev and he was able to negotiate and agree a nuclear test-ban treaty with the Russians. This was a huge step forward in a time of paranoia and mistrust on both sides, but Jack was determined to calm the waters and to find an amicable way to ease the tension between the two super-powers. This conviction is perhaps best summed up in his speech at the American University of Washington on June 10th 1963, where he announced his agreement to negotiate a test-ban treaty and told the world that he would co-operate with other nations in the search for peace.

"I am talking about genuine peace," he announced to the crowd. *"The kind of peace that makes life on earth worth living and the kind that enables men and nations to grow, and to hope, and to build a better life for their children. For in the final analysis, our most basic common link is that we all inhabit this small planet; we all breathe the same air, we all cherish our children's futures, and we are all mortal."*

President Kennedy had shown that he could be a strong and decisive leader and that he was prepared to work tirelessly to help make the world a safer place, in spite of Khrushchev's persistent provocation. In August 1963, he visited Berlin to see for himself the way the people of that city had been divided by the infamous Berlin Wall and how the Russians had set up barbed wire fences and machine-gun towers to stop the flow of refugees fleeing to the west. The President stood before the wall and delivered his milestone speech in which he condemned the actions of the Russians and praised the people of both East and West Berlin for their courage and conviction in fighting for their freedom.

"Freedom has many difficulties," he said, *"and democracy is not perfect. But we have never had to put up a wall to keep our people in."*

The speech was met with rapturous applause, and he ended it with.

"All free men, wherever they may live, are citizens of Berlin. And, therefore, as a free man, I take pride in the words; Ich bin ein Berliner."

The bitter rivalry of the Cold War was not confined to earth but was fought in space, too. In 1957 the Russians launched their Sputnik satellite, and this shocking development rocked the free world to its core. If the Russians could put a satellite into space then they could also launch missiles to any target around the world, and that was a very worrying prospect for the people of America. In response, the United States launched their own program of space exploration but the Russians beat them every time by sending the first man into space, closely followed by the first man to orbit the earth, and then the first woman in space later.

The Americans needed an appropriate response and in 1961, President Kennedy committed the nation to land a man on the moon and return him safely to the earth before the decade was out. This gave them just 9 years to achieve what seemed an impossible objective but, against all the odds, they accomplished this goal when the men of Apollo 11 landed on the moon in July 1969. The irony here is that the President in 1969, and so the man in office when Kennedy's goal was achieved, was his arch-rival, Richard Nixon. It was Nixon who would speak to the astronauts on the moon from the telephone in the Oval Office and it was Nixon, not a Kennedy, who would bask in all the glory.

President Kennedy had shown that he was willing to take risks in his political actions and decision-making but he was more than happy to take risks in his personal life, too. Jack Kennedy was, from his early teens until the end of his short life, a compulsive and obsessive womaniser. He was every bit as promiscuous as his illustrious father and was by far the most active and adventurous of the Kennedy brothers in this respect; quite an accolade in a peer group such as his. We have already seen how girls and sex dominated his school and college years and how he would neglect his studies in pursuit of these pleasures, and he carried these habits on into Congress, the Senate and even into his presidency.

It has been said by many that Jack married Jackie out of political expediency and that he should really never have married at all, but a President without a wife and family was an unthinkable prospect, so he really had no choice. There is no doubt that Jack did love Jackie, but he was biologically incapable of maintaining a monogamous relationship with anyone and Jackie knew from the start that she would never change him. He was his father's son and he was a compulsive sexual predator all his life. This was all well and good for your average man on the street or even for a high-profile businessman like his father, but for the most powerful man in the free world, it was potential dynamite.

The Kennedys had made enemies everywhere and there were plenty of bitter, disgruntled people just waiting for an opportunity to bring them down; not least FBI Director, J Edgar Hoover. Hoover was a tyrannical, overbearing control-freak who had had everything his own way under the Eisenhower administration but his new boss, Robert Kennedy, kept him on a tight leash and he hated him for it. Hoover was a bitter and vindictive man and few would ever dare to cross him, but his bully-boy tactics had no effect on Robert Kennedy. He cared nothing for Hoover's tough guy reputation and the two men held each other in complete contempt. Hoover thought Bobby a spoilt brat and in turn, Bobby christened Hoover, J Edna, in mocking reference to his homosexuality and his penchant for cross dressing. To make matters worse, Hoover had learned that the Kennedys were planning to retire him from his job as head of the FBI, and that was something that her just could not countenance.

The relationship between the Kennedys and Hoover was a strained one from the start, but Jack and Bobby failed to see just how powerful and dangerous he could be. Hoover had spies everywhere and he used them to good effect. The very reason he had remained in power so long was because he had made a career out of digging up the dirt on key political figures, then blackmailing them to get what he wanted. He knew that everyone had their dirty little secrets and he knew that Jack's main weakness was his continuous and compulsive womanising. He knew that whatever the risks, Jack just could not help himself and that he would play right into his hands.

Jack dated everything from call-girls and prostitutes to politicians and heiresses, and Hoover made sure he knew all about it. Hoover knew that, whatever the risks, Jack just could not help himself and that he would play right into his hands in providing him with ammunition. A good example of this was Jack's affair with socialite, Mary Pinchot-Meyer, wife of a former CIA agent and one of the leading lights on the Washington social scene. It was claimed that Jack would acquire LSD for them both and that he would reveal secrets to her during their passionate liaisons. Hoover had their rooms and telephones bugged and when confronted with this, Jack was forced to end the affair. Pinchot-Meyer was mysteriously killed shortly after the death of JFK and a recent book by Peter Janney claims that she was killed by the CIA because she knew too much about the assassination of the President.

Another of Jack's dangerous and notorious affairs was with Judith Campbell Exner. The couple were introduced by Frank Sinatra and had a long and passionate affair but, once again, Hoover intervened. He learned that Exner was also sleeping with Chicago mobster, Sam Giancana and when Hoover played recordings of their sexual liaisons back to Bobby, Jack was again forced to end the affair. Hoover would always claim he was just looking out for the President by warning him of potential security risks, but both Jack and Bobby knew exactly what Hoover was doing. He had them over a barrel, and they knew it.

Jack Kennedy was a sex-addict all of his life and he was prepared to risk all to fulfil this need. He would hold wild, all-night parties at the Whitehouse when Jackie was away and would meet girls at the homes of Frank Sinatra and brother-in-law, Peter Lawford. On official tours he would get his Secret Service men to procure attractive young women for him and send them up to his hotel rooms. One of his agents described how, when he first joined the service, the President told him laughingly not to forget about him when they were fixing up their own dates for the night. The agent thought he was joking and laughed this off but he said Jack grabbed him by the arm and said, "I mean it, don't forget the boss."

Jack had an understanding with the Whitehouse security men that if he had female company and Jackie came home unexpectedly, the agents would warn him and would quickly rush the women, in various stages of undress, out through the back door. Jack would never go a day without some form of sexual encounter, whether in the Whitehouse or anywhere else, and he once commented to a friend, "If I don't get a fresh piece of ass every day, I get a migraine."
Jackie knew all of this, of course, but she suffered in silence for the sake of Jack's career.

Other people would arrange girls for him too, including Bobby and even his own father. Joe Kennedy would use his contacts in Hollywood to line up starlets and chorus girls for his son and, once through with them, Jack would often pass them on to Bobby. Jack Kennedy loved the glitz and the glamour of Hollywood and he loved to court danger by associating with known criminals and with people he knew might pose a risk. He dated big screen stars like Lana Turner and Grace Kelly and even Frank Sinatra's wife, Ava Gardner, but it was his tumultuous affair with Marilyn Monroe that would become the most talked about after his death.

Marilyn Monroe was by this time a troubled, tormented soul and that made her very dangerous. It is not known for certain when Jack and Marilyn first met but by 1962, the couple were already involved in a deep and passionate relationship. To Jack, this was just another casual fling but Marilyn came to believe it was much more than that and she became obsessed with him, calling him constantly at the Whitehouse and even telling friends of their affair. She believed that Jack really loved her and she had convinced herself that he would leave Jackie and marry her and that they would raise a family together. Jack knew none of this until much later in their relationship and in the early days he enjoyed their every moment together and saw her as often as he could. It soon became an open secret that Jack was dating Marilyn and they flaunted this to the world when Marilyn, in a sequin dress she had to be sewn into, sang *Happy Birthday* to him in her low, husky voice at Maddison Square Gardens in May 1962.

Jackie had turned a blind eye to most of Jack's affairs but his association with Monroe bothered her a great deal. She could see just how unstable Marilyn had become and she was concerned that the affair might explode into the media and ruin her husband's political career. In time, Jack saw this too and he eventually ended the affair with Marilyn and passed her on to Bobby, with disastrous consequences for them all.

It seems incredible to us today that the world knew nothing of President Kennedy's sordid personal life until long after his death, but Jack enjoyed a special relationship with the media that few others have been able to achieve. They knew that the voters wanted to see the President in an idyllic, family environment and the Kennedy PR machine was more than happy to oblige. They had a kind of trade-off in which Kennedy would allow them access to his home and family life in return for their silence on the more sinister side of his administration, and that was an arrangement that seemed to work for everyone.

The Road to Dallas

As the Kennedy administration entered its third year it was clear there would be a lot of ground to cover if Jack was going to be successfully re-elected in '64. He had fared well enough in foreign affairs and with his stance against the Soviets, but he was still under heavy criticism for his inertia on Civil Rights and for his lack of progress on public health and social reform. His popularity was on the slide and he knew he would have to campaign hard if he was to stand any chance of winning a second term, so he planned a busy schedule of "meet the people" tours for the fall of 1963. This had been Bobby's main strategy for the 1960 election and it had served them well, so they planned to use same approach again this time.

But all was not well in the Kennedy camp. Jack and Jackie's marriage was under severe strain and Jack's health was again causing concern. Both Jack and Jackie were struggling with the pressures of living in the media spotlight and both used all kinds of drugs and medications to help them cope. They used uppers to keep them awake and sedatives to help them sleep, and they were spiralling into a world of drug and alcohol abuse. Jack was in constant pain with his back and Jackie was smoking heavily and was very unhappy, so they both turned to the notorious and infamous, "Dr Feelgood" for help.

Max Jacobson, aka Dr Feelgood, was a shady medical practitioner of questionable credentials who offered his dubious, high-priced services to the rich and famous. He began treating Jack in the late 1950's and continued to do so until Jack's death. He would inject him with a dangerous cocktail of amphetamines and other unknown chemicals to ease the pain in his back and help keep him awake and alert. He is said to have administered three such injections for Jack before his summit meeting with Khrushchev and Jack kept him close by his side all through his term in office. Jacobson also administered similar treatment to Jackie and he became a constant companion to them both, whether at home or abroad. Jack would go nowhere without him and although the public knew nothing of this, the FBI and the CIA were well aware of Jack's dependency on these drugs and were growing ever-more concerned. Bobby, too, was anxious as he knew that Hoover would use Jack's drug-habit to blackmail him in the coming campaign, but even he could not dissuade Jack from using Dr Feelgood's potions. When asked by a close friend, "Have you any idea what's in those shots that guy is giving you?" Jack said, "I don't care if it's horse-piss; it makes me feel good."

Jack's first term in office had taken its toll. He was tired from all the hard work and this had had a detrimental effect on his health and on his private life. He had known triumph and disaster in equal measure and had suffered a good many personal tragedies along the way. But he had learned the art of statecraft and had developed a genuine desire to make the world a better and safer place. There was still so much he wanted to do, and he was determined to carry on this fight in a second term.

As he hit the campaign trail in 1963, President Kennedy knew he would need all the help and support he could get. The campaign would take in all the major states and cities in America but, once again, it was in the south that he would have to fight the hardest. He was disliked and mistrusted in the southern states, where they bitterly resented his stance on Civil Rights and his so-called soft-touch approach with the Soviets. They felt that Lyndon Johnson should be President and they shared Johnson's own frustration at his being relegated to the ineffective and insignificant Vice-Presidency slot. Jack and Bobby knew they were playing with fire in touring the south, but they knew that they had no choice if they were to stand any chance of winning there.

There had been numerous threats on the President's life long before Jack and Jackie took that fateful trip to Dallas, and others have come to light since. Whilst in prison in 1985, Carlos Marcello confessed to an FBI informant that he had arranged Jack's murder and that he and his mob associates had planned and abandoned two assassination attempts on JFK before they finally succeeded in Dallas. The first attempt was to be in Chicago on November 2nd 1963. The President and First Lady were to ride in a motorcade through town and, as in Dallas later, the parade would pass directly below a warehouse building with windows overlooking the route. Marcello claimed he had hired a gunman and had set up an ex-marine named Thomas Vallee, a man with a very similar background to Oswald, to be the so-called "Lone Nut" who would take the rap. This plot was discovered and the motorcade was cancelled. The official reason given was that the President had a cold.

The second attempt was to be in Tampa, Florida on November 18th. Again, the mob had set up a left-wing extremist named Gilbert Lopez. He, too had a similar background to Oswald and was supposed to take the rap for the professional hit-men who would do the shooting. The difference with Lopez was that he was a keen gun enthusiast and, being somewhat over-enthusiastic, he was arrested on the morning of the parade with a car full of guns and ammunition. The motorcade went ahead but as their "Patsy" had been taken out, the operation was cancelled at the last minute. The plotters had one last chance, and the next attempt would be in Dallas on November 22nd.

On November 9th 1963, just two weeks before the assassination, FBI informer, Willie Somerset secretly taped a conversation with right-wing activist, Joseph Milteer in Miami. In the conversation, Milteer speaks openly and with authority on plans to assassinate President Kennedy in the fall of 1963 and during the meeting, the tape recorder captured the following exchange.

Milteer   Kennedy is coming here on the 18th, or something like that.

Somerset   He'll be well protected.

Milteer   The more bodyguards he has, the easier it is to get him.

Somerset   Well how the hell do you figure would be the best way to get him?

Milteer	From an office building, with a high powered rifle.
Somerset	Do you think he knows he's a marked man?
Milteer	I'm sure he does, yes.
Somerset	Are they really going to try to kill him?
Milteer	Oh yes, it's in the working.
Somerset	Hitting this Kennedy, I'll tell you, is going to be the hardest proposition, I believe. You may have figured it out, how to get him from an office building and all that, but I don't know how them Secret Service…. I mean, they'd check out all them office buildings and anywhere he's going. Do you know whether they'd do that or not?
Milteer	If they had any suspicions they would, of course, but without suspicion the chances are they wouldn't. You wouldn't have to take a gun up there, you could take it up in pieces. All them (sic) guns come knocked down and you can take them apart.
Somerset	Boy, if Kennedy is getting shot we've got to know where we're at.
Milteer	Oh yes, it's coming.
Somerset	That would be a real shake if they could do that.
Milteer	They wouldn't leave any stone unturned, no way. They'll pick up somebody within hours after anything like that should happen, just to throw the public off.

> Somerset   Well, somebody is going to have to go to jail if
> he gets killed.

Reading this transcript it is clear just how uncannily similar this scenario is to actual events in Dallas, so it is easy to assume that Milteer was heavily involved in the plot. In fact, he later bragged to friends that he had been in Dealey Plaza to watch the assassination and a man closely resembling Milteer has been spotted in photographs taken at the scene. Milteer was interviewed by the FBI following the assassination but despite the evidence cited above, he was released without charge. He died in a mysterious house fire some years later.

There were clearly some very serious concerns over the safety of the President but they needed the southern vote so in the end, it was decided that the tour would go ahead. By mid-November, Dallas was firmly added to the itinerary.

Six Seconds in Dallas

At 9.15 on the morning of Thursday, November 21st 1963, John F Kennedy said goodbye to his children for the last time. He attended a brief meeting at the Whitehouse before travelling with Jackie by helicopter to Andrews Air Force base, where they boarded a plane for San Antonio, Texas. At San Antonio, the President attended a ceremony at Brooks Air Force base before moving on again to Houston. In the afternoon he addressed a dinner at the Rice Hotel before taking the short flight to Fort Worth, where he and Mrs Kennedy were to spend the night at the Texas Hotel.

The President was awoken at 7.30am on the morning of Friday, November 22nd and after a quick coffee, he went down to meet some of the crowd who had gathered in the rain outside the hotel to get a glimpse of him. After that, he went back inside and attended a breakfast function with Vice President Johnson and Texas Governor, John Connolly where he joked about Jackie being late because she took longer to get ready than he did. Jack looked comfortable and relaxed as he smiled for the cameras and joked with the guests but beneath that relaxed and carefree veneer, he was nervous. The Dallas morning news had that day published a, "Wanted for Treason" ad in protest of his visit and flyers had been distributed condemning his policies on Civil Rights and communism.

"We're heading into nut country today," he had jokingly said to Jackie earlier and he even knelt down and mimicked a sniper taking aim to demonstrate how easy it would be to take him out from an office building or a bridge. He had made similar comments to Dave Powers following the motorcade through Tampa on the 18th and it was clear he was well aware of the danger.

After breakfast, the party boarded Air-Force One for the short flight to Dallas, landing at Love Field at 11.40am. It had been raining earlier in the day but by the time they arrived in Dallas the sky had cleared and they emerged into bright, warm sunshine and the bullet-proof bubble had been removed from their limousine. In newsreel footage of their arrival, Jack and Jackie can be seen smiling as they shake hands with well-wishers, and Jackie holds a bouquet of red roses given to her by someone in the crowd. She held them close by her side all day and she kept one as a most treasured possession 'til the day she died. She gave some to close friends (including Bobby) as keepsakes and later that day she would place one in the coffin with Jack's body.

When the motorcade was ready, they set-off for the short ride to the Dallas Trade Mart, where a lunch had been arranged in their honour. The crowds waved and cheered as the motorcade passed slowly by and the newsreels show what appears to be a warm and friendly welcome. But Senator Ralph Yarborough, riding two cars back with Lyndon Johnson, remembers it quite differently and says he felt distinctly uncomfortable riding through Dallas that day. He said that the crowds at the kerb-side were waving and cheering but when you looked up at the office windows, it was quite different. He later said.

"People were just standing there, staring down and I didn't see a single friendly face. They just stood there, looking at the President and they weren't saying anything. I'd look up there on the second or third floors and I'd see people through glass windows, just standing back. They were just looking down at the President with what seemed to me like positive hate."

But Jack and Jackie saw none of this as they rode on by and waved back at the adoring crowds. They seemed relaxed and happy and especially close. They were coming to terms with the loss of baby Patrick, who had been born in August but died shortly after, and they were looking forward to a second term in the Whitehouse. The up-coming election was going to be tough, but Jack was confident he would win. He had served his time as a rookie President and he had learned his trade well and they both felt they had a lot to look forward to in the coming months and years. Jack had gained a lot of experience and had grown in confidence during his first term in office, and the next four years were going to be different.

The crowds thinned out as the motorcade reached the end of Main Street and as they left the danger of the high-rise buildings behind them, the President and his bodyguards breathed a sigh of relief. Ahead were the wide open spaces of Dealey Plaza and beyond that, the triple underpass leading to the relative safety of the Stemmons Freeway.

At around 12.30pm the President's limousine reached the corner of Main and Houston, where it slowed to take a 90 degree right turn along the top of the plaza towards the Texas Schoolbook Depository building (TSBD). They then drove the very short distance along Houston before the car slowed again to take the even sharper left turn that would take it into Dealey Plaza, passing directly beneath the open windows of the TSBD. Jack Kennedy had just minutes to live.

The warm Texan sun shone down from a now clear blue sky and as the limousine drove slowly through the plaza, the eager spectators waved and raised their cameras for that photo opportunity of a lifetime. A little girl in a white coat and red dress ran excitedly alongside the President's car as Mary Moorman pointed her Polaroid camera at the grassy knoll opposite, ready to shoot her now famous grainy picture. Charles Brehm held up his five year old son for a better view and on a concrete outcrop of a colonnaded portico, Dallas dressmaker, Abraham Zapruder was about to shoot one of the most shocking and controversial home movies ever taken.

The crowd had been waving all the way from Love Field and as the motorcade turned onto Elm Street Nellie Connolly, riding in front of Jack in the Presidential limousine, turned around and said, "Well, Mr President, you can't say that Dallas doesn't love you."

At that moment, the plaza echoed with the loud crack of a rifle shot, and everyone froze. The little girl in the red dress stopped running, the President stopped waving and the limousine slowed almost to a standstill as the shocked and confused driver hit the brake.

A shot had been fired, and it had missed. The Zapruder film shows the President begin to turn in his seat as another shot is fired and at that moment, his limousine disappears behind a road sign. When the car emerges from behind the sign, the President is raising his hands to his throat as he leans slightly forward and over to his left. Governor Connolly, sitting in front of the President, has also been hit and he, too falls over to his left. Had he not been wearing his back-brace, President Kennedy may well have slumped down into Jackie's lap but the brace supported his back, as it was supposed to, and he remained more or less upright. He was a sitting duck for the third shot which struck him in the head, exploding into a halo of blood and brain tissue as horrified by-standers looked on. At that moment, the limousine driver finally opened the throttle and the car sped off towards Stemmons Freeway. Agent Clint Hill ran after it and as Jackie leaned over to pick up a piece of Jack's skull, he pushed her back into her seat and hung on for dear life as the car accelerated out of the plaza.

The driver put his foot to the floor and raced off at high speed to get the mortally-wounded President and Governor Connolly to Parkland Hospital, whilst the police and some of the motor-cycle escort began to react to what had happened. Some of the spectators looked back to the TSBD building, but most ran up towards a picket-fence on top of a grassy knoll, overlooking the scene of the shooting. Many witnesses stated that they heard shots from that area and some saw smoke and could smell gunpowder. But if someone had fired from there, they were already gone by the time the police arrived.

Finding nothing in the grassy knoll area, the police soon focussed their attention back onto the TSBD and the first officer inside was Marrion Baker, who began a search of the building with the manager, Roy Truly immediately after the shots had been fired. As they rushed into the building and up the stairs, Baker and Truly encountered Lee Harvey Oswald on the second floor. He was holding a Coke he had just bought from the machine and he seemed in no way troubled or out of breath. This was just 90 seconds after the shots had been fired and this evidence would prove crucial and controversial in the days and months ahead and would be debated and deliberated for many years to come.

Meanwhile, at Parkland Hospital staff had already been alerted and they were ready and waiting when the casualties arrived. Jackie's dress was covered in Jack's blood and she refused to let go of her husband as she held his shattered head in her arms. Dave Powers ran up to the limousine as it pulled up and later stated that:
"From his forehead down, Jack's head looked so beautiful. Jackie cradled Jack in her arms and she looked up at me and said, 'I have tried to hold the top of his head down.' I knew right away he was dead."

They eventually persuaded Jackie to let go of her husband and Clint Hill threw his coat over Jack's head as they placed him on a trolley and wheeled him into the hospital. Dr Malcolm Perry tried to get Jackie to wait outside whilst they worked on the President, but she insisted on going in and she would not be deterred.
"I'm not going to leave him," she said. "He's my husband, his blood and his brains are all over me"

A priest was called to deliver the last rites and as the President lay under a sheet, Jackie pulled it back to expose his face.

"His mouth was so beautiful," she later said, "and his eyes were open."

She then took his hand and held it all through the service.

In Trauma Room 1, the team of experts led by Dr Malcolm Perry and Dr Kemp Clark got to work in a vain attempt to save the President's life. Dr Robert McClelland later stated that the President's head had been, "almost destroyed" but that the face was intact. "We knew the President was dead," he said. "Dr Clark just looked into the wound and shook his head."

The Dallas doctors tried frantically to resuscitate the President but it was clear they could do no more and at 1pm, Central Standard Time, the 35th President of the United States was pronounced dead. In a press conference shortly after, it was stated that, "The President died at 1pm Central Standard Time, from the simple matter of a bullet right through the head."

It was the opinion of the Dallas doctors that both the neck and the head wounds had come from the front. Dr Perry stated three times that he used a small bullet entry hole on the front of the President's throat to perform a tracheotomy but this was ignored by the Warren Commission, who described this hole as an exit wound. When asked by reporters about the location of the fatal shot, the hospital spokesman clearly pointed to the right front of the head to indicate that the shot had come from the front.

There then began a frantic and undignified struggle for possession of the President's body. The doctors at Parkland claimed that, as the President had been killed in an act of homicide in their city, then they should be the ones to conduct the autopsy. But the Secret Service would have none of it. They insisted that the body go back with them to Washington and despite the angry protestations from the Dallas doctors, that's exactly what happened. Secret Service agents began wheeling the President's body out to a waiting ambulance and as Dallas doctors stepped in to stop them, they were pushed back against the wall and held at gunpoint. There was nothing they could do as the body was placed in a casket and taken out to the ambulance for transferral to Air Force One, where the handles of the casket had to be removed in order to get it through the door.

Back in Dealey Plaza, the police tried frantically to gain some semblance of control, but the catalogue of errors for which the case would become so famously notorious had already begun. On finding nothing on the grassy knoll, the police soon turned their attention to the TSBD, but they failed to secure the building until almost 30 minutes after the shooting and up to that point people were free to leave, as many of them (including Oswald) did. We have already seen how Officer Baker went immediately into the TSBD building, but he was acting purely on impulse and had no real reason at that time to stop people going in and out as he was looking for no one in particular. Oswald claimed that around this time he asked someone what had happened and they told him that the President had been shot. He then left the building and strolled casually down to a bus stop to catch a bus home to his rooming house in the Oak Cliff district of Dallas. He said he did this because he thought there would be no more work done that day and he saw no point in hanging around.

Once the police had decided that the shots had come from the TSBD they eventually got around to conducting a roll-call of who was in the building at the time of the shooting, and the only person missing and unaccounted for was Oswald. They put out a description of Oswald as a suspect in the murder and as officers took statements from the people outside, they resumed their search of the building, where they found the so-called "Sniper's Perch" at the south east corner of the sixth floor. They also found some chicken bones and a half-eaten lunch which they thought had been left by the assassin, but they later learned that these had been left there by Bonnie Ray William, a TSBD employee.

Further searching revealed a rifle hidden amongst some book cases on the same floor as the Sniper's Nest. The weapon was found by Deputy Sheriff Eugene Boone and was initially reported to be a German-made Mauser with a telescopic sight. This was later claimed to be a mistake and by early afternoon, the police were stating that the rifle they found was, in fact, an Italian-made Mannlicher Carcano of World War II vintage. In the SE corner of the building, the window overlooking Elm Street was half open and behind the boxes of the Sniper's Perch they found three spent cartridges.

Oswald was now suspect number one and the hunt was on to find him. By now he had gone back to his rooming house in Oak Cliff, put on a brown zipper jacket and picked up a pistol. He said goodbye to his landlady then walked out to catch a bus back into town (or, so she claimed). The landlady said she told him that the President had been shot but he showed no emotion and said nothing, which she thought strange. She said he just came in, put on his jacket and left.

What happened next is unclear, but what is known is that Dallas Police officer, J D Tippet was driving around the Oak Cliff district when, at around 1.15pm, he stopped to apprehend a man walking quickly down East Tenth Street. Witnesses said that the policeman got out of his car to speak to this man but as the officer walked towards him, the man turned and shot him in the chest. Tippet fell to the ground and the man shot him again in the head, before running off. Witness statements on the subject are confusing and contradictory but a massive search was begun and the suspect was eventually traced to the Texas Theatre cinema, where he was arrested by Dallas Police officers. The suspect resisted arrest, claiming harassment, and he pulled a gun on the officers who had to forcibly restrain him, cutting his face in the process. On arrival at Police Headquarters, the suspect gave his name as Lee Harvey Oswald and was detained on suspicion of shooting officer Tippet.

By now the President's body had been loaded onto Air Force One, but Lyndon Johnson would not allow the plane to take off until he had been sworn-in as President. He wanted Jackie to stand next to him for the ceremony and after much persuading, she reluctantly agreed. She can be seen in photographs, a tragic, shattered figure in a blood-spattered pink suit, staring aimlessly through blood-shot eyes as Lyndon Johnson lays his hand on a Bible. She had had blood over her face too, but she agreed to wipe this off for the pictures. Jackie later said that she regretted having cleaned her face for the ceremony as she wanted the world to see the horror of what had happened and to know the strength of her feelings. When the ceremony was over, Jackie retreated to the back of Air Force One where she sat by her husband's coffin, drinking whisky with Kenny O'Donnell and Admiral

Berkley. It was suggested that she should change out of her blood-stained clothes but she refused, saying, "No, let them see what they have done."

As the President's body was flown back to Washington, the police in Dallas began to question Oswald. He protested his innocence from the start and emphatically denied having killed either Kennedy or Officer Tippet. He was questioned for more than 30 hours but was given no legal representation and despite the seriousness of the accusations against him, no notes were taken of the interviews. The police told Oswald that they would keep him away from the angry mob but Oswald declined their offer, saying he would face the world as he had nothing to hide. He was paraded before the press a number of times during the weekend and each time he strongly protested his innocence, asking for a lawyer to come forward and give him legal representation.

"I'm just a Patsy," he cried as he was ushered through the crowded hall, and that may well have been true?

Meanwhile, in the early hours of Saturday morning Bobby and the others returned to a quiet and empty Whitehouse, bringing Jack's body with them. Some of the mourners had arranged a traditional Irish wake and were drinking heavily late into the night, but Bobby did not join the party. Milt Ebbins saw Bobby standing alone with his hands on the coffin, his head was bowed and he was crying.

"I thought it strange," said Ebbins, "as Bobby never showed his emotions. He was a cold fish." Ebbins said that he thought Bobby's suffering that weekend was almost "Biblical."

Bobby eventually returned to the group and urged everyone to go to bed. He then asked George Spalding to go with him to the Lincoln Room where, after taking a sleeping pill, he said he was going to sleep.

"All this time he had been completely under control," said Spalding. "Then after I had left him and closed the door, I just heard him sobbing and saying over and over, 'why God, why?' He was just wracked with sobs."

Back in Dallas, Oswald was eventually charged with the murder of both Officer Tippet and President John F Kennedy. He continued to deny the charges and insisted that he knew nothing of either crime and he continued to ask for legal representation, which he had still not been granted. By late Saturday evening, Police Chief, Jesse Curry finally acknowledged that they were making no real progress with Oswald, so he decided it would be better to move him the short distance to the County Jail. There was a lot of angry feeling towards Oswald and it was thought that he would be safer there until a date could be set for his trial.

That trial was never to be. At 12.20pm on Sunday, November 24th Oswald was led out into the basement of the Dallas Police Headquarters where he was to be put into a car for the short ride to the Dallas County Jail. Chief Curry had wanted to move Oswald in full view of the press to show that he had not been mistreated whilst in custody and he allowed a crowd of press and TV reporters into the basement to witness the transfer. When Oswald was brought out, handcuffed to detective Jim Leavelle, the transfer car was not quite in position and they were forced to pause for a minute to wait for it. It was at that moment that small-time crook and nightclub owner, Jack Ruby stepped out and shot Oswald once with a .38 revolver as the shocked nation watched on TV. As policemen wrestled the gun from Ruby's hand, Oswald let out a short grunt then fell silent to the floor. He died in the ambulance shortly after, on his way to the same hospital that had treated Jack Kennedy just two days before.

Following the official post-mortem at Bethesda Naval Hospital, the President's body was laid in state before the grand state funeral which was to take place on Monday, 25th November; John Junior's 3rd birthday. The coffin was draped with the American flag and was carried on a gun carriage to its final resting place in Arlington National Cemetery. The world watched on TV as the young John Junior saluted his father's coffin and his proud mother looked on from beneath a black veil. The guard of honour fired a volley in salute and as the nation buried its 35th President, Lee Harvey Oswald was lowered into his own lonely grave in Rose Hill Park, Fort Worth; the only cemetery in Dallas that would take him.

That should have been the end of a tragic episode in the turbulent history of a young and troubled nation, but it would prove to be only the beginning. From the moment the shots had been fired, there were doubts and suspicions and many were already questioning Oswald's guilt and criticising the police handling of the case. The new President, Lyndon Johnson wanted desperately to silence these doubters and to close the book on the case quickly so he assigned Chief Justice, Earl Warren to head-up a Commission to investigate and deliver a verdict. The Warren Commission (as it became known) would prove to be a complete and utter travesty of justice and has since been totally and completely discredited. Its investigation was steeped in controversy from the very beginning and Chief Justice Warren had originally tried to distance himself from it from the start, only accepting the post at the insistence of President Johnson.

The Investigation and Cover-Up

As Lyndon Johnson settled into his coveted new seat in the Whitehouse, the official investigation began in earnest. Oswald was dead so there could be no trial but within days of the shooing, rumours and accusations began to spread. Lyndon Johnson and J Edgar Hoover were both keen to reach a verdict in order to ease tension at home and abroad and it was clear from the start that Earl Warren had been persuasively steered towards a conclusion that Oswald had committed the crime and that he had acted alone.

The Warren Commission's report was published on September 24th 1964 and its conclusion was that no-one but Oswald had been involved in the shooting. It also concluded that Jack Ruby had acted alone in killing Oswald and that he did so out of grief and sympathy for Jackie and to save her from the emotional distress of a difficult and very public trial. These two simple facts were to form the very fabric of the Warren Commission's findings and both have since been disproven. Oswald was not the Lone Nut the Commission had portrayed him to be, and Ruby did not kill Oswald on impulse. The likelihood is that President Kennedy was killed as a result of a complex conspiracy and that Oswald was either involved in, or had some knowledge of it, so Jack Ruby was sent to silence him before he could talk. Ruby was known to have had links with organised crime and he and Oswald were no strangers to one another. We have a number of credible witnesses who claim to have seen Oswald in the company of Jack Ruby in the weeks leading up to the killing and recently released records have shown that they had some very interesting mutual acquaintances. Ruby later said that he had more to tell and he asked to be taken to Washington where he felt safe to talk, but his request was denied and he was never allowed to divulge what he knew.

The Commission studied the assassination in minute detail and interviewed hundreds of witnesses. They considered all of the evidence and visited the scene of the crime, even re-enacting the shooting. They studied the ballistics and fingerprint evidence and they delved deep into Oswald's past; but still they got it wrong. Their conclusion was that Lee Harvey Oswald fired three shots from the south east corner of the Texas School Book Depository, killing President Kennedy and wounding Governor Connolly; but not everyone agreed. Commission member, Hale Boggs had been unhappy with the way the Commission had been managed from the start and he later went on record to say that witness statements had been altered and evidence tampered with. This bothered him a great deal and he did not sign the official report until shortly before its publication. He said that, "Hoover lied his eyes out to the Commission on Oswald, on Ruby, on their friends, the bullets, the guns; you name it."

In order to make their scenario work, the Commission concluded that one shot had missed and that only two shots actually struck the President and Governor Connolly. But there was a problem with this proposal; there were too many wounds for just two bullets. The solution to this problem came from a junior Commission investigator named Arlen Specter and his incredible and highly controversial theory has since come to be known as, "*The Magic Bullet Theory.*"

Specter proposed that if Kennedy and Connolly were sitting in just the right position relative to one another, then the two bullets that actually struck them could indeed have inflicted all of the wounds sustained by the two men. Specter theorised that the first bullet missed and hit a kerb-stone close to the triple-underpass, a piece of which wounded spectator, James Taig in the cheek. This was the bullet that caused people to react and the limousine to slow down, as seen in the Zapruder film. The second bullet hit the President in his upper back, exited through his throat and went on to hit Governor Connolly in the back, exiting through his chest and shattering his wrist before finally coming to rest in his thigh. The third bullet, claims Specter, also came from behind and hit Kennedy in the head, shattering his skull in a halo of blood and bone. But there are several significant problems with this version of events.

Firstly, looking at all the evidence that has come to light over the years it is hard to see how there could have been only three shots fired, and anything more than three shots would mean that there must have been more than one gunman. Many witnesses said they heard four shots and some said there were many more. Secondly, the Warren Commission claimed that the fatal head shot came from behind, snapping Kennedy's head forward when it struck. But the Zapruder film, which had been hidden away in the vaults of Time-Life until subpoenaed by Jim Garrison in 1967 and was not shown to the American public until 1975, showed the President's head thrown sharply backwards when the bullet struck; thus suggesting a shot from the front.

We also now know that the Warren Commission lied about the location of the wound in Kennedy's back. Pictures later unearthed by vigilant private investigators show that the Commission placed the hole in Kennedy's back higher than it really was, and they did this to make the magic bullet theory work. This was later admitted by former Commission member and one-time President, Gerald Ford in a 1997 interview. An entry wound lower down (as it actually was on the body) would not correspond with an exit wound in the throat, and for the magic bullet theory to work the bullet in the back had to exit through the hole in the throat. Even then, Kennedy would have had to have been leaning forward when shot in the back, but the Zapruder film clearly shows him sitting upright. There are those who claim to have proved that the magic bullet theory does work, but the evidence seems to show that the shot that hit Kennedy in the back could not possibly have exited through the hole in his throat; the hole that the Dallas doctors had identified as an entry wound. The bullet in question (WC exhibit No 399) was allegedly picked up from a stretcher at Parkland Hospital after falling out of Kennedy's body but despite the damage it was supposed to have caused, it was in almost pristine condition. Also, Governor Connolly has always sworn that the bullet that struck him was not the same one that had struck the President, and he has remained adamant about that all along.

The first serious attack on the Warren Commission came within weeks of the assassination, and long before the report was issued, when Mark Lane published an article in the Guardian on December 19th 1963. Lane had been hired by Oswald's mother to represent her son's interests in the Warren Commission investigation. Marguerite Oswald maintained until her death that her son was innocent of the crime and that he was actually working for US intelligence at the time and had been set-up. These views were further developed in a book entitled, *Oswald; Assassin or Fall-Guy* by Joachim Joesten, an excellent and well-crafted appraisal of the facts, published in 1964. These early works soon opened a floodgate and the Warren Commission was subjected to severe and heavy criticism long before it was ever put to the nation. It was clear from the start that the investigation was only interested in proving Oswald's guilt and establishing the Lone Nut theory and would not consider any evidence that might refute these findings.

So if it wasn't Oswald, then who else could have committed such a shocking and heinous crime, in broad daylight and in full view of the public and got away with it? Whoever it was, they must have had inside knowledge of the President's movements that day and they must have known how they would escape capture and set-up someone else to take the rap. They would have to have known the route that the President would take through Dallas and be ready and waiting in just the right spot for just the right time to act. But there is strong evidence to suggest that the motorcade route was changed at the last minute and this begs the question, who would have the authority to do this and why?

On the day of the assassination, the Dallas Morning News printed a map of the planned route which showed the motorcade going directly down Main Street and onto Stemmens Freeway before going on to the Trade Mart. It did not show the sharp right and left turns into Dealey Plaza as happened on the day, so it must have been changed at the last minute. It is interesting to note here that the Mayor of Dallas at the time was Earle Cabell, brother of former CIA Deputy Director of Operations, General Charles Cabell, who was forced to resign from his job along with Allen Dulles following the Bay of Pigs fiasco. Cabell had good reason to hate the Kennedys and would have been very well placed to change the motorcade route if asked to do so.

If the motorcade had gone straight down Main Street as planned, it would not have had to slow down to make the two sharp turns onto Houston and then onto Elm Street and, more importantly, it would not have passed directly below the TSBD. Dealey Plaza is a wide open space of grass banks and lawns with a railway bridge underpass in front and a picket fence to the right, on top of a grassy knoll. It offered a perfect location for a triangulation of fire and as the crowds here were far fewer in number, it would be a good place for a gunman to hide, do his job and get away quickly. Dealey Plaza was the perfect place for a well-planned ambush, and the motorcade had to drive through it for the plan to work.

Another strange and baffling feature of the motorcade that day was the apparent lack of security. There were no Secret Service agents on the ground in Dallas, although many people claimed they were shown Secret Service credentials by men who told them to "move on." The only Secret Service personnel assigned to protection duty that day were those riding in the motorcade and Fletcher Prouty, a former US Colonel and Chief of Special Operations has gone on record to express his sheer disbelief that this was ever allowed to happen. He said that the arrangements on that day were a shameful farce and that they should have had Secret Service men all along the route, watching the crowds, and he said that he would never have allowed, "All those open windows." Dallas police, too were told to back off and to take no part in protecting the President during his ride through town.

There seems to have been a deliberate attempt to expose the President to danger and this started as soon as the motorcade left Love Field. Newsreel footage shows Secret Service men stepping onto the running boards of the President's car as it pulls away from Air Force One, only to be ordered off again. This is most unusual and in the newsreels we can clearly see an agent looking surprisingly over his shoulder and holding out his hands in protest as the President's car drives off unprotected. The Secret Service bodyguards who would normally ride on the running boards of the President's car are forced to ride in the follow-up car.

This is even more incredible when we consider just how unpopular President Kennedy was in the oil-rich city of Dallas, where he was planning to abolish certain tax reliefs enjoyed by the Texas oil barons and worth billions of dollars to them. Add to this the right-wing extremists who resented his stance on Civil Rights and who thought him soft on communism and we can clearly see that Jack Kennedy was going into a hornet's nest in Dallas that day.

So what really did happen, and how can we know? The crowds in Dealey Plaza were much thinner than those downtown but there were still plenty of witnesses for the Warren Commission to call, but they were rather selective about who they chose to interview. Some of those closest to the President when the shots rang out were never called before the Warren Commission as the investigators seemed to be interested only in those who said they heard only three shots and that they came from the TSBD. Many people said they heard shots from the grassy knoll area to the right of the motorcade and newsreel footage shows people running in that direction immediately after the shots were fired, including a motorcycle cop who drops his bike and runs up the bank with his gun drawn. But as events unfolded and the police began to take control, the story being fed to the world was that the President had been shot from behind, by an assassin located somewhere in the Texas School Book Depository. This version of events gathered momentum with every passing hour and by early afternoon the Dallas Police were sure that the shots had been fired from the TSBD and that the man they now had in custody had pulled the trigger.

But what about the dozens of witnesses who swore that they saw and heard something very different? At least 50 witnesses said they heard shots fired from the grassy knoll and most of these were never even interviewed by the Warren Commission. Of those that were interviewed, many said that their statements had been altered and many more were badgered and bullied into changing their stories.

The Witnesses

So if we are to believe the Warren Commission, there were three shots fired at President Kennedy that day and they were all fired from the TSBD by Lee Harvey Oswald. But there were dozens of witnesses who would always bitterly contest this scenario.

Abraham Zapruder, who shot the now famous colour footage of the assassination was standing on a ledge on the grassy knoll and he said he was sure that the shots came from behind him, as did William Newman, who was also standing on the grassy knoll. Off-duty soldier, Gordon Arnold said he heard shots fired from the picket fence behind him on the grassy knoll and he even felt the whiz of a bullet fly past his ear.

Beverly Oliver was standing at the kerb facing the grassy knoll when the shots were fired. She was filming with her movie camera when the President was hit and she said in her statement that the shots came from behind the fence, right in front of her. "There was a figure there," she said, "and I saw smoke."

The FBI took the undeveloped film from her camera, promising to return it within a few days, but she has never seen it since. If there really was a gunman behind the fence, Ms Oliver's film would surely have shown him.

Charles Brehm, standing close to the President's car when the shots rang out, thought they came from the President's right front. So did Virginia Baker. She was standing on Elm Street, close to the TSBD and she said that the shots came from the direction of the triple underpass in front of the motorcade and that she saw something bounce from the roadway close to the President's car. Also standing just outside the TSBD was Depository employee, Bill Lovelady. He stated categorically that the shots came from the direction of the triple underpass. He told the Warren Commission, "I heard several loud reports, which I first thought to be firecrackers and which seemed to me to come from the direction of the Elm Street viaduct, just ahead of the motorcade. I did not, at any time, believe the shots had come from the TSBD."

William Newman was also standing on the north side of Elm Street and said that the shots came from "the garden area," behind him. Ochus Campbell, the Vice President of the TSBD said that he ran towards the fence on the grassy knoll where he, "thought the sniper was hidden."

Travelling in the follow-up car immediately behind the President's limousine, Whitehouse staff members Ken O'Donnell and Dave Powers, both close friends of Jack Kennedy, were well placed to see what was happening. In his official statement O'Donnell testified that the shots had come from the rear. Powers agreed but added that, "I also had a fleeting impression that the noise appeared to come from the front, in the area of the triple underpass."

This testimony remained unchallenged until Tip O'Neal, a well-known and respected politician claimed in his memoirs that both men had told him that they had, in fact, heard shots from the grassy knoll. O'Neal said he had never questioned the findings of the Warren Commission until having dinner one evening with Kenny O'Donnell and Dave Powers. He says that during the dinner, O'Donnell said he was sure that he heard at least two shots fired from the grassy knoll, and Powers agreed.

"That's not what you told the Warren Commission," said O'Neal.

"That's right," replied O'Donnell. "I told the FBI what I had really heard and they said it couldn't have happened that way and that I must have been imagining things. So I testified the way they wanted me to. I just didn't want to stir up any more pain and trouble for the family."

Secret Service agents, Paul Landis and Forrest Sorrels were also travelling in the follow-up car and they, too said the shots came from the front. Some people even claim to have heard multiple shots coming from all directions. Roberta Parker was standing at the entrance to the TSBD and she said that the first shots came from the cement memorial to the north of the building (where Abraham Zapruder was standing) and as she looked over in that direction, she heard two more shots which seemed to come from the TSBD. A J Millican, standing on Elm Street, went even further. He said he heard three shots come from the direction of the TSBD then he heard two more shots come from the arcade between the TSBD and the underpass. He then went on to say that he heard three more shots come from the same direction, but further back.

There were also witnesses who said they could smell gunpowder in the air at ground level at the time of the shooting. Patrolman, J M Smith said he could smell gunpowder in the area of the parking lot behind the picket fence and Senator Ralph Yarborough, riding two cars behind the President, said he could smell gunpowder in the air. If they really did smell powder, it could not have come from a rifle fired six floors up in the Texas School Book Depository.

There were, of course, many witnesses whose testimony supported the Warren Commission's conclusion that three shots were fired from the 6th floor of the TSBD. Some of those on the 5th floor even said they could hear the rifle-bolt being worked above them and shells falling onto the wooden floor. The police argued that any other shots reportedly heard by witnesses were simply echoes, and that became the official line. However, in 1975 the House Select Committee on Assassinations carried out acoustic tests in Dealey Plaza that showed that there were, in fact, more than three shots fired in the plaza that day and that, consequently, there must have been more than one gunman.

The evidence for more than one gunman is overwhelming. Lyndon Johnson, Admiral George Berkley and former CIA Director, John McCone all later stated privately that they believed there had been more than one gunman. Add to this the testimony of the numerous witnesses who swore they saw or heard shots fired from the grassy knoll and it is hard to accept the Warren Commission's "Lone Nut" theory which, after all, is just a theory like all the others and has never been contested in a court of law.

If there were two or more gunmen in Dealey Plaza that day, then they must have had men on the ground, and there were certainly people in the area whose presence cannot be easily explained. Some witnesses claim to have seen a man in a police uniform behind the fence on the grassy knoll and some even encountered bogus Secret Service agents in the vicinity. We now know that the Secret Service had no men on the ground that day but many people said they were shown Secret Service ID by officious-looking men in suits who told them to stay away from the picket fence area. Sam Holland was trying to find a good spot from which to view the parade when he was "moved on" by a man in a smart suit who showed him Secret Service credentials. Similarly, immediately following the shots, 2 policemen, Deputy Seymour Weitzman and Officer Joe Marshall were also shown such credentials by men in suits close to the fence on the grassy knoll. Marshall later said that in hindsight he should have been more vigilant because he noticed that one of the men had dirty fingernails, more in fitting with a mechanic or a manual worker than a Government agent.

The fence on the knoll was clearly a key focal point on the day and has continued to be so ever since. Following the assassination, two Dallas police officers came forward to say that they had seen several men with rifles acting suspiciously behind the picket fence in Dealey Plaza just days before the shooting. They approached the men but they got away, so the officers reported the incident to their superiors. The FBI were informed but the lead was not followed up and this strange encounter was never mentioned in the Warren Commission's report.

Lee Bowers was working in a railroad control tower to the north of the car park behind the grassy knoll and had a clear view of the area behind the picket fence and he stated that shortly before the shooting, he saw three suspicious looking cars enter and leave the area. Mr Bowers knew his cars and he had a good eye for detail. At around 11.55am he saw a 1959 Oldsmobile Station-Wagon enter the car park behind the fence and drive slowly around before leaving. The car had out-of-state plates and was driven by a middle-aged white man. He then said that at around 12.15pm he saw another car enter the area, this time driven by a white man aged about 25 to 35. This was a 1957 black Ford and also had out-of-state plates. The driver seemed to be holding a microphone or radio up to his mouth and as he drove off, yet another car pulled into the area and stopped. This was a 1961 Chevrolet Impala, white and dirty with mud up to the windows. The driver was white with long blonde hair and this car hung around a short time before leaving at 12.25pm, just 5 minutes before the shooting.

After being moved on from the grassy knoll area, Sam Holland found his way to the triple underpass to get a good view of the President as his car passed underneath. He stated that when the shots were fired, he looked over to the grassy knoll area and clearly saw a puff of smoke from the trees behind the fence. And he was not the only one to claim to have seen this.

Another key witness, often overlooked, was deaf mute, Ed Hoffman, who had also positioned himself on the triple underpass. He had an even more incredible story to tell and claimed to have witnessed the whole scenario of the shooting from his vantage point on top of the railroad bridge. He was interviewed in 1988 by the producers of *The Men Who Killed Kennedy* documentary series, where he told his story through sign-language, expressing his deep frustration at being ignored by the authorities.

Hoffman claimed that at the time of the shooting, he saw two men standing behind the picket fence on the grassy knoll, one holding a hand-gun and the other a rifle (it is interesting to note that some witnesses said that at least one shot sounded different to the others, as if it had come from a different type of gun). Hoffman stated through sign language;

"I saw two men behind the fence who looked suspicious. Both were white male. One wore a dark suit and a hat and the other wore a blue jacket and looked like a railroad worker. I saw a puff of smoke (being deaf, he heard no sound) and I thought it was a cigarette, but it wasn't. The man had a gun and he walked back towards the railroad. He tossed the gun to the second man then he turned around, straightened his jacket, adjusted his hat and walked casually away. The man in the striped shirt, the railroad shirt, then walked over to the electrical box with the gun. He took the gun apart and put it into a toolbox then he walked slowly away, in the direction of the railroad tracks."

Hoffman said that when the motorcade sped by underneath him he realised the President had been shot and was horrified. He went straight to the FBI to tell them what he had seen but they did nothing.

It has been suggested that Hoffman's disability may have led the FBI to somehow take him less seriously or that it may have affected their ability to understand what it was he was trying to say, but there is another side to this story. Hoffman was interviewed again by the FBI in June 1967 and there is no record of him giving this version of events at that time. His father and brother were also interviewed and both said that Ed had a tendency to lie and to make up stories. Hoffman's father has said that he never believed Ed's story, but friends and family members have suggested that he may be saying this to protect his son from dangerous and powerful forces.

Whatever the truth, it would appear that there was some strange and unexplained activity in the area behind the picket fence at the time of the shooting. There clearly were some suspicious vehicle movements in the area and the police failed to search any of the cars in the parking lot. They did, however, search the railroad cars parked in the sidings and found three so-called "hobos" who, on closer scrutiny, may not have been quite what they seemed?

On searching the empty railroad cars the police found three men who were arrested and questioned. There are very few photographs of these so-called tramps in existence but those we do have show three healthy, well-fed and rather affluent looking men with neatly groomed hair, good clothes and expensive-looking shoes; hardly what we would expect to see in people sleeping rough. But perhaps the strangest thing about these three men is that, despite their unusual appearance and the fact that they were found in the immediate vicinity of the shooting, they were quickly released without charge and no notes were ever taken of their interrogation. We don't even have their names.

The identity of these men has been argued over for many years. It is widely believed that one of them was E Howard Hunt, a notorious CIA operative who would later be convicted for his part in the Watergate scandal. Hunt has long been suspected of involvement in the Kennedy assassination and he even made a death-bed confession to that effect in January 2007. He was known to have been involved in CIA plots to kill Castro and he headed up the CIA's own team of assassins, known as ZR/RIFLE.

Another of the tramps was thought to be Charles B Harelson, a high-profile professional hit-man who has openly admitted to killing at least 5 people during his illustrious career. In 1988 the producers of *The Men Who Killed Kennedy* documentary series found him serving a life sentence for killing a federal judge in San Antonio, Texas. Harelson was interviewed on camera where he can be seen offering a very unconvincing, almost tongue-in cheek denial that he is one of the three men in the photos.

The Suspect

So who did kill President Kennedy and who was this Lee Harvey Oswald? The Warren Commission would have us believe that Oswald was a screwed-up, angry young man who killed Kennedy out of a deep-rooted allegiance to communism and Castro's Cuba and a sad and lonely desire for fame and notoriety. But if that were so, why did he protest his innocence so vehemently to the end?

Oswald was certainly a very complex and multifarious character and the final solution to this case may still lie somewhere with him? Born in New Orleans, he spent his early years in Dallas and then New York where he soon showed his unruly, rebellious side. He would skip school and spend his time in libraries and riding the subway and his delinquency would often land him in trouble. His was a difficult childhood in the school of hard-knocks and as soon as he was able, he achieved his boyhood ambition and joined the US Marines.

During his time in the Marines, Oswald developed a strong fascination with communist Russia, subscribing to left-wing journals and even learning the Russian language. Yet in spite of this, he was given top security clearance and posted to a highly sensitive and top secret radar and tracking facility in Japan. This shows a curiously high level of tolerance for a left-wing sympathiser in the most right-wing arm of the US military establishment at the height of the Cold War, and this has never been fully investigated or explained.

Oswald would appear to have become disgruntled with the Marines and in 1959 he was granted an early discharge, supposedly to care for his sick mother. He then claimed to have become disillusioned with the US in general and later that year, he defected to the Soviet Union. The Soviets claimed that they never really saw much value in Oswald and he was given what was said to be a menial job in a factory in Minsk. The truth was that Oswald lived a very extravagant lifestyle in Minsk, renting a luxury apartment and living way beyond the means of his so-called menial job in the electronics factory. He mixed freely with the locals and he led a very active social life and it was here that he met his Russian wife, Marina.

Oswald then decided he would like to return to the United States with his new wife and baby and despite his having betrayed his country by defecting with potentially damaging top-secret information, he was not only allowed back into the country at Government expense, but his application was actually fast-tracked and he returned to the United States with the minimum of fuss or bother. What we are being asked to believe here is that a United States Marine with top secret military clearance could defect to the Soviet Union, mix openly with known KGB agents there, take a Russian wife and then return freely to the United States without even being interviewed by the FBI!

On returning to the United States, Oswald lived for a short time in New Orleans, where he was very publicly arrested in the summer of 1963 for causing a disturbance whilst handing out "Fair Play for Cuba" leaflets and he was later interviewed on local radio claiming to be a Marxist. By contrast, Oswald had also been linked to right-wing extremist groups planning to remove Castro from Cuba and he is known to have had links with Guy Banister and David Ferrie, both right-wing fanatics and both later implicated in the plot to kill Kennedy. David Ferrie was a known right-wing anti-Castro activist and he was a key player in Operation Mongoose, the CIA's secret plot to eliminate Castro and impose a US friendly Government in Cuba. He was also a close associate of crime boss, Carlos Marcello and we shall see the significance of this later. Ferrie was to be a key witness in Jim Garrison's case against New Orleans businessman, Clay Shaw but he was found dead in his apartment just days before he was due to testify. The cause of death was alleged to be suicide through a drug overdose, but the circumstances surrounding it were highly suspicious. Ferrie had expressed fears that his life was in danger and had been under police protection and Garrison was convinced he had been murdered in order to prevent him giving evidence at Shaw's trial.

Lee Harvey Oswald was an enigma, and we may never really know exactly who or what he really was or what he really believed in. The US Government is still holding hundreds of documents on Oswald, including his service records and even his tax files and there have even been suggestions that he was an agent for the CIA. He was a complex mix of left and right-wing personas that were completely at odds with one another and this is a clear indication that he may well have been working for US intelligence. On reflection, and with the benefit of hindsight, one might suppose that Oswald's left-wing sympathies may have been a cover for his role as an agent for one or more of the US intelligence agencies and that his mission was to infiltrate these left-wing groups in order to gain their trust and establish their intentions. It is just possible that he may have been groomed in this role by rogue elements within US intelligence and led unwittingly into a trap. They could have used his left-wing, pro Castro persona (which they had created) to portray him as a Lone Nut with a grudge and then set him up to take the rap for killing Kennedy. Oswald's mother has always believed this to be the case and it may be that Oswald was exactly what he said he was; "Just a Patsy."

There can be no doubt that Oswald was in the TSBD on Friday November 22nd and that he was even on the 6th floor, but there is no real hard evidence that places him there at the time of the shooting; quite the contrary. We have already noted how he was seen, apparently calm and unruffled and drinking a Coke he had just purchased from the Coke machine in the first floor lunch-room, within minutes of the shooting. He later stated that he had been there all the time, and the evidence would seem to support that claim. This scenario is also supported by the testimony of office worker, Victoria Adams. She was watching the motorcade from a window on the 7th floor of the TSBD when the shots were fired and she immediately ran down the back staircase with a colleague to go out into the plaza. She stated that she saw or heard no-one else on the staircase and, as the stairs were old and rickety, she certainly would have known if there had been anyone else there. This was the only staircase available and the elevator was inoperative at the time, so if Oswald had gone from the 6th floor to the first floor lunch-room in time for Truly and Baker to have seen him, he would have had to come down those stairs, and very quickly. There was just no other way down. Adams has always sworn that there was no one else on that staircase when she came down it and she has never wavered from that belief.

Add to this the fact that Oswald would have had to hide the rifle amongst the boxes after wiping it clean of prints, and this lengthens further the time it would have taken him to reach the lunchroom in time to be seen by Truly and Baker. And ask yourself why? Why would an escaping assassin, having done his job, wipe his gun clean of prints and hide it in a place he knew it would be found, before fleeing the scene? Especially as the gun in question could be so easily and obviously traced back to him. This just makes no sense.

The fact is that there is no hard evidence to place Lee Harvey Oswald at the 6th floor window at the time the shots were fired. The descriptions given by witnesses who saw men in that window do not match Oswald and many witnesses say they saw two people up there in the seconds before the shots were fired. Movie footage shot by spectator, Charles Bronson shows two men moving from window to window on the 6th floor moments before the motorcade appears, and neither of them fits Oswald's description. Consider also the fact that Oswald was seen on the first floor immediately after the shooting and that he could not be placed on the staircase at that time and this shows that the case against him is not just unproven but is, in fact, most unlikely.

Shortly after the assassination, the ONI (Office of Naval Intelligence) conducted their own investigation into Oswald and concluded that he could not have been the guilty party. They then claimed to have destroyed most of their records on Oswald and promptly closed the case as far as they were concerned. Even Dallas Police Chief Curry admitted that the Dallas Police had no real, hard evidence against Oswald. They had no evidence to place him on the 6th floor at the time of the shooting and no evidence that he had even fired a gun that day. In fact, tests showed that he probably had not.

Lee Harvey Oswald was no angel and it is very likely that he was involved in the assassination in some way, or that he at least knew something about it. He did behave in a strange and peculiar way in the weeks and months leading up to the assassination and on the morning of November 22nd he left $170 on a sideboard for his wife, Marina. He also took off his wedding ring and left that in an ornate Russian cup that Marina's mother had given her. Oswald never took off his wedding ring and $170 would have been a lot of money to him at that time, so it would seem he knew something was going to happen. Was he led to believe that he was working for US intelligence and then set-up as a Patsy, or was his role more sinister? We will probably never know.

The Gun

The rifle that was alleged to have been used to shoot President Kennedy was a WWII vintage Mannlicher Carcano with a telescopic sight, but even that was not so simple. The police found the rifle stashed amongst some boxes on the 6th floor of the TSBD within a short time of the shooting but the rifle they found was at first claimed to be a German Mauser, and not a Mannlicher Carcano. Only when the police came out to show the gun to the press later was it identified as a Mannlicher Carcano, a strange choice of weapon for someone planning the crime of the century. The Mannlicher Carcano was an old, antiquated weapon of Italian make and of World War II vintage. It fired old, 6.5mm bullets that were, by then, very hard to get and it would jam more often than it would fire. It was also slow and difficult to load. Oswald's gun had no ammunition clip, which meant that each round had to be loaded separately and this would surely have been a consideration for anyone planning a shooting that would require a quick-fire operation and a quick getaway. In a state where people knew their guns, the Carcano was known to be a cheap, unreliable weapon of very poor quality and no one with any sense would even consider using it to kill the President.

So just how was this weapon linked to Oswald, and how did he come by it? For a man who so strongly protested his innocence whilst in custody, Oswald had left a surprisingly strong and visible trail of damning evidence, and there seems to have been a deliberate attempt to incriminate him in the weeks leading up to the assassination. He was allegedly seen test-driving a car like a mad-man when the real Oswald couldn't even drive. He was reportedly seen shooting at targets on a firing range saying he was imagining that they were Kennedy and a gunsmith in Irvine said he had fitted a sight to a rifle for a man named Oswald just a few weeks before, although the gun Oswald was said to have used already had a sight fitted when purchased. The gunsmith clearly remembered the man giving his name as Oswald but when he produced the receipt for the work it was noted that the name on the receipt was actually, Alek Hidell. When Oswald was arrested he was found to be carrying ID and a library card in the name of A Hidell and when questioned on this, he refused to offer any explanation. Later investigation revealed that the Mannlicher Carcano found in the TSBD was purchased by mail-order from Klein's Sporting Goods in Chicago by a man named A Hidell. He paid just $19.95 for it. Curiously though, Oswald was carrying no Carcano ammunition when arrested and none was found at his house so if he really had bought the gun, why had he not bought ammunition?

None of this made any sense. If Oswald had wanted to cover his tracks, he could easily have gone into any gun store in Texas and bought a weapon anonymously over the counter using fake ID. And in a state where guns are inexpensive and easy to come by, any serious assassin would never have chosen the Carcano for such an important job, and he would certainly not have bought it by mail order. The only possible reason for purchasing the gun by mail-order would be to draw attention to it and to make it easy to trace; in this case, to Alek Hidell. Oswald was carrying Hidell ID when arrested but this could easily have been a set-up, a bogus ID that he had no idea had been used to purchase the weapon that supposedly killed the President. The FBI found no prints matching Oswald's on the gun when they first examined it but they did eventually find a palm-print on it on the Sunday, hours after Oswald had been killed. Dallas Police fingerprint expert, Carl Day said later that he did find a thumb print on the gun and it was not Oswald's, but he was told to keep quiet. Another curious twist to this tale was added by staff working at the funeral home where Oswald's body had been kept. They claimed that on the Sunday night, two plain clothes agents arrived, showed them some Government ID and said they wanted to view Oswald's body, alone and in private. They were shown into the chapel and spent some time with the body before leaving as suddenly as they had arrived.

There would appear to be strong evidence that there were at least two, and possibly even three rifles used in the shooting of President Kennedy. Many claim that the reference to the Mauser was not a mistake at all but was a reference to a second gun found in the TSBD and there was some evidence for yet another, found on the roof. A film taken by Dallas Cinema Associates immediately after the assassination shows police officers descending the staircase from the roof of the TSBD holding up a rifle. This rifle has no telescopic sight so could not have been the Mannlicher Carcano but, like the Mauser, it simply disappeared and was never recorded or entered as evidence.

It seems very likely that had he lived, Oswald would never have been successfully convicted of the murder of John F Kennedy, which is exactly why he had to be silenced so quickly. The evidence against him was just too weak and controversial and any good lawyer could have taken the prosecution apart if the case had ever come to trial. But what about the President's body, would the autopsy offer any clues as to who shot JFK and from which direction the bullets had come? The simple answer to this question is, no. The official autopsy of JFK's body was a complete and utter farce and there is strong evidence to suggest that there were, in fact, two autopsies and that the body had been tampered with before it ever reached Bethesda Naval Hospital for the official autopsy late on Friday night.

The President's body arrived at Bethesda Naval Hospital on the evening of the assassination in a simple, grey casket and was found to be completely naked, except for a white sheet wrapped around the head. This has been confirmed by all present at the time the casket arrived and was described by medical technician, Paul O'Connor as follows.

"The door opened and about 6 or 7 people rushed in carrying a casket, a cheap grey shipping type casket, and the

President's body was in a grey body bag. We took the body out of the casket and placed it on the table. It was nude, with a white sheet wrapped around the head."

However, this was not the casket in which the body was flown out of Dallas on Air Force One. Dallas funeral home attendant, Aubrey Wright testified that in Dallas on that Friday afternoon he placed the body of the President in a large, expensive bronze casket, wrapped all over in white sheets. This casket can be seen being loaded onto Air Force One at Love Field where, the reader may recall, the handles had to be removed to get it through the door. Somewhere between leaving Dallas and arriving at Bethesda, the caskets had been changed and the body tampered with.

The official autopsy at Bethesda would be carried out under the complete control of the military. The procedure was performed by Doctors Humes and Boswell, assisted by Dr Pierre Finck and in the presence of President Kennedy's personal physician, Dr George Burkley. These men had little or no experience of dealing with gun-shot wounds and were woefully unqualified for the task. The room was filled with people and was extremely noisy and the doctors were bombarded with orders and instructions not to do this or that and to skip procedures that would and should have been followed as a matter of routine. Humes was not even allowed to trace the trajectory of the bullets through the body or to probe the entry and exit wounds with his fingers.

Photographs and X-rays were taken of the body but these were never shown to the Warren Commission and witnesses have since sworn that the photographs that did eventually emerge from various sources had been heavily doctored. The wound in the back was shown to be much higher up than it actually was and the head wound looked nothing like the gaping hole seen by witnesses on the day of the autopsy. Witnesses who were present in both Dallas and at Bethesda described the wound in Kennedy's head as a massive, gaping hole with a large part of the brain destroyed, but autopsy photographs released much later show a far less severe wound. They also appear to have been doctored to show a shot from the rear and not from the front, as many witnesses had claimed.

It later emerged that at some point during the autopsy, Dr Burkley was actually removed from the room for being difficult and obstructive and the procedure was continued by junior doctors. One of these doctors, Dr David Osborne later testified that during the autopsy a bullet dropped out of the President's body onto the table and that he gave it to one of the by-standers, who slipped it into his pocket and told him to keep quiet. This bullet was never entered as evidence and would have been at least bullet number 4. In fact, we have yet another bullet found in Dealey Plaza by a police officer, who tagged it and submitted it to the FBI. This bullet was never recorded in the evidence either, and would have been at least bullet number 5.

Whilst the autopsy was being conducted, Jackie and Bobby were in a room on the 17th floor with family members and some close friends, including Jackie's mother and Jack's sister, Jean. Dr Burkley later joined them and it is claimed that the autopsy was really controlled from there, with Bobby giving the orders. Despite the official findings of the autopsy, Dr Burkley always believed that there must have been more than one gunman in Dealey Plaza that day and, amazingly, he was another key witness who was never called before the Warren Commission. His note on the death certificate that the wound in the throat was an entrance wound (suggesting a shot from the front) was never entered into the official record and he was side-lined and ignored. Dr Burkley remained silent for many years but in 1983, he finally unburdened himself by telling researcher, Harry Hurt that he had always believed that Jack Kennedy had been the victim of a conspiracy.

When the autopsy was finished, Dr Burkley went downstairs and removed the wedding ring from Jack's finger and brought it up to Jackie. She then gave him one of the red roses she had been carrying all day, a souvenir he treasured for the rest of his life. Bobby took the slides and photographs, together with what was left of the President's brain and placed them in the National Archive for safe keeping. He also considered taking possession of the limousine but Evelyn Lincoln informed him that it had been sent to Detroit to be "done over" for President Johnson. People in Detroit later claimed that there was bullet damage in the windscreen (which was replaced) and on the front bumper. The damaged windscreen and bumper have never been found.

The Theories

President John F Kennedy was killed in broad daylight and in full public view but although there were hundreds of witnesses to the event, we are no closer to knowing the truth now than we were the minute the shots were fired. Perhaps Oswald did do it after all and maybe he shot Tippet, too? But the evidence would suggest otherwise. It may also be true that shots were fired from the 6th floor of the TSBD but that, in itself, does not necessarily mean that Oswald pulled the trigger. If there were shots fired from that location, they could just as well have been fired by someone else and there have been plenty of possible candidates put forward for this over the years. Some witnesses claim to have seen two men in the SE corner window of the TSBD and some saw figures in other windows on the sixth floor, too. Some even claim that shots may have been fired from the Dal-Tex building, one block away from Dealey Plaza and to the rear of the motorcade. Shots fired from that location would mimic almost exactly the shots that the Warren Commission claimed came from the TSBD and however outlandish, the theory deserves further examination.

Whatever Oswald's involvement, it would appear that President Kennedy was caught in a triangulation of fire, an ambush with as many as three or more shooters firing at him as his car drove slowly down Elm Street. There were dark and powerful forces at work that day and they had determined that Jack Kennedy could not come out of that plaza alive.

Despite all of the evidence and witness testimony it remains difficult to say just who fired the shots at President Kennedy that day, but the truth about who planned it and why is even more elusive. The assassination of President Kennedy has spawned thousands of books and numerous films and documentaries and we have seen all kinds of conspiracy theories put forward over the years. These range from the more serious, well-argued scenarios like the involvement of the CIA or a hit arranged by the mob, to a Secret Service agent accidentally firing his gun at the President from the follow-up car. These and other theories are more than adequately covered in other books and we do not need to examine them in any depth here. We are primarily concerned with how the death of Jack Kennedy fits into the overall pattern of what happened to the Kennedy family but the nature of his death may have its roots in his father's earlier actions, so it is worth considering at least some of the most credible of these theories in order to help gain a fuller understanding of who may have killed JFK and why?

In the 1970's, French drugs trafficker, Christian David filed a letter with his lawyer in which he confessed his involvement in the Kennedy assassination and gave details of how he claimed it happened. Now known as the French or Latin Connection, David describes how he was contacted by members of the US Mafia to plan and carry out the murder of the President, using professional hit-men brought in from France.

David says that he was offered a contract to take out a "leading political figure" in the United States in June 1963. He says that three gunmen were flown from Marseilles to Mexico by an associate of the Chicago Mafia, not named but now generally believed to have been David Ferrie. They then entered the United States through Brownsville before moving on to a safe-house in Dallas, from where they could recce the proposed site of the shooting. David named one of the gunmen as Lucien Sarte, a known drugs trafficker and he says that he wore a police uniform as a disguise on the day (it may be recalled that witnesses reported seeing a man in police uniform on the grassy knoll at the time of the shooting). He did not name the other two shooters and Sarte was killed in a shoot-out with police in Mexico City in 1972. David also volunteered the detail that Sarte had wanted to shoot from the railroad bridge but in the end, fired from behind the fence on the grassy knoll.

David claims that the hit was planned by mobsters, Carlos Marcello and Santos Trafficante in association with rogue elements of the US intelligence services. This has some credence as it is known that Marcello and Trafficante were actively plotting to kill JFK around this time. In a 1962 meeting at his New Orleans headquarters, Carlos Marcello went wild when Kennedy's name was mentioned. "Take the stone out of my shoe," he said; a Sicilian metaphor for removing an enemy, and they all understood what he meant. It was agreed that the real problem was Robert Kennedy, the Attorney General, and some suggested that he should be taken out, but Marcello had a better idea. He said that to kill a dog, you must remove the head and the tail stops wagging, and it was clear to all present that he was advocating the murder of the President, and not the Attorney General. According to David, Marcello said that arrangements had already been made and that a "Lone Nut" had been lined up to take the blame. The plan had been worked out in minute detail, using outside hit-men as they would not be known to the US police and therefore could not be traced. He said that the FBI had been informed of this plan, but they did nothing.

Another, more recently proposed scenario is in some ways similar to the one outlined above, but offers a little more insight into a possible motive. In their ground breaking book, *Ultimate Sacrifice* Lamar Waldron and Thom Martmann claim they have finally established the truth behind the JFK assassination and why it had to be covered up, and their arguments are very convincing. They say that they interviewed over two dozen close associates of Jack and Robert Kennedy, including JFKs Secretary of State, Dean Rusk. This led them to files in the National Archive that show how Carlos Marcello and Santos Trafficante, along with mob leader, Johnny Rosselli did, indeed have Jack Kennedy murdered in such a way that powerful people like

Robert Kennedy, J Edgar Hoover and Lyndon Johnson would be forced to keep quiet and do nothing.

The book claims that the Cuban Missile Crisis never really ended at all as Castro refused to allow US weapons inspectors into the country as agreed in the treaty. This was interpreted by the Kennedys to mean that their pledge not to invade Cuba was no longer legally binding, so they were free to reconsider all the options available to them to remove Castro. Castro was becoming ever-more bold and belligerent but despite years of trying to remove him from power, he was still there and growing stronger by the day. Castro was beginning to look more like a dictator than a man of the people and many of his own aides and advisors were unhappy with the way he was leading the country. In particular, Juan Almeida, one of the original members of Castro's rebel force and now the head of the Cuban army, had become disillusioned with Castro and the revolution and he made overtures to Robert Kennedy that he would be willing to work with the US in eliminating Castro and imposing a more enlightened form of Government in Cuba. In a top secret, covert operation the CIA had made contact with Almeida and were planning a coup to remove Castro and put Almeida at the head of a new Cuban Government prior to holding open, democratic elections. The plan was that once Castro had been removed, the US would step in and invade Cuba on the pretext that they had been invited to do so by the Cuban people. This was all set to take place on December 1st 1963 and Almeida was just waiting for a key phrase in a speech to be delivered by President Kennedy as the signal to move.

This was, of course a very dangerous and risky proposal and if it failed, the consequences could be dire, and the mob used this to blackmail Robert Kennedy into doing nothing following the death of his brother. The book claims that rogue elements of the CIA engaged Marcello and Trafficante to kill Jack Kennedy and that the two crime bosses then forced Bobby and the authorities to hide their involvement in return for their silence on the Almeida plot. President Kennedy was killed just days before this plan was to be put into action and his death put the entire operation on hold. Bobby was forced to comply in order to protect Almeida, who was still in office and remained so for many years after, and to avoid a diplomatic crisis that could easily lead to all-out war. Waldron and Martmann have researched this theory extensively for over twenty years and they present a very detailed and well-argued case in their book. There can be no doubt that the Kennedys never really gave up on the idea of removing Castro from Cuba, or that they worked closely with the CIA and even the mob to achieve that goal. If we consider that point, then the Almeida plot seems entirely credible and this scenario would certainly explain why so many people in high office knew so much and did so little. The threat of all-out nuclear war is a powerful deterrent.

It is clear to us now that a lot of important and very powerful people knew more about the Kennedy assassination than they ever let on. Robert Kennedy had always maintained to close friends that he thought the mob had killed Jack and, privately at least, he never wavered from that belief. Many believe that J Edgar Hoover had some prior knowledge of it and there is a very strong case to suggest that Lyndon Johnson may have been involved, too. Johnson was clearly a very manipulative and unscrupulous character who would stop at nothing to get what he wanted.

Johnson's possible involvement in the assassination of JFK is covered extensively and very convincingly in the book, *The Dark Side of Lyndon Baines Johnson*, by Joachim Joesten, and has been much debated over recent years.

There had been rumours of Lyndon Johnson's involvement in the assassination from the start and when Johnson died in 1973, more evidence began to emerge to support that hypothesis. Johnson's former attorney went on record to say that he knew for a fact that Lyndon Baines Johnson had President Kennedy killed and even LBJ's former mistress and life-long confidante, Madeline Brown said she believed that Johnson arranged the killing of the President and that he was in on the plot. She claims that she was at a party with Johnson and J Edgar Hoover the night before the assassination when Johnson turned to her and said.

"Those Kennedy SOBs will never embarrass me again. That's not a threat, it's a promise."

These claims have been substantiated by other witnesses.

Johnson's lust for power began when he cheated his way into the Senate in 1948 and he won that election by the narrowest of margins in what we now know was a rigged ballot. The incident became known as the Box 13 scandal and it was the start of a long and successful political career based on bribery, corruption and intimidation that would earn Johnson the nickname, Lying Lyndon. Lyndon Johnson was a ruthless, dangerous man who would do anything to get what he wanted, and he wanted the presidency more than anything else in the world.

In 1984 Billy Sol Estes, former business associate of Johnson testified to a grand jury about his dealings with Johnson and other officials, and his claims were a shattering revelation. He gave evidence of Johnson's corrupt dealings with leading figures in business and in politics and he listed at least 8 people that he said LBJ had had killed, including John F Kennedy and Johnson's own sister. This, he said, was achieved through Johnson's close association with a known hitman named Malcolm Wallace.

Wallace was named as one of gunmen in the JFK assassination in Mark Collom's book, *The Men on the 6th Floor* and he was certainly involved in a number of controversial murders in the 1960's. In 1961, Government official Henry Marshall was investigating LBJ and others on charges of bribery and corruption and it is alleged that when bribery failed, LBJ gave the order to "get rid" of Marshall. In June of that year, Marshall's body was found next to his car. His head had been battered and he had a high level of carbon monoxide in his bloodstream and he had been shot 5 times with a bolt-action rifle. It was widely believed that Wallace had done the deed but the official verdict was that Marshall had committed suicide. And this was not the first time Wallace had escaped justice on such a charge. In 1951 he had been convicted of the murder of John Douglas Kinser and received just a 5 year suspended sentence. It is believed by some that LBJ ordered the killing and that he pulled strings to get Wallace off.

By 1961, Johnson's past was catching up with him. He was in a powerless position as Vice President and he was under investigation from a number of different directions. Kennedy was pulling out of Vietnam, he was attacking the oil barons' generous oil depreciation allowance and he had curtailed the activities of the CIA and one theory is that all of these people got together to do something about it. Johnson had a lot of good reasons for killing Jack Kennedy and it is believed by many that he ordered the assassination, or that he at least knew about it and was involved in some way.

There is strong evidence to suggest that Wallace may well have been one of the shooters in the Texas School Book Depository on November 22nd and if that is so, then there may be good cause to suspect Lyndon Johnson's involvement. When checking fingerprints in the vicinity of the sniper's perch, the police came across one print they could not identify. This was later shown to one of the top fingerprint experts in the country and he was able to state quite categorically and without any doubt that this print belonged to Malcolm Wallace. He found a 34 point match, which is about as good as it gets, and he was certain that this was a print from Wallace's little finger. The print was re-examined by the FBI and after deliberating for 18 months, they came back and said it was not a match.

Another theory, seemingly put forward by mobster, Johnny Rosselli was that President Kennedy had been killed by members of his own Secret Service, who had been programmed by Castro to do so. The Kennedys had become obsessed with Castro and worked closely with the CIA to eliminate the Cuban leader throughout the whole of Jack's presidency. Rosselli claimed that Robert Kennedy sent a hit squad to Cuba to take out Castro but that they were captured, tortured and brain-washed to return to the US and hit Kennedy. This scenario has been given some credence by some but most researchers dismiss it as pure fantasy and when we consider the likely source, we can see why.

There have been a number of serious attempts to establish the truth behind the assassination of John F Kennedy but none of them have really answered the key questions in any convincing way. The scenarios outlined above are just the tip of the iceberg and they may or may not be true. In 1976, the House Select Committee on Assassinations investigated the murders of Jack and Bobby Kennedy and of Martin Luther King and they concluded that President Kennedy had probably been the victim of a conspiracy, but they fell short of naming the culprits.

In his 1972 book, *The Fabulous Jackie*, Christian Cafarakis reveals that Jackie also tried to get to the truth but that she, too was thwarted. He tells how Jackie appointed a famous New York detective agency to investigate the case and that the agency uncovered the plot and was even able to name the four gunmen involved. Jackie was going to give the report to President Johnson but was prevented from doing so by death threats on her and her children. Cafarakis claims that the Kennedy family knew about the report but if they did, they have always maintained their silence.

Will we ever know the truth? In 1992, 4 million pages of information on the JFK assassination were released to the public but the Washington group, OMB Watch determined that over 1 million records relating to the assassination are still being withheld by the CIA alone. It is likely that the FBI and other investigative and law-enforcement bodies are holding many more. We may never really know for certain who killed JFK and why. Years go by, memories fade, witnesses pass-on, interest dwindles. But it is important that those die-hard researchers continue to seek out the truth. This was not just a murder gone unpunished, it was an audacious and vicious attack on democracy that sends out the message that no-one is safe and that there are dark forces all over the world that will stop at nothing to achieve their own aims and ambitions.

With the death of Jack, the Kennedys' run of bad luck took on a very different and more sinister dimension. Although undoubtedly pressured by his father, no one had set out to kill young Joe when he took off on his mission in 1944, and the death of Kathleen was just another tragic accident. But with Jack, it was different. The Kennedys had reached the top of the greasy pole, but they had made a lot of enemies along the way. These people would not lie down and play dead and to incur their wrath would be a bitter and fatal mistake. Jack Kennedy was never going to be allowed to ride rough shot over the mob and the CIA and get away with it and his arrogant self-belief had, in the end, cost him his life.

It would appear that Joe Kennedy had made promises to the mob in return for their support and favour, but his sons had failed to keep their part of the bargain. Joe had raised them up to positions of power but he found that once there, they proved hard to control and wanted instead to do things their own way. With this power came confidence and Joe soon realised that he was losing his grip and his influence over them was waning. Their sheer arrogance had blinded them to the dangers that their father knew only too well, and they thought themselves invincible. They played the game and they lost, and they paid dearly for their mistakes.

One might suppose that the Kennedys would learn from this and step back out of the limelight and, for a time, they did. But it would not be long before the next Kennedy hopeful would step up to take his place in on the world stage and make his own impassioned bid for power. Would he fare any better than his brother?

7 BOBBY

Bobby Kennedy was always very different from the other Kennedy boys. Born on November 20th 1925, Robert Francis Kennedy was the third son of Joe and Rose Kennedy, and from the very beginning he had to fight for his place in a family where only the toughest survived. It was never going to be easy following in the footsteps of his older brothers and Bobby's wife, Ethel once said of him, "The main difference between Bobby and his brothers is that Bobby had to fight for everything." He was a weak and scrawny boy and his father unkindly dubbed him the "Runt" of the family.

Bobby was always the gentlest and the shyest of the Kennedy boys and his fondness for sitting with his sisters at family meals caused his grandmother to worry that he was becoming a "sissy". Lifelong friend, Lem Billings said that Bobby was, "Just the most generous little boy," and his nurse, Luella Hennessey called him, "The most thoughtful and considerate of his siblings." Bobby could not have been more different from his overbearing father and by the time he started school, Joe had pretty much written him off. But he would go on to surprise them all.

Like his brothers before him, Robert Kennedy attended a number of prestigious schools including Riverdale, Portsmouth Primary and the Milton Academy. He was a hardworking, if somewhat unremarkable student and he applied himself to his studies with a determination and vigour that would later become his trademark. A friend recalled how he once gave Bobby a copy of the following day's Latin exam paper that he had stolen from the Master's study. Bobby was horrified and the friend later found the paper in the bin and said that he never really knew whether Bobby had used it or not. He said that Bobby always demonstrated a very serious demeanour; a kind of Alter-Boy disposition.

From a very early age, Robert Kennedy displayed a very strong sense of right and wrong and he was a devout and sincere Catholic. He was very close to his mother and at Portsmouth Primary he was known as, "Mrs Kennedy's little boy," due to the fact that he once proudly introduced his mother to his class-mates. On one particular occasion a long-standing friend made a joke about a picture of Rose Kennedy in a magazine and Bobby went "ballistic," chasing the boy out of the room. Another friend said that Bobby had, "This streak of loyalty to his entire family and the merest slight sufficed to set him off."

But Bobby's devotion to his mother was not born out of any wimpish, Mummy's Boy disposition but rather was a true and sincere show of love and affection. Young Robert Kennedy was no sissy. He was a tough, resilient, hard-nosed fighter who refused to accept failure or defeat in anything. He once said of being the 7th child in a large, competitive family, "When you come from that far down, you have to struggle," and his eldest brother, Joe once described him as a person with, "Either a lot of guts or just no sense." He was always being picked on by his older brothers and this made him very strong and determined. Life was tough and demanding for young Bobby Kennedy and he always swore that when he had kids of his own, he would bring them up differently.

There was no place like the Kennedy nursery for learning the hard lessons in life. In a bid to prove himself in a tough, dog-eat-dog world the young Robert Kennedy soon showed a feisty spirit that would stay with him all of his life. At 4 years of age he would repeatedly wade into a rolling sea and have to be rescued by Joe or Jack as he disappeared beneath the waves. When he was just 5, his sister Eunice once threw a plate of pudding at him and he jumped from his chair and leapt across the table at her with such ferocity that he needed 15 stitches in his head.

At Milton School people remembered Bobby for his shyness, determination and self-mocking sense of humour. He tried hard to be more confident around girls but fellow-student, Mary Piedy recalled that, "He just walked around with his head way down, buried in his neck like a bird in a storm." He would stand on one foot with the other resting on top, his hands way down in his pockets, "Moon-faced and with a forelock that dropped down over his right eye."

But over time, Bobby's shyness with girls passed. Former class-mate, Samuel Adams recalled how at one time he and Bobby both liked the same girl and both wanted to ask her out. Bobby convinced Sam that they should dismiss such thoughts from their minds as they had too much studying to do to allow themselves to be distracted, and Adams agreed. He later discovered that while he was busy studying for his exams, Bobby had taken the girl out himself.

Bobby tried hard to succeed at school but these were difficult times for him. Class-mate, David Hacket later said that Bobby was neither a natural athlete nor a natural student, and neither was he a natural with the girls. He said Bobby had no natural gift for anything and nothing ever came easy for him. Bobby's school report once said.
"He writes poorly and needs to learn the elements of expression, but he has a refreshing habit of asking how and why?"

Bobby himself later remembered that in his younger years, "I was very awkward and dropped things, and I fell down all of the time. I had to go to hospital a few times for stitches in my head and leg and I was pretty quiet most of the time. I never minded being alone."

Joe Kennedy was hard on all of his boys but there can be no denying that, despite the pressures of growing up a Kennedy child, Bobby did have a privileged and somewhat sheltered upbringing. He worked hard to compete with his fellow-students and older brothers but the family wealth and influence was never far away. That's not to say he was frivolous with money; far from it. He once loaned a school friend five dollars that he never repaid and when the two met up much later in life Bobby greeted his old friend with, "Hey bud, how you doing? And where's my five bucks?" And he wasn't joking! Bobby liked to make out he was just one of the guys, but it was never really quite like that. After all, how many of those other "guys" would take a job delivering newspapers from the back seat of his Daddy's limousine?

When Joe Kennedy was appointed US Ambassador to Great Britain, Bobby moved to London with the rest of the family but he returned to the United States at the outbreak of war in Europe. When the US later entered the war on Britain's side Bobby desperately wanted to follow his brothers into action but to his great disappointment, he was too young for active service, so he joined the Naval Reserve and was sent to the V-12 Navy College at Harvard. In December 1945 the Navy commissioned a destroyer, the *Joseph P Kennedy Jr* in honour of young Joe, who had been killed in action the year before and Bobby served in this vessel for a short time in 1946.

In May 1946 Bobby received an honourable discharge from the Navy and returned to Harvard to continue his studies and he was still a full-time student when he found the love of his life in Ethel Shakel, the daughter of a wealthy Chicago businessman and a former class-mate of his sister, Jean. The romance blossomed and the two were married in a lavish, high society wedding on June 17th 1950. Bobby and Ethel were well-matched and the couple were very happy together and they would go on to have 11 children before Bobby's tragic and untimely death. Meanwhile, Bobby continued to study for his Massachusetts Bar Exam and he graduated from the Virginia Law School in 1951.

In late 1951, Bobby embarked on a 7 week tour around Asia with Jack (who was by then a Congressman) and their sister, Pat. This was the first time that Bobby and Jack had spent any meaningful time together and they formed a deep, strong bond that would serve them both well in the years to come. But Bobby knew that at some point he was going to have to choose a career for himself and in November 1951 he and Ethel moved to Georgetown, Washington where he took his first job as a lawyer in the Internal Security section of the US Department of Justice. He soon proved his worth in this role but he resigned in June 1952 to manage Jack's campaign for the Senate.

Getting Bobby to run Jack's campaign was their father's idea and was a stroke of genius. Bobby threw himself full-force into the task of ensuring Jack's election to the Senate and he proved to be a formidable and unstoppable force. He planned every aspect of the campaign in minute detail and he spent Daddy's money wisely. From dawn until dusk he was there, leading from the front and driving the campaign workers hard, every minute of the day and long into the night. Bobby had at last been presented with an opportunity to show his father just what he could do, and he didn't disappoint. Jack Kennedy was elected Senator for Massachusetts and they all knew that his success was largely due to Bobby's relentless, untiring management of the election campaign.

Having achieved his objective of getting Jack elected to the Senate, Bobby turned again to his own career. In December 1952 his father pulled strings to get him a job as Assistant Counsel on the US Sub-Committee on Investigations under close family friend, Senator Joseph McCarthy. However, Bobby clashed with fellow committee member, Roy Cohn and he resigned from this post in July 1953.

After working for a short time with his father, Bobby returned to Washington where he wrote a report condemning McCarthy's allegations of communism in the US Army and openly criticising McCarthy's tactics. He later gained notoriety for his work on Senator John McClellan's Senate Sub-Committee on Racketeering, where he fought vice and corruption in the Trade Union movement.

Robert Kennedy was a straight-talking, no nonsense totalitarian with a very strong sense of right and wrong. To him, the world was black and white, with no grey area in between. There were good guys and there were bad guys and in Bobby's ideal world, the good guys had to win and the bad guys must be punished. Life Magazine's Paul O'Neil once wrote of Bobby.

"He is motivated by a stern and literal belief in concepts of good and evil which most humans abandon after childhood and by a sense of duty to family and country which overrides his own considerable ambition."

He was, as Jack often said, incorruptible.

Bobby held a sincere and almost naïve belief that good must prevail, and this drove him to pursue vice and corruption with the relentless passion of an all-out crusade. He made it his mission in life to root out evil and corruption, in any place and at any level and to Robert Kennedy, the very personification of corruption and evil was Teamsters Union leader, Jimmy Hoffa.

Jimmy Hoffa was a tough and aggressive power-hungry tyrant who had gained his position in the union through violence and intimidation and he maintained it by doing deals with the mob. He was used to getting his own way and was feared by friends and enemies alike, but he had more than met his match in Robert Kennedy. Hoffa had come from the school of hard knocks and he saw Robert Kennedy as nothing more than a spoilt brat who had used his father's money to gain a position of power and the two of them harboured a mutual hatred of one another that would only intensify over the ensuing years. They were both fiercely competitive and they would watch each other's every move in an effort to ensure that no one gained the upper hand. Once when Bobby was being driven home after work, he saw the lights still on in Hoffa's office. "Turn the car around," he said to his driver. "If Hoffa is working late, so are we."

In January 1957 the US Senate created the Select Committee on Improper Activities and Bobby used this forum to showcase his skills as a tough prosecutor of mobsters and criminals like Hoffa and Mafia boss, Carlos Marcello. The sessions were shown live on TV and Bobby became a national hero as he ferociously attacked gangsters and hoodlums that no one else dared touch. He was fiercely aggressive with his intimidating style of questioning and he,

"Just went for them like something possessed." One reporter wrote how on the Tonight show on June 23rd 1959, the audience saw Bobby change "From a shy, quiet boy to a fierce fire-spouting religious zealot when the subject of Hoffa came up."

"They think they are above the law," Bobby spouted. "They think they can fix judges and juries and they say that every man has his price. This country can't survive if you have somebody like that operating, and they won't win in the end."

Bobby had taken his place on the world stage and he had made his position quite clear. He would stop at nothing to ensure that crime and corruption would not go unpunished and there were no exceptions to this rule. Even his own father and his brother, Jack were surprised at his relentless, unflinching determination that all these vile, corrupt people should be tracked down and punished; whoever they may be. High and low, rich and poor, friend or foe, it made no difference to Robert Kennedy. A bad guy was a bad guy and he would answer for his crimes.

If Bobby had made an enemy in Jimmy Hoffa, he made an even bigger one in J Edgar Hoover and this, too would prove to be a life-long battle. One might have thought that as head of the FBI, Hoover would have backed Bobby to the hilt, but he opposed and blocked him in any way he could. Hoover had refused to accept that the Mafia even existed at all and he denied that the US had a problem with organised crime, but Bobby just worked around him. He proved that not only did the Mafia exist but that it was deeply entrenched into American society at every level and that it controlled business and Government interests everywhere. This made Hoover look out of step with the world and he was bitterly resentful of the success Bobby was having in tackling organised crime. Hoover hated the Kennedys with a passion that he found hard to repress and he was not a man to cross. In chairing these sessions, Bobby had made enemies of some very dangerous people with very long memories and he cared nothing for their threats and their scorn.

In 1959, Bobby quit his job at the Justice Department in order to manage Jack's campaign for the presidency. He had done a terrific job in getting Jack elected to the Senate and he was the obvious choice to head up Jack's campaign against Richard Nixon. He visited more than 300 homes per day and shook hands so many times he had blisters. Dave Powers later said that when Bobby asked people to vote for Jack, "You would have thought he was inviting them to enter the Kingdom of Heaven."

Jack's bid for the Whitehouse was, of course, successful and once there, Jack bowed to pressure from his father to appoint Bobby as Attorney General. Jack was not keen on the idea and Bobby certainly didn't want the job but he soon became Jack's closest advisor and would be his rock throughout his term in office.

"If I want anything done and I want it done right away," Jack once told a reporter, "I rely on the Attorney General."

Bobby's role as Attorney General was unique in the Government as he was closer to Jack than any of his other advisors. He became known as the second most powerful man in Washington and he was given full autonomy to act on his brother's behalf in many key areas of Government. He helped steer Jack through the troubled waters of the Bay of Pigs fiasco, the Cuban Missile Crisis and the struggle with the Soviets and he had his finger in every pie, sometimes with damaging effect. Bobby became obsessed with the idea of removing Castro from Cuba and he conspired with the CIA in secret plots to assassinate the Cuban leader. He ran covert operations and worked closely with various Government agencies and organisations to eliminate Castro or to have him overthrown. But he was playing a dangerous game and this would have serious ramifications later on.

Robert Kennedy had a very strong and engaging personality and he brought a fresh new approach to the role of Attorney General. He was more relaxed and unconventional than previous incumbents and he breathed new life into the stuffy old Justice Department of the Eisenhower regime. He would sit back in his chair with his feet up on the desk, his tie hanging loose and his sleeves rolled up as he talked on the phone to officials up and down the country. He would bring his pet dog into the office with him and the walls were decorated with pictures that his kids had drawn for him. He would interrupt important meetings to talk on the phone with Ethel or the kids and he was relaxed and informal whenever prudence would allow. Most of his staff found this approach both refreshing and inspiring, but there were still those who did not approve.

As Attorney General, Bobby was now Hoover's boss and the FBI chief hated Bobby's casual, informal style. This was made even worse when Bobby installed a buzzer on his desk to summon Hoover to his office whenever he wanted to see him and Hoover found this both demeaning and disrespectful. No one had ever treated Hoover that way before and this only fuelled the bitter hatred that Hoover felt for the Kennedys. J Edgar Hoover was a vain and petty man who bore lifelong grudges and in making an enemy of him, Bobby was playing with fire. Hoover was one of the most powerful men in the country and he was not going to be pushed around by these cocky little rich kids from Massachusetts.

It was during this time that Bobby began to develop a real awareness of the plight of black people in America and of the need for social reform. His role in Government had given him a unique insight into the social problems facing the nation at that time and he saw for himself how the country was being torn apart by poverty and inequality in certain quarters. Bobby was slow to respond to the issue of Civil Rights but as the black people of America began to fight back against segregation, he saw that this would soon become a major problem for his brother's administration and he opened Jack's eyes to what was happening. Jack was like a rabbit caught in the headlights as he deliberated what he should do and once again, it was Bobby who stepped in to take charge.

The black people of America were rising up in protest against segregation as the so-called Freedom Riders boarded whites-only buses and rode through the southern states in total defiance of the segregation laws. Bobby urged restraint but riots ensued and the National Guard were called out, attacking the protesters with tear gas, dogs and water cannon. The nation was in crisis and it was Bobby who intervened, negotiating on the phone with the authorities and with Martin Luther King for a safe resolution to the conflict. This then opened the door for reform and in 1962, Bobby was instrumental in getting black student, James H Meredith admitted into the University of Mississippi.

The black people of America had at last found a voice, and people were beginning to listen. Bobby used the law to force the change that was so badly needed and he began the long and arduous process of national desegregation that would continue for many years to come. When discussing the Supreme Court School Desegregation Act during one of his many speeches on the subject, he said.

"We will not stand by or be aloof, we will move on. I happen to believe that this decision was right, but my belief does not matter; it is the law. Some of you may believe the decision was wrong? That does not matter; it is the law."

Robert Kennedy had always been utterly fearless in everything he did and he believed totally in his own convictions. Whether it be organised crime and union corruption or foreign policy and Civil Rights, Bobby worked tirelessly to right the many wrongs that he saw all around him. He cared nothing for what other people might think and he was always more than willing to take the flack for his brother.

"I'm not running a popularity contest," he once said. "It doesn't matter if they (the politicians) like me or not. Jack has to be nice to them but somebody has to be able to say no. If people are not getting off their behinds and working hard enough, how do you say that nicely? Every time you make a decision in this business, you make somebody mad."

The tough guy was getting tougher and as time went on, Bobby became even more aggressive in his pursuit of what he felt was right. On one occasion, the Cabinet were discussing the release of prisoners taken by Cuba during the Bay of Pigs invasion when George McBundy suggested that conceding to Castro's demand for $62m dollars in ransom would cost them votes. Bobby was playing with a yellow pencil and when McBundy made this comment Bobby threw the pencil on the table, stood up and glared at him, saying.

"As long as I am Attorney General, we have a moral obligation to those people in that jail and I don't care if we lose every election that will ever be held, we're going to get those guys out."

With that, he stormed out of the meeting.

Bobby felt a huge sense of responsibility for the plight of the Bay of Pigs prisoners and this was typical of his strong moral fibre, but not everyone believed these dramatic displays of impassioned sincerity. Philip Hoff, Governor of Vermont once said, "My initial reaction to Bobby Kennedy was that there didn't seem to be one ounce of warmth in him. He was direct, he was to the point and he was absolutely humourless and almost chillingly cold."

But Civil Rights campaigner, James Farmer saw it slightly differently, although he was still less than flattering.

"The Kennedys meant well but they didn't feel it," he said. "They didn't know any blacks growing up, there were no blacks in their communities or going to their schools. But their inclinations were good."

With the benefit of hindsight, these comments about Bobby seem somewhat harsh and unfair, even at that time in his life. The Kennedys did mean well and Bobby did care, especially later in his career. But he was a deep and complex character, hard to read and almost impossible to know.

"Robert Kennedy was a strange, complex man," wrote Kennedy aid, Pat Anderson. "Easier to respect than to like and easier to like than to understand. In all, he was a man to be taken seriously. His love for humanity, however real, seemed greater in the abstract than in individual cases. He was no intellectual but he was more receptive to other men's ideas than most intellectuals. But even as you made excuses for his weaknesses, there was the feeling that you were doing more than he would do for you."

The simple fact is that Robert Kennedy was a man of extremes. If you were privileged enough to be called a friend, he would prove passionately loyal and you were a friend for life. On the other hand, cross him and he would neither forgive nor forget. As former associate, Oleg Cassini once said, "JFK liked to charm his enemies; RFK wanted to vanquish them."

"People say I'm ruthless," Robert Kennedy once mockingly said. "I'm not ruthless, and if I find the man who says I am, I will destroy him."

But there was another, more gentle and compassionate side to Bobby, too and his mother could always see this in him. She would call him her, "own little pet" and Jackie Kennedy always said that Bobby was the least like Joe of any of the Kennedy boys and this was never more apparent than in the way Bobby was with his own children. Robert Kennedy valued family above all else and having had a hard and strict upbringing himself, he always swore it would be different for his own kids. He and Ethel would have eleven children and although quite demanding of them academically, they allowed them an enormous amount of freedom around the house. When holding meetings at his home Bobby would listen intently to the speaker and if one of his children walked by, he would sit and hold their hand whilst still focussing on the matter being discussed.

Family friend, Gerald Tremblay once said, "Bobby could be very demanding on his kids. He didn't cuddle his children. He didn't raise them so they would come up and whine to him if something happened to go wrong. He never tolerated his kids crying or complaining. But he always treated them well and gave them a lot of affection. I never saw Bobby lose his temper with his children."

Bobby raised his children with a curious mix of hard-nosed discipline and genuine, caring affection. Real estate agent, Phil Stanton once recalled how hard Bobby could be on his kids, saying.

"During the winter the family would go skiing in New Hampshire. After the children had come down the slope Bobby would look at them and if they weren't bruised, he'd send them back up. He wasn't happy until they were black and blue."

"Kennedys never cry," he would say. "And Kennedys never give up."

Bobby and Ethel made their home at Hickory Hill, an old Civil War mansion in Virginia where they would raise their children and the name became a by-word in Washington for anarchy and mayhem. Hickory Hill was Robert Kennedy's retreat from the strains of public office and on arriving home in his old Mercedes car he would leave his cares and woes well and truly at the gate. It was a special place with no set rules and everyone, including the kids, could do pretty much as they liked. The house was filled with unruly children running around all over the place and with animals of every kind. Jackie Kennedy once drew a cartoon of Hickory Hill showing kids and animals running about and hanging out of the windows and a cook walking away down the path. Ethel loved it and she pinned it on the refrigerator.

All of this made life very hard for their neighbours and there would be no end of complaints and confrontations. They would often complain to Bobby that his kids had broken their windows or caused some other nuisance but although always respectful, Bobby paid little attention.

"Those kids thought there were two sets of rules," one neighbour said, "one for us and one for them."

There would be noise, too. Bobby and Ethel would hold loud parties late into the night and again there would be no rules or formality. The kids and animals would be running around everywhere and Ethel had a particular liking for pushing their distinguished guests into the swimming pool. They enjoyed childish games like hide and seek and they would play touch-football as if their lives depended on it. Neighbour, Larry Newman said that when watching their football games you would notice their bloody noses and Ethel even played during her frequent bouts of pregnancy.

"They were a pretty competitive bunch," said Newman, "and they would just beat the hell out of one another."

Hickory Hill was a crazy, chaotic and unruly madhouse, which is why they had so much trouble keeping domestic staff. It was a never-never land where kids could be kids and grown-ups could be kids, too. But Bobby liked it that way. In his black and white world of extremes he could be a leading political figure during the week and an unruly child at weekends. Bobby worked hard and he played hard and Hickory Hill would be his own personal sanctuary until the day he died.

Robert Kennedy cared a great deal about the things that he felt really mattered in life, but he was no saint. For all his differences he was, after all, a Kennedy and he shared the family weakness for women. There can be no doubt that Bobby really loved Ethel very much and she would always be the number one woman in his life but there were countless others, too. Like his father and brothers before him, Bobby saw no wrong in dating other women or indulging in one night stands with call-girls, actresses and anyone else who might be willing. Ethel knew all about this but, as Jackie had with Jack, she turned a blind eye and accepted it. It was what Kennedy women did. Bobby had numerous affairs with some famous and high profile stars like Jayne Mansfield and Candice Bergen but, again like Jack before him, it was his tempestuous affair with Marilyn Monroe that would prove the most controversial.

Bobby had become romantically involved with Marilyn Monroe after she had been cast off by Jack and the affair was to prove disastrous for both of them. To Bobby, Marilyn was nothing more than a casual fling but again, Marilyn saw it differently. She became increasingly demanding and Bobby ended the affair but Marilyn refused to give in. She was spiralling out of control and she began pestering Bobby, telling friends how much they loved one another and that they were planning to marry. She had acted in a similar way with Jack but with Bobby it was far more intense. She would continually call the Justice Department and when she couldn't reach him there she would even call Ethel at Hickory Hill. Marilyn was on self-destruct and Bobby knew that something had to be done. He asked brother-in-law and close friend, Peter Lawford to intervene but he could do nothing with her, either.

All of this changed with the shocking news that Marilyn had been found dead in her Hollywood home on August 5th 1962. The official story was that she had become depressed at the failure of her most recent film project and by problems in her personal life and had overdosed on sleeping pills and barbiturates, but there are many who dispute that to this day. Leading LA Coroner, Dr Noguchi later testified that this scenario was extremely unlikely and that he believed that Marilyn had been murdered, and some have laid the blame for this at the door of Robert Kennedy.

These claims have never been substantiated but many believe that Marilyn's death was orchestrated by the Kennedys because she was about to tell the world of her affair with Bobby and that he had agreed to marry her. It is claimed that Robert Kennedy and Peter Lawford went to visit Marilyn at her home shortly before her death to dissuade her from this course of action, but the meeting ended in a fight between a drunken Marilyn and Bobby. Bobby's movements that weekend are unclear and many witnesses said they saw him around Marilyn's home on the night of her death, but these claims were never made public at the time and have only come to light in recent years.

Marilyn had become a problem for Robert Kennedy, and there can be no doubt that her sudden and untimely death was more than just a little convenient for him. With her out of the way he was free to move on but there would soon be another death, closer to home, from which he would never fully recover.

JFK Killed

On Friday, November 22nd 1963 Robert Kennedy had spent the morning discussing judicial appointments with Nicholas Katzenbach before returning home to Hickory Hill for a working lunch meeting with the US Attorney for New York and his chief of criminal division. They both later said that Bobby had called the meeting to tell them he was resigning from his post as Attorney General to manage Jack's up and coming re-election campaign.

They were joined by Ethel and were sat around the pool enjoying soup and sandwiches when at 1.34pm, the phone rang. Ethel answered the phone and, covering the receiver with her hand, she called out to Bobby that J Edgar Hoover was on the phone. Bobby took the phone and Hoover told him, bluntly and to the point that the President and Governor Connolly had been shot whilst riding in a motorcade through Dallas. Bobby asked the President's condition and Hoover replied, "I think it's serious," then hung up.

Bobby put his face in his hands and, turning to Ethel, said, "Jack's been shot. It may be fatal?"

Bobby ran into the house and began to ring frantically around for more news, until he eventually reached agent, Clint Hill at Parkland Hospital in Dallas.

"Is it serious?" asked Bobby.

"I'm afraid it is," replied Hill.

There was a pause then Bobby asked, "Is he conscious?"

"No," replied Hill.

Bobby then asked, "Has a priest been called?"

"Yes, sir," replied Hill. "We're doing everything we can."

Bobby asked Hill to keep him informed but at 2.10pm Hoover called Bobby again to tell him the President had died.

Bobby just could not believe what had happened. He wandered aimlessly through the grounds of Hickory Hill with his head down, his shoulders hunched and his hands deep in his pockets. He was entirely alone, except for his favourite Newfoundland dog, Brummus, who followed faithfully at his heels. In time, Bobby began to realise that he was now the head of the family and he knew he had to be strong. He was worried for his ailing father and he called his mother and asked her to keep him away from the television or the radio as he had asked Teddy to go and give him the news in person. He then made urgent arrangements to travel to Washington to meet the plane carrying Jackie and his brother's shattered body. He was completely broken and at the point of collapse but knew he could not show it as he wanted so desperately to be there for everyone else. John McCone said of those first few hours, "Throughout this ordeal, as severe a trial as a man can go through, he never cracked. He was steely."

As events quickly unfolded that day, Bobby became especially concerned for Jackie and for her children. Bobby had always been very fond of Jackie and the two were very close. Jackie saw qualities in Bobby she knew were lacking in Jack and she found his warm and caring nature a welcome and refreshing change from Jack's aloofness and lack of sensitivity. Bobby later moved Jackie and the children into an apartment in New York and he devoted all of his time and energy into looking after them, visiting them almost daily. There was even talk that Bobby and Jackie might get together, but Ethel proved too strong a force to allow that to happen. They were just two sad and lonely people, brought together by a shared sense of grief and monumental loss and they both knew the time would pass.

Following the death of his brother, Bobby withdrew into a dark, deep abyss where no-one, not even Ethel, could reach him. He was completely shattered by the loss of his brother and this feeling was made even worse by an overwhelming sense of guilt that it may have been his fault. Bobby had always been the fearless, hard-nosed fighter and he had never been afraid to make enemies. Jack and Bobby had known only too well that they had crossed some very dangerous people, but Bobby always felt that if they ever sought retribution it would be him they would come after, not Jack, and he was prepared to take that risk. But now that Jack had been killed, he felt it had all backfired. He couldn't help feeling that his attacks on the likes of Hoffa and the mob may have provoked a backlash for which Jack had paid the price; and he was right.

The Kennedys had been warned of a threat in Dallas, but it was Bobby who urged Jack to go ahead with the visit. Senator William Fulbright had already declined several invitations to visit Dallas as he thought the place too dangerous and he pleaded with Jack to do likewise. He wrote to Bobby on November 4th telling him he was worried about JFK's planned visit to Dallas and urging him to reconsider, but Bobby refused to cancel the trip.

Bobby's world had been turned upside-down. He had devoted every day of his life to his brother's cause and now his very reason for being was gone overnight. Worse still, he was still Attorney General but was now serving a man he loathed and despised. He became a virtual recluse and stayed away from his office and he would do all he could to avoid contact with just about everyone. He did keep one or two engagements that were important to him and one of these was a charity dinner at an orphanage in December of 1963. He had long been a supporter of the orphanage and he was determined to attend, but it was clear to all present that he was reeling from the pain inside. The other guests tip-toed carefully around him until a young boy stepped up to him and with the innocence of a child, said, "Your brother is dead."

The room fell silent and the boy, sensing he had said something wrong, began to cry. But Bobby just bent down, picked the boy up in his arms and said, "It's alright, I have another."

It was a touching example of how, even in his darkest grief, Bobby could still be kind and thoughtful when the need arose.

In the months following JFK's death, Bobby tried hard to continue his brother's work and to ensure that Jack's policies were carried through to fruition but in the end, it proved an impossible task. Lyndon Johnson was now President and Bobby was just another Attorney General, with none of the power and influence he had enjoyed under his brother's regime. And Hoover was kicking back, too. The situation had become untenable and Bobby felt he had no choice but to resign from his post, and most were sorry to see him go.
"It had been exciting at the Justice Department," one staff member said, "then all of a sudden, it wasn't."

Moving On

So where now for Robert Kennedy? On leaving the Justice Department, Bobby became even more reclusive and withdrawn and many feared he would never recover from the traumatic and devastating loss of his brother. He began to look back on his life so far and to analyse every aspect of it in minute detail. He became more thoughtful and reflective and he distanced himself even further from the people around him, but he was dealing with his grief in the only way he knew how; head-on and alone. It was a hard and difficult journey for Bobby but he eventually began to emerge a more caring and compassionate man than he had been before. He searched desperately for some meaning to it all and he sought wisdom in the writings of Shakespeare, Homer and Aeschylus. For her part, Ethel took solace in her religion and in her genuine and unshakable faith she could often be heard saying, "Jack will take care of that. Jack is in Heaven and he will take care of that."

The Kennedy family seemed doomed in some way, and their resolve was being tested to the limit. There seemed no end to the tragedies that had befallen them over the years and this was made worse when in 1964, Ted was involved in a plane crash. Two of the occupants of the plane were killed and Ted was badly injured and once again, Bobby's thoughts were for those closest to him as he worried for his parents.

"How much more can they take?" he said, adding, "Somebody up there doesn't like us."

By the middle of 1964, Bobby had begun to come to terms with what had happened and looked again to his own career. He considered law or perhaps teaching but in the end he decided he would continue his career in politics by running for the Senate as representative for the state of New York. His opponent was Republican incumbent, Kenneth Keating who tried to portray Bobby a Carpet Bagger, an outsider with no real ties to the state of New York and no business running for office there. Keating would be hard to beat but Bobby came out fighting and through hard work and diligence he managed to convince voters that he really did care about the people of New York and that he would do all he could for the underprivileged and the minorities if elected. He wanted people to believe that he was going into politics because he really believed he had a lot to offer, and not because he felt he had to.

"Well, I could have stayed on relief or I could have retired," he told one reporter with a smile. "And my father has done very well, so I could have lived off him. I don't need the money and I don't need the office space."

Bobby won his seat in the Senate and would keep it until he died. He had learned a lot about politics and about life in general and he just wanted to put that experience to good use. He proved to be as passionate about helping the people of New York as he had been about racial equality and fighting crime. He initiated a number of major projects to improve the lot of the poor and underprivileged of that state, the most significant and successful of these initiatives being the Bedford Stuyvesant renovation project. This was a project to renovate and improve what was once a deprived and run-down area of New York into what became known as Restoration Plaza, holding the Bedford Stuyvesant HQ, The Billie Holiday Theatre and the Skylight Gallery. The project proved enormously successful and its legacy continues to this day.

Bobby tried hard to accept what had happened to Jack but he was never the same after his death and people close to him said he remained a broken man, grieving every minute of every day. He tried to convince the world that he had moved on and that he was now his own man with his own views and convictions, but Jack was never far from his thoughts. In March 1965 he climbed Mount Kennedy, a peak in the Saint Elias Mountains in Yukon, Canada that had been named after Jack. He found the experience both difficult and unpleasant but he had committed to doing it and he never gave up on anything, so he battled on through the snow and the ice. He made the final leg of the climb alone and he left some personal items at the summit when he got there. He never told anyone what he had left up there or what his thoughts had been, but we can be fairly certain that for that short time, he felt closer to Jack than he had ever been since his death.

By the spring of 1968, Bobby felt recovered enough to consider running for the Democratic nomination in the upcoming Presidential elections. He had been advised that it would be difficult to beat Lyndon Johnson at that time and to wait until 1972, but he felt sure that the time was right. And besides; he had a score to settle. He had been to hell and back and had survived and he had come out of it all a stronger, more mature politician. He had finally shaken off the yoke of being Jack's right-hand man and had an agenda of his own and people were beginning to take notice. The country was ripe for change and was crying out for strong and decisive leadership, and Bobby was ready to answer the call.

"I do not run for the presidency merely to oppose any man but to propose new policies," he told a press conference in May 1968, and those policies would prove to be contentious and controversial.

Bobby was one of the first high profile political figures to speak out openly against the war in Vietnam and by early 1968, he had become bitterly opposed to America's involvement in the conflict. Many Americans at that time supported their country's involvement in the war but Bobby was one of the first people to stand up and oppose it, and his campaign gained momentum and support over the coming weeks and months. He openly questioned America's right to pursue the war in the way that it was and its right to send young Americans into combat for what he felt was a questionable cause. He was very vociferous on the subject and would often express his strong views in interviews with the press and on TV. He questioned America's motives in pursuing a war that was killing countless innocent people and he pulled no punches when interviewed on the subject.

"We're going in there and we're killing South Vietnamese," he once said. "We're killing children, we're killing women and we're killing innocent people because we don't want to have the war fought on American soil, or because they are 12,000 miles away and they might get to be 11,000 miles away."

In another television interview he related how an Army commander had tried to justify his actions by saying he had to destroy a whole village in order to save it. This was a ludicrous statement and was indicative of just how crazy the situation in Vietnam had become. It made no sense at all and Bobby held out a pointed finger and said, angrily.

"38,000 people; killed for no reason! I'm not blaming him. I'm blaming me and I'm blaming you. We are the American people and we allowed that to happen."

The pressure was on and in his usual, tenacious way Bobby refused to let go, and President Johnson had no choice but to respond. Johnson eventually engaged with Bobby on the subject of Vietnam and was forced to concede that he would review and reconsider his stance on the issue. Bobby was gaining support and Johnson was feeling the pressure and this fuelled their mutual hatred of one another even more. When commenting on these discussions, Bobby once jokingly said.

"We talked about pacification, we talked about a ceasefire and we talked about ending the struggle. It was a nice conversation and he told me that if I came back next week we might talk about Vietnam."

It was one of Bobby's endearing qualities that he could joke about himself in this way, and the people loved him for it.

Despite what some people might have thought or said, Robert Kennedy did have a rather mischievous, self-mocking sense of humour and he would often joke about the bitter rivalry between himself and Lyndon Johnson. He once told an audience that President Johnson had recently advised him to, "Go west, young man." "Mind you," he added with a smile, "I was in San Francisco at the time."

On another occasion, he was on a plane with a group of campaign workers when it was severely buffeted by bad weather and turbulence.

"You know," he said to them, "if we go down, you guys are all going to be in small print."

Besides the war in Vietnam, the other real passion for Bobby during his Presidential campaign was again the issue of Civil Rights. This had been a thorn in the side of Jack's administration and had continued to be so for Lyndon Johnson, and it was clear that this problem was just not going to go away. There had been some progress and some new legislation passed but these measures were nowhere near enough and the country was still deeply divided on the issue. The black people of America still felt bitter and resentful about the way they had been treated and they turned to their charismatic leader, Dr Martin Luther King Jr to champion their cause. Bobby had been suspicious of King during the race riots and freedom rides of the early 1960's but he now supported him fully and the two worked closely together to fight segregation and inequality across the US.

Bobby had developed a deep and sincere understanding of the Civil Rights issue and of the need for racial equality and he spoke openly about injustice and prejudice, especially in the south. He urged people of all races to be more tolerant of one another and to accept that they should all live in harmony, blacks and whites together.

"Suppose God is black?" he once asked. "What if we go to Heaven and we, all our lives have treated the Negro as inferior and God is there and we look up and he is not white? What then will be our response?"

Wherever possible, Bobby would combine his views on the war and on Civil Rights into the same simple message of peace and harmony. To him, the two issues were closely linked as they both questioned the morality of the political and social climate of the country. Both issues were indicative of the hypocrisy and injustice in America at that time and he would use them to promote his call for change. He was brave enough to face these issues head on, without fear or compromise. He once said.

"How can we put a man in a uniform and send him off to war telling him he is a citizen of the United States but after that, tell him he is a second class citizen of Jackson, Mississippi?"

He then added, "Any man who says the Negro should be satisfied with his lot in life, let him say he would willingly change the colour of his skin and go and live in any of the major cities in the United States."

He was giving the American people some long-overdue home-truths, and there were many in the country who found that uncomfortable.

Robert Kennedy was able to connect with the black people of America in a way that few white politicians ever could, and he felt a real empathy with the poor and underprivileged. He travelled the length and breadth of the country, visiting the slums and the ghettos to see the hardships these people suffered and to experience for himself what these places were like.

Charles Evers, brother of murdered black activist, Medger Evers described how he once visited a ghetto in New Orleans with Bobby and described Bobby's reaction to what he saw. Evers said that the people lived in dirty, smelly hovels and that the smell was so bad it made him retch, but

Bobby didn't flinch. He went straight inside one of these dreadful houses and saw a black child sitting on a dirt floor, playing with some grains of rice. The child was starving and his stomach was sticking out and Bobby went over to him and picked him up. He sat on the bed, gently rubbing the child's stomach and he said, "My God, I didn't know this kind of thing existed in the United States. How can a country like this allow it?"

Evers said that Bobby tried to get a response from the child by tickling his chin, but there was nothing. He said, "Tears were running down Bobby's cheeks and he just sat there and held this little child. Roaches and rats were all over the floor."

Very few politicians have been able to demonstrate such a sincere and heart-felt compassion for the poor and disadvantaged and in Robert Kennedy, it was all very real; you just can't fake that.

Pat Anderson of *Esquire Magazine* travelled with Bobby on his campaign and wrote of how he loved children. On a visit to a municipal pool he was mobbed by black children, all calling his name and reaching out to touch him. "Bobby loved it," she said, "and his face lit up. He would rub their heads and reach out to the smaller ones at the back."

As the election campaign gathered momentum, so did Bobby's burning desire to bring about change in a country torn apart by injustice and inequality. He believed more than ever that right would prevail and he was prepared to take on the most deadly of foes to make that happen.

"Fear not the path of truth for the lack of people walking on it," he once said, adding, "Each time a man stands up for an ideal or acts to improve the lot of others, he sends forth a ripple of hope. And those ripples build a current which can sweep down the mightiest walls of oppression and resistance."

How can anyone fight a conviction like that? Well the fact is that in the end, Lyndon Johnson couldn't. Johnson fought tooth and nail with Bobby and it looked as though he would go all the way, but on March 31st Johnson shocked the world by announcing that he was pulling out of the race and that he would not accept his party's nomination for President. Bobby was surprised by this news and he never fully understood the reason behind Johnson's withdrawal, but it meant that the road was now clear for him to challenge Herbert Humphry for the Democratic nomination.

Bobby hit the campaign trail harder than ever and he subjected himself to a gruelling schedule of public appearances and interviews across the country. He wanted to get up-close with the ordinary people and for that reason, he insisted on minimal security. He would have his clothing torn and his cufflinks taken (on one occasion, even losing a shoe) but he would not allow any police or security to get in the way. He was advised against this policy but he would have it no other way, and this was to prove a major headache for his security advisors on the campaign trail. He never stopped for a moment, sleeping in cars and eating at fast food restaurants and his campaign workers struggled to keep up, but Bobby refused to slow down. He had an election to win and he was going to win it.

On April 4th 1968, Robert Kennedy was en-route to Indianapolis when he received the shocking news that Martin Luther King had been killed. Dr King had been assassinated on the balcony of a Motel in Memphis by a white man who had, for the time being, escaped capture. A crowd had gathered in Indianapolis to hear Bobby speak and when he finally arrived, it was clear that they had not heard the news. There were fears for Bobby's safety and he was urged to go straight to his hotel, but he insisted on facing the mostly black crowd head-on. He stepped up on the back of a truck, took hold of a portable microphone and bluntly announced that Dr King had been assassinated that night and that his killer was a white man.

There was a gasp from the crowd as the news sunk in and many feared a riot, but Bobby urged restraint. He told them he knew how they felt as he, too had lost a loved one to an assassin's bullet and he asked them to resist the temptation to seek revenge. His speech was unscripted and unrehearsed but it was perhaps the most emotional and heart-felt speech of his life. He let them know that he felt their pain in a way that very few white men could, and he quoted his favourite Greek poet, Aeschylus.

> *Even in our sleep, pain which cannot forget*
> *Falls drop by drop upon the heart*
> *Until, in our deepest despair and against our will*
> *Comes wisdom, through the awful grace of God.*

The effect of these words was shattering. The crowd drifted slowly and quietly away and as the hours passed into days, the people of America began to realise that something had to be done to bring harmony and understanding between blacks and whites. Once again, Bobby had shown that even in times of danger and crisis, he could empathise and relate with people on both sides of the divide and from all walks of life.

But despite his popularity with the ordinary people, Bobby knew he had made some very dangerous enemies along the way and that they were always there, lurking in the shadows. He refused police protection as he felt they might form a barrier between him and the people and he had only a few private security men with him through the whole campaign. They were dedicated and loyal and were more than capable but they all knew that if someone wanted to kill Bobby, there would be very little they could do to stop them. "I fear that a gunman stands between me and the Whitehouse," Bobby once told one of his aids. The aid later said, "I was stunned because here we were, only three days after King's death, and he was talking like that. Almost two months to the day later, he was gone."

There were reports that people were plotting to kill Robert Kennedy from the very start of the campaign. On June 4th 1968, Harold Weisberg interviewed some of Bobby's friends on TV and they told him that they feared there were guns waiting for Bobby everywhere he went. When he asked them who was behind these guns, the implication was that it was the CIA, but there were others, too. The FBI had picked up reports that Jimmy Hoffa had been plotting to have Bobby killed from inside his cell in Lewisburg Penitentiary, where he had finally ended up once the law had caught up with him. When asked what precautions he was taking to protect himself Bobby said, "There's no way to protect a candidate who is stomping the country, no way at all. You've just got to give yourself to the people and trust them."

Jackie worried about Bobby more than most. She had already lost her husband to an assassin's bullet and, believing there were dark forces out to get all of the Kennedys, she worried for Bobby too. She once told Arthur Schlesinger.

"Do you know what I think will happen to Bobby? The same thing that happened to Jack. There is so much hatred in this country and more people hate Bobby than hated Jack. I've told Bobby this but he is not fatalistic like me."

These feelings were widespread and there were a lot of people who believed that Bobby would never make it to the Whitehouse. French writer, Roman Gary once remarked to Pierre Salinger, "You know, your guy will get killed."
"Why do you say that?" asked Salinger.
Gary smiled and replied, "He's too rich, too young, too attractive, too happy, too lucky, and too successful. He arouses in every persecuted type, a deep sense of injustice."

Similarly, in a conversation over drinks one night Jimmy Breslin asked of John Lindsey, "Do you think he has the stuff to go all the way?"
"Yes," replied Lindsey, "of course he has the stuff to go all the way; but he is not going all the way. Somebody is going to shoot him. I know it and you know it. He's out there now, just waiting for him."

Death in LA

By early June 1968, Bobby's campaign was reaching a dramatic climax with the hotly contested California primary. The omens were good and on June 4th Bobby and his family were staying at the beach-front home of film director, John Frankenheimer whilst waiting for the results to come in. The kids played on the private beach and they all went swimming in the ocean and at one point, Bobby had to rescue young David from a roaring sea, sustaining a cut over his right eye for his trouble.

At 6.15pm Bobby and Fred Dutton were driven by Frankenheimer to the Ambassador Hotel in Los Angeles where they were to celebrate the expected victory and where Bobby could meet and thank his campaign workers. Frankenheimer was driving his Rolls Royce very fast and Bobby joked, "Hey John, take it slow. I want to live long enough to enjoy my impending victory."

They arrived at the hotel at 7pm and took the elevator to their suite on the fifth floor where Ted and their sister, Jean were already waiting for them. Ethel was to follow on a little later.

On the morning of the same day, a young Palestinian immigrant named Sirhan Sirhan crawled out of bed in his mother's bungalow in Pasadena and climbed into his pink and white 1956 Desoto car to drive the short distance to the shop to buy a newspaper. Sirhan was a compulsive gambler and enjoyed going to the races but having studied the form for that day he decided to go to the shooting range instead. He took his Iver Johnson .22 revolver and set off to do some shooting, calling in for some ammo on the way. He stayed at the shooting range until it closed at around 5pm, then he met up with some friends for a coffee and a chat at the end of what seemed like a normal day.

Sirhan was a quiet, unassuming young man; 24 years of age, 5′ 2″ tall, wiry build with bushy dark hair and there appeared to be nothing unusual about his behaviour on that day. He was the sort of man no one would notice and on June 4th 1968, there seemed no reason to suppose that would ever change. But later that day, he took his gun and his Desoto car and headed off towards the Ambassador Hotel, where he would become a leading player in events that would change the course of history.

It is thought that Sirhan arrived at the Ambassador at around 7.30pm, when a guard recalls directing him up to the

Embassy Ballroom where Kennedy campaign workers were waiting to greet their hero. There were several confirmed sightings of Sirhan at various times throughout the evening and many who saw him later said he was acting quite strangely. At around 9.30pm Western Union operator, Mary Grohs saw him staring at a teletype machine, transfixed and in a trance. She asked if she could help him but she got no response, Sirhan simply stared at the machine and ignored her. He was seen again later talking to a young lady standing by a coffee machine and a security guard recalled seeing him hanging around the backstage area at around 11.00pm and sending him back into the Ballroom.

At around 11.30pm campaign worker, Sandra Serrano (who we will meet again later) went out onto the fire escape to get some air and said that a man resembling Sirhan came past her, up the stairs, with a girl in a polka-dot dress and another young man in a gold sweater. At 11.45pm Sirhan was seen going into the kitchen at the back of the Ballroom and asking staff if Kennedy was to be coming through there later. There can be no doubt that Sirhan was at the Ambassador all evening and that he was acting strange. He seemed lost and bemused and many who saw him said he looked a little out of place; a serious, solemn face in a crowd of happy people.

Just after midnight, a group of kitchen workers gathered around a TV set in the pantry to watch Senator Kennedy take the stage in the Embassy Ballroom just a short distance away whilst, unnoticed by anyone, Sirhan placed himself on a tray stacker by the ice machine. Bobby gave a short speech thanking everyone for all their hard work, ending at 12.15am with.

"Mayor Yorty has just sent a message that we've been here too long already... So my thanks to all of you and now it's on to Chicago and let's win there."

He then put up his thumb, gave the victory sign and, flicking back his hair, he turned to leave the stage as the jubilant crowd chanted, "We want Kennedy. We want Kennedy. We want Kennedy."

For a brief moment Bobby seemed unsure which way to go so hotel worker Kark Uecker took hold of his right arm and led him through a door behind a curtain at the back of the stage. They were headed for the Colonial Room where Bobby was to hold a press conference and they took a short cut through the kitchen pantry to avoid the crowds in the Ballroom. But this area was every bit as crowded as the Ballroom and in the confusion Bobby became separated from his security men, who could only look on as he disappeared into the teeming mass of well-wishers. They pushed frantically to get through to Bobby but he was in the pantry before they knew it and they could get nowhere near him. Bobby pushed through the crowd and as he moved slowly along he saw a group of kitchen workers lining up to shake his hand, and he was only too happy to oblige. People were pushing and shoving in all directions and as kitchen worker, Juan Romero stepped forward and held out his hand to Bobby, all hell broke loose.

High school student, Lisa Urso was standing by a tray stacker when she saw a movement out of the corner of her eye as a slight young man with dark hair, stepped out in front of her and raised his arm. She saw that he was smiling and thought he was going to shake Bobby's hand but he held out a snub-nosed revolver and shouted, "Kennedy, you son of a bitch," before firing it directly at Bobby.

Romero felt a hot flash on his cheek as the gun was fired and he saw Bobby put his hands up to his face and fall backwards onto the floor. Uecker leapt forward and grabbed Sirhan around the neck, taking hold of his arm and bashing it down onto the steam table to try and make him drop the gun, which kept firing until it was empty. Bill Barry then charged through the crowd and struck Sirhan twice in the face as George Plimpton and Jack Gallivan tried to get the gun from his hand.

"I have never hit anybody in my whole life as hard as I hit Sirhan," said Barry, "and he didn't even move. I tried to get the gun down but the gun wouldn't move. It was like he was catatonic."

All those present said that Sirhan had a sick smile on his face as he fired the gun and Plimpton later said he was struck by his eyes; dark and emotionally peaceful.

"I came face to face with Sirhan," he said, "and he looked like the devil himself. As long as I live I shall never forget those utterly cold, utterly expressionless eyes."

People were clamouring to get to Sirhan shouting, "Kill him, Kill him," as others shouted to lock the doors and called for a doctor. CBS cameraman, James Wilson turned his camera away but soundman, John Lewis urged him to keep filming so Wilson turned his camera back onto the stricken Bobby, but he could not bear to look through the viewfinder. Meanwhile, radio reporter, Andrew West turned on his tape recorder and began to commentate.

"Senator Kennedy has been shot, Senator Kennedy has been shot. Is that possible? Is that possible?"

Others in the pantry were hit by flying bullets, too. Ira Goldstein felt a sharp pain in her hip as student, Irwin Stroll felt something strike his shin. ABC newsman, William

Weisel felt three thumps in his side and fell to the floor as behind him, Elizabeth Evans bent down to pick up her shoe and felt blood running from a wound in her head. Campaign worker, Paul Schrade was also hit in the head and at one point someone placed a straw hat over his face, thinking he was dead.

Hotel busboy, Juan Romero was the first to reach the stricken Senator and as he cradled Bobby's head in his hands he could feel the warm blood running through his fingers. Blood was oozing from a wound behind Bobby's right ear and Romero could see he was trying to speak. Romero leaned in closer and as he lay there bleeding, one eye twitching and the other one wide open, Bobby whispered.
"Is everybody alright?"
"Yes," said Romero. "Everything will be OK."

Private security guard, Eugene Cesar, who had been standing behind Bobby when the shots were fired and had fallen with him to the floor, leapt back onto his feet and pulled his gun as student, Paul Grieco took off his jacket and placed it under Bobby's head to try to stop the flow of blood.
"Is everybody alright? Is Paul alright?" Bobby asked again.
Don't worry, Robert," replied Grieco, "you'll be alright."
Meanwhile, Fred Dutton loosened Bobby's collar and belt and removed his shoes and cufflinks. He hung on to those shoes for the rest of the night, refusing to let them go.

Ethel finally pushed her way through the crowd and bent down by Bobby's side, cradling his bleeding head in her lap. Romero asked her if he could give Bobby his Rosary Beads and, getting no reply, he placed them into Bobby's hand, wrapping them around his thumb as he was unable to grip them himself.

It was clear to everyone that Bobby was in a serious condition. His breathing was shallow and his pulse was low and Doctor Abo, who happened to be at the hotel at the time, probed the wound in the back of his head with his finger to stop the blood from clotting and to prevent a build-up of pressure in the brain. A call was made to the emergency services and at 12.22am an ambulance arrived, closely followed by the police. At Bobby's insistence, there had been no police presence at the Ambassador that night so when LAPD officers, Travis White and Arthur Placenia duly arrived in response to the call, they were taken upstairs to where a group of people were still wrestling with Sirhan as he was punched and kicked by the crowd. Sirhan was protesting that his leg was hurting and the officers had to forcibly peel people off of him to apply the handcuffs. They quickly pulled him away and took him down the spiral staircase to the waiting car, people lashing out and grabbing at his clothes all the way.

"I did it for my country," said Sirhan as they bundled him into the police car.

All those who grappled with Sirhan that night commented on his seemingly super-human strength and they all said that he was smiling the whole time. Placenia said that Sirhan had a sick smile on his face as he bundled him into the squad car and when he shone a light into his eyes he saw that his pupils were dilated and did not respond, as if he were drunk or high on something.

Sirhan was taken to Rampart Police Station in downtown LA where, as he refused to give his name, he was booked as John Doe. It was only when Sirhan's brother came in later in the day having seen news reports on the TV that the police had a name for their suspect. Sirhan was booked and charged with assault with intent to commit murder and detectives began to question him in earnest. He was calm and polite but would offer very little information. He enjoyed talking to the detectives and seemed to wallow in all the attention but he would offer nothing of any worth. He seemed distant and detached and he showed no remorse for what he had done. In fact, he had no recollection of doing it. Detectives later said that he seemed to be playing a game and enjoying it.

Back at the Ambassador Hotel, paramedic, Max Berhman rushed in to find Ethel kneeling down beside her husband, holding an ice pack on his head as she cradled it in her lap. Ethel at first refused to let Berhman touch Bobby but they eventually got her to agree and as they tried to lift him, Bobby cried, "Oh no, please don't move me, please don't."
They put Bobby into the ambulance and as Ethel got in the back with him, Bill Barry climbed in the front with the driver. Berhman took out his notebook and began to question Ethel but she grabbed the book from his hands and threw it out of the window. He then tried to apply a dressing to Bobby's head and Ethel yelled, "Get your dirty, filthy hands off my husband," and slapped him across the cheek, shouting, "Bill, come back here and throw this guy out."

On arrival at the hospital, Bobby was taken into the emergency room where six surgeons fought hard to save his life. They worked on him for nearly four hours, but it was clear from the start that there was no hope. Bobby had sustained three wounds, the most serious being a bullet that had entered behind his right ear and fragmented in the brain. Press aid, Frank Mankiewicz said that the doctors took him to one side and told him that they had taken some bullet fragments from the brain but could not get them all.

"They were as gloomy as doctors can be," said Mankiewicz, "and it seemed to me that this was the end."

As Mankiewicz walked into the bathroom at the hospital he saw Ted Sorensen standing over a sink, splashing his face with water. Ted looked up and Mankiewicz said, "I have never seen so anguished a look on anyone's face in all my life. It tore me up."

At around 2am on June 6th, Frank Mankiewicz stood before a crowd of reporters at the Good Samaritan Hospital in Los Angeles and, choking back the tears, said.

"I have a short announcement to read. Senator Robert Francis Kennedy died at 1.44am today, June 6th, 1968. With Senator Kennedy at the time of his death were his wife, Ethel, his sisters, Mrs Stephen Smith and Mrs Patricia Lawford, his brother-in-law Stephen Smith and his sister-in-law Mrs John F Kennedy. He was 42 years old. Thank you."

Meanwhile, back at Rampart station the police were making little progress with Sirhan. They had found his car at 4pm on the day of the shooting with a parking ticket on it from 9.35 that morning. In the car they found 2 expended .22 calibre slugs on the front seat, underneath a copy of the Los Angeles Times. There was an empty box of CCI Mini-Mag hollow-point .22 calibre bullets and a wallet containing just under $400 and some ID. There was an unused rifle bullet and a receipt for 4 boxes of .22 calibre bullets from the Lock Stock and Barrel gun shop in San Gabriel and there was a book entitled, *Healing; the Divine Art.* When questioned about these items, Sirhan refused to comment.

Sirhan Sirhan was an enigma from the start. He knew he had shot Robert Kennedy, but he consistently and adamantly claimed that he had no memory of doing it. He said he could remember going to the Ambassador Hotel to see the Senator but he had no recollection of shooting him, and he has never once wavered from that conviction. He said he liked and admired Senator Kennedy and claimed he could not understand what might have driven him to shoot him and the police tried everything they could think of, including hypnosis, to try and unlock his memory.

Despite Sirhan's protestations, the LAPD were sure that they had their man and when they searched Sirhan's home they found even more incriminating evidence. In particular, they found two notebooks filled with vicious, rambling notes stating that Robert Kennedy must die and that RFK must be killed before June 5th 1968. The notes would appear to be written in Sirhan's own handwriting but, again, he claimed he had no recollection of writing them. He said he did not feel that way about Robert Kennedy so could not understand why he would write such things. The police also found literature from the Mystical Order of the Rosicrucians and other readings on the occult as well as an envelope on which was written, "RFK must be disposed of, like his brother was."

Bobby's funeral was held on Saturday, June 8th at St Patrick's Cathedral in New York. The church was full to capacity and people lined the streets outside as Teddy, the last surviving Kennedy son, stepped up and in a shaky voice, delivered his now famous eulogy for his dead brother.

"My brother need not be idealised or enlarged in death beyond what he was in life. Let him be remembered simply as a good and decent man who saw wrong and tried to right it, who saw suffering and tried to heal it, who saw war and tried to stop it. As he said many times in many parts of this nation, to those he touched and to those who sought to

touch him; *Some men see things as they are and say, why? I dream things that never were and say, why not?"*
The service ended with close family friend, Andy Williams singing *The Battle Hymn of the Republic.*

After the service, Bobby's coffin was loaded onto the last car of a slow moving train for its final journey to Washington DC and as the train pulled out of New York, news came through that James Earl Ray, the alleged assassin of Martin Luther King, had been arrested in London.

Thousands of people turned out to line the tracks as the train rolled slowly by and in some places the police had difficulty in controlling the crowds. In Elizabeth, New Jersey a group of people stepped onto the track to get a better look and were hit by a train coming the other way. Two people were killed and six others injured.

The journey turned out to be a long one and Bobby's coffin did not arrive in Washington until 9.10pm. Floodlights were placed around the grave and 1,500 candles were distributed to the mourners as the coffin, borne by 13 pallbearers including Bobby's eldest son, Joe, astronaut, John Glenn and Bobby's brother, Ted was brought to the graveside. There was a short service delivered by Terence Cardinal Cooke, Archbishop of New York then Bobby's coffin was lowered slowly into his grave at Arlington National Cemetery, close to that of his brother, Jack.

That should have been the end of it; another state funeral for another murdered politician and the killer safely behind bars. But Bobby was a Kennedy, and it was never going to be that simple.

A Second Shooter?

From the very beginning there were those who questioned the LAPD's conclusion that Sirhan had acted alone in killing Robert Kennedy and the evidence to support those doubts is overwhelming. Leads were left unfollowed, key witnesses were never called to testify and the physical evidence was, at best, misinterpreted. There were injuries and bullet holes that could not be accounted for given the number of bullets Sirhan's gun could hold and the wounds sustained by Bobby suggest shots from behind, when Sirhan was standing in front of him when firing.

Like that of his brother before him, the autopsy of Robert Kennedy was mismanaged and was steeped in controversy. On examining the body, Dr Noguchi, chief medical examiner for the county of Los Angeles found that there were three separate wounds from three separate bullets. The cause of death was determined to be a gunshot wound to the right mastoid bone, one inch behind the right ear, penetrating the brain. Noguchi described the path of the three bullets as follows;

Bullet 1 penetrated the right mastoid bone and travelled upwards to sever the branches of the superior cerebral artery. The bullet exploded and fragmented on impact.
Bullet 2 entered the back of the right armpit in a left to right direction and exited through the front of the right shoulder.
Bullet 3 entered the right armpit, one inch below bullet 2 and travelled in a near parallel path, burrowing through the muscles in the back of the neck and lodging close to the 6th cervical vertebrae, where the neck meets the back.

The interesting point here is that Dr Noguchi states quite clearly that all three shots were fired from behind and at a steep upward angle. He also stated that the head shot was fired at point blank range, no more than one or two inches, which he ascertained from the powder marks on Bobby's right ear. Yet despite this, the LAPD came to the staggering conclusion that all three shots were fired by Sirhan, who was standing in front of Bobby, some feet away and with his arm raised to chest height when firing.

The police argued that the shots were not fired at point blank range but from two or three feet away and they attributed the rear entry wounds to Bobby's turning as the shots were fired, but this is in direct conflict with witness testimony. Almost all of those present said that Sirhan was standing in front of Robert Kennedy with his arm out level with the floor when he fired the shots. And although Bobby may well have turned as the shots were fired, none of the witnesses saw him turn to any degree and when he hit the floor, he landed on his back.

Karl Uecker, who was standing very close to Bobby at the time said, "The gun was one to two feet away. There is no way that the shots described in the autopsy could have come from Sirhan's gun. Sirhan never got that close."
Another witness, Peter Hamill said that he saw Sirhan standing in front and to the left of Senator Kennedy when he fired the gun, seven or eight feet away with his arm extended.

Frank Burns, who was standing at Bobby's right shoulder and was one of the people who grabbed Sirhan said, "I don't believe that Sirhan's gun got within a couple of inches of Kennedy's head as the powder burns showed. I have never been able to reconcile that, and I was standing right there."
"What it all comes down to for me," he added, "is that the official story is just not believable, nor are other explanations

and theories for who could have killed him. It is still an unsolved mystery in my mind."

There is also the question of how many bullets were fired that night? Sirhan's gun had a capacity of 8 bullets and after close examination of the crime scene and the wounds sustained by other people, the LAPD said they could account for each and every one of them. According the their version of events, the order and trajectory of the bullets was as follows;

Bullet 1 entered Kennedy's head behind the right ear. This bullet fragmented in the brain and was partly recovered and booked as evidence.

Bullet 2 passed through the right shoulder pad of Kennedy's coat without entering his body and travelled upwards at an angle of 80 degrees, striking Paul Schrade in the head. This bullet was recovered and booked as evidence.

Bullet 3 entered Kennedy's right rear shoulder and came to rest in his neck. This bullet was recovered and booked as evidence.

Bullet 4 entered Kennedy's back, one inch to the right of bullet 3 and exited through the front of his chest. It then passed through a ceiling tile, hit the concrete ceiling and was lost.

Bullet 5 struck Ira Goldstein in the right buttock and was later recovered and booked as evidence.

Bullet 6 passed through Goldstein's left trouser leg and struck the concrete floor, ricocheting off to strike Irwin Stroll in the left shin. This bullet was later recovered and booked as evidence.

Bullet 7 struck William Wiesel in the left abdomen and was later recovered and booked as evidence.

Bullet 8 passed through a ceiling tile, ricocheted off the ceiling and struck Elizabeth Evans in the forehead. This bullet was later recovered and booked as evidence.

Apart from Robert Kennedy, all the victims later recovered from their injuries.

So, there it was; all 8 bullets accounted for and all of the injuries explained. But there were more bullet holes and more shots. Witnesses described hearing more than 8 shots and later acoustics tests suggested there were at least 13. FBI agent, William Bailey said that when he examined the crime scene he saw a set of double doors with a centre-post in between them and on close examination he saw two freshly made bullet holes in the wood at about chest height. He probed them with his finger and could feel the slugs still inside and he has never been in any doubt that they were bullet holes. Several other officers also said that they saw these holes and there are crime scene photographs of police officers pointing at the holes, which have been circled to pick them out on the photographs. If these were bullet holes then the unavoidable conclusion is that there were at least two shots unaccounted for in the LAPD version of events.

The door frame was removed for further investigation but was never entered as evidence. The LAPD concluded that the holes were not bullet holes and so were not relevant to the case. They later destroyed the post, saying that it was really just a piece of rubbish and they needed the space. They also destroyed over 2,500 crime scene photographs once Sirhan had been successfully convicted.

To add further weight to the argument for a second shooter, key witness, Vincent DiPierro recounted an interesting story when interviewed in 1987. DiPierro said that when he went to wash the blood from the sweater he was wearing that night, he found two small holes in the upper left sleeve. He showed this to detective, John Howard and he confirmed they were bullet holes. He told DiPierro to keep the sweater as they might need it but he was never asked about it again.

The evidence for a second gunman is overwhelming and if we are looking for a likely candidate, we may do well to start with Eugene Cesar? Robert Kennedy had not wanted police protection at the Ambassador that night but instead hired private security firm, Ace Security Services and Cesar was one of the guards assigned to the detail. But his assignment may not have been all that random?

Thane Eugene Cesar had a regular day job and worked part time as a guard for Ace Security. On the night of the assassination, Cesar had been the one who escorted Robert Kennedy from the Ballroom to the pantry and he was behind him and holding his arm the whole time. Cesar fell backwards with Bobby when the shots were fired and it is widely claimed that as the shots that hit Bobby came from behind and at low level, they must have been fired by him. This has never been proven or even challenged in a court of law and Cesar may well be completely innocent, but there is ample evidence to support this theory and it deserves further scrutiny. Cesar was interviewed within minutes of the shooting and when asked where Kennedy had been hit he replied, "In the head and the chest and the shoulder." No one knew at that time where Bobby had been hit and it was not until doctors examined Bobby later that the position of the wounds on the body became apparent, so one has to wonder how Cesar could have been so accurate in describing them so soon after the event? This was just one of the strange and unexplained facts regarding Thane Eugene Cesar and his behaviour on that night.

Cesar was standing immediately behind Robert Kennedy at the time of the shooting and would have been ideally placed to have fired the shots described in Dr Noguchi's autopsy report. Noguchi stated in his report that the shots were fired from behind, at close range and at a sharp, upward angle and by his own admission Cesar was himself in such a position at the that time. He told police that when the shooting started he was behind Kennedy and in contact with him and that when he heard the shots, he dropped down into a crouching position and pulled his gun. He later changed his story, claiming he had not pulled his gun at all but there were witnesses who had seen him do so, and that gun would later become the subject of much debate.

Sirhan's gun was a .22 calibre Iver Johnson and the shots that killed Bobby were of a .22 calibre, but Cesar claimed that on the night in question he was carrying a .38 calibre weapon. He said he had owned a .22 calibre pistol but that he had sold it to co-worker, Jim Yoder three months previously, in March 1968. However, in 1972 authors, William Turner and John Christian tracked down Mr Yoder and he still had the receipt for the sale of the gun, which he showed them. The document stated that Yoder had paid Cesar $15 for the gun, serial No Y13332 but the date was September 6th 1968; three months after the assassination and not three months before as Cesar had claimed. This was never revealed in the official investigation and the lead would never be followed. When Turner and Christian asked to see the gun they were told it had been stolen in a house burglary shortly before their visit.

There are many questions to be answered here and none have been asked in any official capacity. Why did Cesar tell police he had worked for Ace Security for 6 months when in fact he had only worked 3 assignments for them, and why change his story about whether or not he drew his gun? Why did he lie about the date he sold his .22 revolver to Yoder and how, when interviewed within minutes of the shooting was he able to give a staggeringly accurate description of the wounds when no one had even examined the body? Why was he even there at all?

If Ace Security had been entrusted with the life of Robert Kennedy, then Thane Eugene Cesar was an odd choice of guard for the assignment. Cesar hated both Jack and Robert Kennedy with a passion and he made no secret of his contempt for them both. He held some extremist right-wing views and once worked for pro-segregationist, George Wallace but this was never made public at the time. Cesar has been interviewed several times in the years following the assassination and has always been eager to express his views and political opinions. On one such occasion he stated.

"I definitely would not have voted for Bobby Kennedy because he had the same ideas as John did, and I think John sold the country down the road. He gave it to the commies and he gave it to whoever else you want him to. He gave it, literally gave it to the minority. He says, here, you take over, I'm giving it to you. You run the white man."

On another occasion he said, "The black man has been cramming this integrated idea down our throats so you learn to hate them. And one of these days there's gona be civil war in this country, white against black; and the black will never win. I think the white man will try to do it with the voting card but if he can't get the right figure in office, I think he will take it into his own hands."

Of course, none of this makes Cesar a murderer, but these are hardly the ramblings of an enlightened, tolerant man. Cesar has always protested his innocence but there is surely enough circumstantial evidence to warrant further investigation, if only to clear his name. He was never called to give evidence at Sirhan's trial and his gun was not even test-fired, and this has led to accusations of a cover-up by the LAPD. There were reports of other people with guns that night but these were never followed up or investigated so until they are, Cesar is likely to remain in the frame.

There can be no doubt that despite their assertions that they did not want *another Dallas*, the LAPD handled the investigation very badly and left themselves wide open to criticism. They failed to follow up important leads and they ignored any evidence or witness testimony that did not support their hypothesis that Sirhan had killed Bobby and that he had acted alone; a chilling reminder of the defiant stance of the Warren Commission. Richard Lubic, who was standing close to Bobby at the time of the shooting says that he was visited shortly after the assassination by members of "Special Unit Senator," a task force set up by LAPD to investigate the case but that they did not want to hear what he actually saw. He said they seemed more like "Government People" and when he asked why they thought Cesar did not raise his gun and aim at Sirhan he was told that was none of his business and he was not to mention it again.

Another key witness who was brow-beaten and bullied into changing her story was campaign worker, Sandra Serrano.

As we saw earlier, Miss Serrano was sitting on the fire escape staircase taking some air when she heard a faint popping sound from inside the hotel. Shortly after, two people came running down the stairs shouting, "We shot him, we shot him." When she asked, "Who did you shoot?" they replied, "We shot Senator Kennedy."

Serrano related this story in a TV interview within minutes of the shooting and she also told the police what she had seen. She said that two people had come down the stairs saying they had shot Kennedy. One was a young woman with dark hair and wearing a white polka-dot dress and the other was a male Mexican American, about 23 years old. The police took a statement from Serrano but dismissed her story, saying she was hysterical or perhaps just mistaken?

Some days later, LAPD investigator, Hank Hernandez took Serrano out to dinner after which he took her back to police headquarters to conduct a lie detector test, to which she readily agreed. In the audio tapes of this session we can hear Hernandez bullying Serrano into changing her story and admitting she had been mistaken about what she saw and heard. Serrano continues to insist that she has been telling the truth but in the end, after a gruelling 50 minutes of relentless pressure from Hernandez, she finally agrees she must have been mistaken. However, almost immediately after the interview she retracted that admission saying she had made it under duress and she has continued to stick to her original story ever since.

If Serrano had been the only witness to see the girl in the polka-dot dress we may well wonder whether she may have been mistaken, but there were others who saw her, too. In the hotel parking lot a couple in their fifties ran up to LAPD Sergeant Paul Sharaga, hysterical and clearly trying to tell him something. He urged them to calm down and they told him how a young couple had just run past them shouting, "We shot him, we shot him." When asked who they had shot they replied that they had shot Senator Kennedy. This incident took place within minutes of the shooting and a good distance away from the fire escape, so this couple could not possibly have known that Serrano had recounted a similar story just minutes before.

Sergeant Sharaga took their names and their details then tore the sheet from his notebook and gave it to a courier, asking him to take it right away to detective, Bill Jordan. Sharaga later recalled that the couple's name was Bernstein but that was the only detail he could remember and his notes never reached Bill Jordan. Jordan denied any knowledge of the event and the LAPD withdrew Sharaga's statement from the record without his knowledge. They denied the incident had ever happened and the Bernsteins were never traced.

In an interesting postscript to this story, investigative reporter, Fernando Forar interviewed a man who claimed to have spent that day with the girl in the polka-dot dress and that she predicted everything to him, just as it happened. Forar gave his tape to the police and on investigation, the story the man gave of his movements that day checked out. But the lead was never followed and the girl was never found.

But the polka-dot dress story just would not go away, so the LAPD had to do something to quash it. Eight months after the shooting, they said that they had found the girl in the polka-dot dress and that her name was Valerie Shulty, a Kennedy campaign worker who was at the Ambassador that night. However, Shulty was the wrong height and build, had the wrong hair colour and on the night in question she had her leg in a plaster cast and was on crutches. Valerie Shulty could not have been the girl described by Serrano and the Bernsteins, but the LAPD insisted that she was and they promptly closed that avenue of investigation.

If witness testimony could not help, then surely photographic evidence could? There were a lot of pictures taken in the pantry that night but none that have survived help in resolving the question of a second gunman, but that does not necessarily mean that there were none. Scott Enyart was a 15 year old high school student at the time and had gone to the Ambassador with his camera to take pictures for his school magazine. He spent the evening taking pictures of the celebrations in the Ballroom then some of Bobby giving his short speech from the podium. He then followed Bobby and his entourage into the pantry to get some more shots of him there.

Enyart was standing about 8 feet from Bobby when the shooting started and he immediately jumped up onto a steam table and began clicking his shutter. After the shooting, he returned to the Ballroom to load his third roll of film when he saw two men in suits looking at him strangely. He moved and they moved with him, eyeing him up all the time and this made him feel uncomfortable, so he ran. The men chased and caught up with him and they emptied his pockets, taking his film and his camera. He was then taken to Rampart police station where he was questioned about the photos he had taken and told that the film and camera were needed as evidence, but that he would get them back.

However, the photos were not returned and when he asked for them he was told that he could not have them as they had been locked away as evidence and were classified. He continued to fight for their release and in 1988 he again wrote to the police demanding their return, but he was told they could not be found. He then filed a law suit against the LAPD and the photos were eventually found in Sacramento, but they were not complete. He received one roll of film when he had, in fact shot three and the film he got back was Ilford when he had been using Kodak, so they had clearly been doctored. There were pictures of the celebrations and of Kennedy giving his speech but nothing in the pantry, where he says he took several from his vantage point on the steam table.

To add further intrigue to this story, in 1996 a courier said he was hired to carry some negatives from Sacramento to the courthouse in LA and on arriving in LA he picked up a hire car at the airport. He said that when he went to drive the car off, he found that his tyres had been slashed and he had to go to a callbox to call breakdown. While he was making the call, the briefcase containing the negatives was stolen.

Something is not right here. If this was an open and shut case then why did the LAPD ignore witness testimony and dismiss evidence from the crime scene, and why did they lie about the number of bullets and the wounds they inflicted? The bullet taken from Paul Shrade's head was supposed to have ricocheted off the concrete ceiling but was almost pristine when recovered and there were problems with the other bullets, too. Police investigator, Dewayne Wolfer fired a test shot from Sirhan's gun and stated that this bullet and those recovered from the crime scene matched that gun, but he later admitted that this was not so. The bullets did not match and were, in fact, two different kinds of ammunition altogether.

There are so many problems and unanswered questions in this case that it just cries out for a fresh, new look. There are many witnesses still living today who could shed new light on these questions if a new investigation were to be launched, not least Sirhan himself. He may still hold the key to this controversial and contentious case and perhaps we should start with him?

Sirhan's trial began on February 12th 1969, and he was doomed from the start. His defence entered a guilty plea in an effort to avoid the death sentence and they made no real effort to defend him at all. The prosecution argued simply that Sirhan had been there that night and he had fired his gun so he must be guilty, and the defence just went along with it. They failed to cross examine key witnesses or to challenge the way the evidence had been handled, and they failed to follow leads that may have proved that a second gunman had been involved. For his part, Sirhan took the stand to say that he knew he had fired his gun but that he still had no recollection of doing it, but he was unable to convince the jury. The prosecution argued that Sirhan knew exactly what he was doing and that the murder was well planned and pre-meditated. On April 17th 1969, Sirhan Sirhan was convicted of the murder of Senator Robert Kennedy and was given the death sentence, which was later commuted to life imprisonment.

Sirhan's movements and behaviour in the days and weeks leading up to the assassination are strange, to say the least. Gun shop owners, Ben and Donna Herrick gave a statement to the police that Sirhan and two other men had called in their shop about 6 weeks before the shooting and asked for some armour-piercing tank ammo which, of course, they didn't have. They.say that shortly after giving this statement, the police came around and tried to get them to change their story and when they refused, they were told they would not be required to testify after all. There were other strange sightings of Sirhan, too, some of which may not have even been him at all?

On June 1st 1968, a man claiming to be Sirhan supposedly went to the Corona police pistol range and behaved in a way that was bound to attract attention, just as Oswald had done in 1963. However, on further investigation the description of this man did not match that of Sirhan and so could not have been him. In addition, the man in question carried his gun in a zipper case, which Sirhan never did. The following day, Sirhan was allegedly seen entering the Kennedy campaign headquarters and when asked if he needed any help he pointed to the man next to him and said, "I'm with him." The man in question was claimed to be Khaliber Khan, who had strong connections with the CIA and was at that time one of the most notorious intelligence agents in the world. These sightings may or may not have been Sirhan and they may never have happened at all, but they are on record and should be fully investigated, if only to rule them out as nonsense and hearsay.

Having got nowhere by conventional means, the LAPD tried to unlock Sirhan's memory through hypnosis but that, too, failed. Sirhan was especially susceptible to hypnosis and doctors said he was a perfect subject, but their sessions failed to produce any results. However, Sirhan's susceptibility to hypnosis has raised some intriguing questions over the years and there are many who believe that he may have been a Manchurian Candidate; a subject hypnotised by military intelligence to kill on a given trigger or command. The theory is that a suitably susceptible person is taken under the wing of the intelligence services and hypnotised to kill a particular person in a particular way and at a given time. It may seem an unlikely scenario but if that was, in fact what happened it may well explain why Sirhan has been unable to recall what took place that night. The CIA has admitted that they did run such a program in the 1960's and there are some who claim to have been involved and that it was used to assassinate some key political figures. If this were the case, then there is a cruel irony in the fact that Bobby was staying with close friend and Hollywood director, John Frankenheimer the night before he was killed. In 1962, Frankenheimer had directed the film, *The Manchurian Candidate*, in which a soldier is hypnotised to carry out just such a killing in exactly this way.

Sirhan has never been given a fair trial and has been languishing in prison, protesting his innocence since the day of his arrest. As recently as 2012, Sirhan's lawyers were still campaigning for a new investigation but to date they have been unsuccessful. Sirhan has been refused parole at every attempt and his requests for a re-trial have been repeatedly denied. There can be no doubt that Sirhan Sirhan fired a gun at Senator Robert Kennedy that night, but his bullets did not kill him. All the evidence would suggest that someone else killed Robert Kennedy and we need to know who, and why?

Despite the best efforts of the LAPD's Special Unit Senator, they were unable to quell the rumours of a conspiracy in the death of Robert Kennedy. The evidence for a second gunman is overwhelming and a second gunman would, of course, constitute a conspiracy of some kind, and there is no shortage of likely candidates.

Like his father and brother before him, Robert Kennedy had made enemies of some very dangerous and vindictive people and they were just queueing up to get their revenge. There have been claims that the Mafia had arranged the killing in revenge for Bobby's treatment of them when Attorney General, and some said that Jimmy Hoffa may have arranged it from his prison cell. There were suggestions, too that the CIA had used Sirhan as a Manchurian Candidate and some even claimed that President Johnson may have been involved, as they said he had been with JFK. Bobby had been an outspoken opponent of the Vietnam War and many believe this had been the cause of his downfall as the multi-million dollar defence industry wanted to continue the conflict in Vietnam.

Another very powerful argument is that Bobby was killed because he was close to winning the presidency, and that could never be allowed to happen. Although silent on the subject in public, Bobby told close friends that if he were elected President, he would re-open the investigation into his brother's murder and go after the killers, whoever they were. This was not widely known at the time but in recent years, new evidence has emerged that this may well have been the case.

Whoever killed Bobby and whatever the reason, he was gone and his dream was gone with him. We have every reason to believe that had he survived and been elected, Robert Kennedy may have been one of the finest Presidents the United States has ever had and his tragic death was a great loss to the nation and to the world. For a brief moment in the summer of 1968, there was a glimmer of hope for a brighter future for the United States, but that all changed with the death of Robert Kennedy. The nation was plunged once more into darkness, and the forces of evil loomed large once again. The minority groups had lost their voice. Young men were still dying in a far off war that could never be won and with Bobby out of the race, it was Jack's arch-rival,

Richard Nixon who would win the coveted seat in the Whitehouse.

Joe Kennedy had lost another of his precious sons to the pursuit of wealth and power and by now he must surely have been asking himself, "Was it really all worth it?"

8 TED

By the summer of 1968, Joe Kennedy's dream had become a nightmare. Confined to a wheelchair and in failing health, the 80 year-old former Ambassador could only look on in grief-stricken frustration as yet another of his precious sons was taken away from him. The death of Bobby had left only one surviving son and even Joe must have known that young Ted was a most unlikely candidate for the presidency, but that would not prevent him from trying.

Edward Moore (Ted) Kennedy was born on February 22nd 1932 at St Margaret's Hospital in Boston; the fourth son of Joe and Rose Kennedy and the youngest of their nine children. Ted was a quiet, timid boy and although much loved by his parents, they had a tendency to compare him unfavourably with his brothers. Ted had a happy childhood and enjoyed the company of his older brothers and he was especially close to young Joe, who always treated him as a favourite.

Ted was frequently uprooted as the family flitted between Boston, New York and London and this had a detrimental effect on his schooling. By the age of eleven, Ted had attended ten different schools and he found it hard to settle, making him, at best a very average scholar. He found schoolwork hard and frustrating so he turned his attention to athletics instead and he was especially good at football. His headmaster at Milton described him as, "absolutely fearless" and he once received a recruitment offer from the Green Bay Packers, but he declined the offer in favour of a career in politics.

Like his father and brothers before him, Ted attended Harvard College but he failed to live up to their high standards. He copied answers from other students in tests and in May 1951, Ted persuaded a friend to take his place in a Spanish language exam. But his ruse was discovered and he was expelled for cheating.

Undeterred by this set-back, Ted enlisted in the US Army in June 1951. His father had pulled strings to ensure that Ted was not sent off to fight in Korea and on completing his basic training, Ted requested a posting to army intelligence in Maryland. He was accepted but was dropped after just six weeks. He then trained in the Military Police Corp. and in 1952, he was assigned to the honour guard at the SHARP Headquarters in Paris where he had a grand time, seeing the sights and attending parties. Ted had signed up for a four year term in the Army but again his father pulled strings and in March 1953, Ted was given an honourable discharge after serving just 21 months.

Tired of playing soldiers, Ted returned to Harvard in the summer of 1953, where he worked harder to improve his grades (this time, without cheating) and continued to indulge his passion for football. He graduated from Harvard in 1956 then followed in Bobby's footsteps by enrolling at the University of Virginia Law School. His appointment there caused some controversy in light of his having been expelled from Harvard and, by his own admission, he had to work ten times harder than everyone else, just to keep up.

Like all the Kennedys, Ted had to be tough in order to survive and he suffered a number of knocks and setbacks in his early years that would affect him for the rest of his life. Ted had always been a sensitive, caring child and, being the youngest, he formed a very strong bond with his siblings; especially Joe Junior and Rosemarie. He was just nine years old when Rosemary was sent away following her failed lobotomy and he just could not understand what had happened. One day she was there, the bright and beautiful big sister he loved and adored and the next day, she was gone. No explanation and not even a chance to say goodbye. In his nine year-old mind, his sister had in some way upset their father and this made Ted think he had better do as his father said or he would be next. Then just four years later Ted had to come to terms with the death of Joe Junior before suffering another shattering blow when Kathleen was killed in a plane crash in 1948.

These devastating and traumatic events would have a profoundly disturbing effect on the young Ted Kennedy and they would stay with him forever. He would never fully recover from the loss of Rosemary and Joe Junior and he later found solace in alcohol. The signs were there in his college years where he began to show a difficult, rebellious side to his nature, once being booked for reckless driving and driving without a licence. It was the same old story; dad was Joe Kennedy, and the Kennedys could do whatever they liked.

In October 1957, while still at law school, Ted met college student and former model, Virginia Joan Bennet and the couple were married at St Joseph's Church, New York on November 28th 1958. They would eventually go on to have three children together; Kara, Ted Junior and Patrick. These were happy times for the young Ted Kennedy. He was admitted to the Massachusetts Bar in 1959 and in 1960 he helped manage the campaign that would see his brother, Jack elected President. Meanwhile, he continued to pursue his interest in sports such as skiing and sailing and he also learned to fly, a passion he would later share with his nephew, John Kennedy Junior.

Ted Kennedy found himself at the centre of yet another controversial scandal in his bid for a seat in the Senate. Jack's election to President had vacated his place as Senator for Massachusetts, but Ted would not be eligible to fill the vacancy until his 30th birthday in February 1962. The solution to this was that Jack asked Massachusetts Governor, Foster Furcolo to name family friend, Bill Smith as interim Senator until Ted could contest it, which he duly did, despite his dislike of the Kennedys. In the meantime, Ted took a job as Assistant DA for Suffolk County, Massachusetts on a salary of just $1. People said he earned every penny, but not much more.

Despite yet more allegations of misconduct and dirty dealing, Ted took on and beat Edward J McCormack Jr and then George Cabot Lodge in the 1962 Senate special election to become, at last, Senator for Massachusetts. His expulsion from Harvard had become public knowledge during the campaign and there were many who felt that Ted was just one Kennedy too many. But as it turned out, Ted would eventually mature into a very able politician and would serve as Senator for Massachusetts for many years to come.

Whilst Jack and Bobby were busy running the country from their Camelot on Capitol Hill, Ted was learning his craft in the Senate, where he performed well and showed real skill as a politician. He also took several trips abroad around this time, during which it was claimed he frequented brothels and nightclubs and even had a brief affair with a notorious Soviet spy; a claim he vehemently denied. For all their faults, the Kennedys were generally not heavy drinkers, but Ted was the exception to this rule. Jack and Bobby were never seen drunk in public but Ted turned to drink at an early age and developed a dependency on alcohol that would stay with him for the rest of his life. The pressures of public life had put a severe strain on Ted's marriage too and in time his wife, Joan also took solace in drink. Joan was a quiet, unassuming woman who found it hard to play the role of a Kennedy wife and within just a few years of their marriage, the cracks were beginning to show.

On the afternoon of Friday, November 22nd 1963, Ted was presiding over a meeting of the Senate when a messenger came in and told him that his brother had been shot. Shortly after, Bobby called to tell him that Jack had died and to ask him to go to Hyannis Port to break the news to their father in person. Ted called his mother and asked her to keep old Joe away from the TV and the radio until he arrived and then he and his sister, Eunice boarded the plane for Hyannis. Three days later, Ted and Bobby were leading the funeral procession as they made the slow march to Arlington National Cemetery, where they laid their dearly beloved brother down to rest.

Bobby was now the eldest son and he worried for his father and his mother, but their trials were not yet over. On June 19th 1964, Ted was a passenger on a private plane flying from Washington to Massachusetts when it ran into bad weather and got into difficulty. The plane crashed into an apple orchard on its final approach to Barnes Municipal Airport, killing the pilot and Kennedy aid, Edward Moss. Ted was pulled alive from the wreckage by fellow Senator, Bill Bayh but he had suffered a punctured lung, broken ribs and internal bleeding. He also sustained a serious back injury that would land him in hospital for several months and would trouble him for the rest of his life.

This experience triggered Ted's lifelong passion for health reform and when he returned to the Senate in January 1965, he began to campaign hard for change. He became a strong and influential spokesman for social and healthcare reform and he began what would become a long and successful career as a legislator. Old Joe's plan to create a political dynasty and have a succession of Kennedys in the Whitehouse had been derailed by the death of Jack but within a couple of years, it was firmly back on track. Ted was working hard in the Senate and Bobby, having begun to come to terms with his immense personal grief, was planning his own political future. It was time for Ted to play second fiddle to Bobby as the surviving Kennedy sons positioned themselves for another Kennedy onslaught.

In the spring of 1968 Bobby, now a Senator for the state of New York, announced his candidacy for President in the upcoming elections and he turned to Ted for support. Ted had initially advised against Bobby's running in '68 but once committed, he threw his full weight and support behind his campaign, just as Bobby had for Jack in 1960. Ted was by now an experienced and influential Senator in his own right and he worked tirelessly to recruit allies in the Senate and in Congress. Bobby's campaign gathered momentum with every passing day and by the end of May, many were predicting another Kennedy victory. He seemed certain to become the next President of the United States but once again, the cruel hand of fate intervened.

Ted was in San Francisco when he heard that Bobby had been shot and he rushed to LA to be at his side. He sat vigil with Ethel and Jackie as the doctors did all they could but on June 6th, 1968 Bobby died from his wounds and once again, Ted was left stricken by grief. Frank Mankiewicz saw Ted at the hospital and said, "I have never, ever, nor do I expect ever, to see a face more in grief."

On June 8th 1968, Ted stood before a crowd of grief-stricken mourners and delivered his beautiful and heart-felt eulogy to his dead brother. It was one of the most defining moments in Ted's life.

Ted was now the sole surviving son of Joseph P Kennedy and he knew it would be up to him to keep his father's dream alive. It would be Ted who would carry the Kennedy torch and he knew that the eyes of the world would be on him. He was urged to run for President in Bobby's place but he declined, choosing instead to continue his work in the Senate. He needed more time to prepare, so he set his sights on running in '72 and many believed he would succeed, but all of that was about to change following an incident on the quiet little island of Chappaquiddick.

Chappaquiddick

We may never know exactly what happened at Chappaquiddick but what we do know is that on the afternoon of Friday, July 19th 1969, as Apollo 11 was preparing for the first moon landing, Senator Edward Kennedy took a flight from Washington DC to Martha's Vineyard for a weekend that would change his life forever. He was to take part in the Edgartown sailing regatta and on that Friday evening he had arranged a party at a rented cottage on the small island of Chappaquiddick. The party was to be a reunion of a small group of young, single women known as the "Boiler-Room Girls," all former campaign workers of the late Robert Kennedy, who had been killed just over a year before. The cottage had been rented for the weekend by Ted's cousin, Joe Gargin and the plan was that they would hold a cook-out there; six men (five of them married) and six young, single women, all hanging out in the privacy of the secluded Lawrence Cottage and away from prying eyes.

At 1.30pm on that Friday afternoon, Ted's chauffer, Jack Crimmins drove him from the airport at Martha's Vineyard to the rented cottage on Chappaquiddick Island, which was accessible only by a small, two car ferry from Edgertown. Ted changed his clothes then went down to the secluded beach for a swim with some of the girls before taking the ferry back to Edgertown to take part in the afternoon's racing. He then went back to his room at the Shireton Hotel in Edgertown to change before being driven back to the cottage on Chappaquiddick Island at about 7.30pm.

According to his own testimony, Ted claimed that he decided to leave the party at about 11.15pm as he wished to return to his hotel in Edgertown and he did not want to miss the ferry, which usually closed at around midnight. He said that one of the girls, Mary Jo Kopechne then said that she, too would like to leave and asked if she could go with him. Ted got the car keys from Crimmins and he and Mary Jo set off for the ferry, with Ted at the wheel and Mary Jo in the passenger seat.

Ted claimed that he drove the black Oldsmobile 88 down the dark and secluded main road until he came to the sharp left-turn that would take them to the ferry landing, but he took a wrong turn and went right into Dike Road instead. Dike Road was no more than a rough dirt-track that led to the beach via a narrow wooden bridge and Ted said that before he knew it, the bridge appeared out of nowhere and he was on it. He said he touched the brakes but it was already too late and he lost control. The car toppled off the bridge on the right-hand side and landed upside-down in about 6 or 8 feet of freezing cold water.

The water rushed into the car through the broken windows, but Ted somehow managed to get out and struggled to the surface. He could not see Mary Jo anywhere and as he got no reply when calling her name, he realised she must still be in the car. He said he made repeated attempts to dive down and rescue her from the vehicle but the tide was too strong and he soon became exhausted, so he rested on the bank for about 15 to 20 minutes to catch his breath. Having recovered enough to walk, he then went on foot back to the Lawrence Cottage to get help. He described how he distinctly remembered stumbling around in total darkness, down the deserted road to the cottage. On arriving at the cottage, he saw someone standing outside and he asked them to go inside and fetch Joe Gargin while he, himself waited outside in a rented car that was parked there. He did not go into the house as he did not want to alarm any of the other girls.

Joe Gargin and Paul Markham came out of the house and Ted told them what had happened and asked what he should do. The three of them then drove back to the bridge and Ted claims that Gargin and Markham made several more attempts to rescue Mary Jo but that they, too were unable to do so. Gargin and Markham insisted that the accident should be reported immediately and they urged Ted to go to the police, so they drove Ted down to the ferry landing so he could cross over to Edgertown to inform the authorities of what had happened. According to Gargin, Ted was sobbing and on the verge of becoming crazed.

Ted claimed that when they reached the ferry it had already closed for the night, so he instructed Gargin and Markham to return to the cottage to sort things out that end. He said that he then swam the 500 feet to the other side of the channel, almost drowning in the process. Gargin and

Markham have been heavily criticised for agreeing to this course of action as they effectively allowed a man who had a bad back and had just been involved in a serious accident to swim across the channel in freezing cold water and against a very strong current when they should have considered other options. That is, of course, if this part of the story is true?

Ted had assured them that he was going to report the accident as soon as he reached the other side but instead, he went to his room at the Shireton Hotel, where he promptly fell asleep. He said he was awakened by a noise outside his room and he put on some clothes and popped out to see what it was. He saw what he thought were some tourists and he asked them the time; it was 2.30am.

Ted went back into his room and was not seen again until around 7.30am when he appeared in the lobby of the hotel, casually talking to some fellow contestants about the previous day's racing. He appeared calm and relaxed and he made a series of phone calls from a payphone, borrowing a dime from the receptionist to do so. He was then joined at the hotel by Gargin and Markham at around 8am. How they got across to Edgertown that morning is a mystery, as the ferry operator said he did not take them.

According to Ted's own testimony, the two men asked him why he had not yet reported the accident and they had what he described as a, "heated conversation." He told them how he had swam across the channel in a confused state and how he thought that they were somehow going to tell him that Mary Jo was alright. The three of them then took the ferry back to Chappaquiddick where Ted made several more telephone calls, none of them to the police. Only when he heard that the car had been found and he saw the hearse pass by on its way to Dike Bridge did he realise that the game was up. He crossed back over to Edgertown and went, at last, to the police station to report the accident. The time was around 10am; a full 9 hours after the accident had happened.

Earlier that morning, two amateur fishermen had seen the car submerged in the water and alerted the inhabitants of a nearby cottage, and at around 8.30am they called the police. Edgertown police chief, James Arena arrived on the scene and, borrowing a bathing suit, dived into the water to investigate, but the current was too strong and he was forced to abandon the attempt. He called in local volunteer diver, John Farrar, who arrived on the scene at around 8.45, having changed in the car on the way to save time. Farrar dived into the water and soon discovered the body of Mary Jo Kopechne in the back of the car. The car was upside down in around 6 to 8 feet of tidal water and Mary Jo's head was in an air pocket in the rear footwell, her hands still gripping the back of the front seat.

The body was removed and was examined at the scene by medical examiner, Dr Donald Mills, who stated that Mary Jo was, "The most drowned person I've ever seen." He said that the slightest pressure on the chest brought water out from the nose and mouth and he declared that there would be no need for an autopsy, a decision that would prove controversial later.

The car was recovered from the pond and a quick check revealed that it was registered to Senator Edward Kennedy. Arena knew Ted very well and he put out a call to have him picked up but by that time, Ted was already waiting for him at the station, having insisted he would talk to no one else. Arena went back over to Edgertown to interview Ted as Mary Jo's body was quickly whisked away.

Ted gave his statement to the police then rushed off to the family compound at Hyannis Port for the weekend, where all the Kennedy big-guns had gathered to help sort out the mess. In the end, Ted pleaded guilty to leaving the scene of an accident after causing injury and was told that no further charges would be brought against him. He appeared on national TV on July 25th to admit his guilt and to ask for forgiveness.

Inconsistencies

The story that Ted told during that address was more or less the one related here, but this was not quite what he had said in his original statement. The story Ted gave to the police on the afternoon of Saturday, July 19th made no mention of Gargin and Markham trying to rescue Mary Jo, nor did it describe how he swam across the channel. These details were added later, after the weekend meetings at Hyannis Port. And those were not the only inconsistencies; the whole story was riddled with them. In order to determine, as well as we can, what really happened that weekend, we need to examine Ted's story very closely from the beginning.

Firstly, just what kind of party was it? Ted claimed it was an innocent re-union of a group of respectable, like-minded people and that it was a quiet affair with very little liquor, but that may not have been quite the truth? Five of the six men were married and all of the women were single, and there certainly was plenty of booze, and noise too. There was ample evidence of drink at the house when the police investigated on the Saturday and there were reports of loud noises late into the night, one neighbour almost calling the police to complain. Ted said that it was only ill-health that prevented his wife, Joan from attending the party with him, but few believed that claim as it was known that Ted and

Joan were having problems around that time. Ted also defended the reputation of Mary Jo and insisted that she had been a sweet, innocent girl who would do nothing to tarnish the good name of herself or her family, and all who knew her seemed to agree. Friends said she was respectable to the point of prudish and that she hardly ever drank and when asked if there had been any relationship between them, Ted stated.

"There is no truth whatever to the widely circulated suspicions of immoral conduct that have been levelled at my behaviour and hers regarding that evening. There has never been a private relationship between us of any kind."

Relationship or not, at some point in the evening Ted and Mary Jo left the party together and we may never know why. Ted claimed they were going back to the hotel in Edgertown but if Mary Jo had intended to leave for the night, why did she not tell any of the others? She also left her purse at the cottage and she never asked her room-mate, Esther Newberg for the key to their hotel room. Ted had always claimed that the intention was for all of the party-goers to return to the hotel in Edgertown after the party and not to stay at the cottage overnight. But if that were the case, why did no one else leave to catch the last ferry, as Ted claimed he and Mary Jo had?

Local Deputy Sherriff, Christopher Look testified that at around 12.15am on July 19th he saw a dark coloured car with two people in the front seat and what he thought may have been another person or a bundle of clothing in the back. He said that the car passed directly in front of him and into his headlights and he continued on but then stopped, as he noticed the car was backing up towards him. He thought they were stopping to ask him for directions so he got out of his car and started walking towards them when the car sped off down Ferry Road before turning right into Dike Road. Look testified that the car had a licence plate beginning with L7. The registration plate on Ted's car was L78207, but Look could not have known that at the time. When the car was pulled out of the water later that day, Look positively identified it as the one he had seen.

We already have a number of troubling contradictions here. Ted claimed to have left the party at 11.15pm, but Look did not see the car until 12.15am. In addition, Ted said he turned into Dike Road by mistake but Look has him turning in there quite deliberately, as if trying to avoid the police. Ted claimed to have been unfamiliar with the road but he knew the area well and had been driven down that road in broad daylight just hours before. Dike Road is a narrow dirt track off the main road and it would be almost impossible to turn into it by mistake, even at night. The main road has a tarmac surface and clearly goes around to the left towards the ferry, whereas Dike Road is a simple dirt track on the right. The change in road surface would have become apparent to the driver immediately. In addition, the main road to the left is indicated by a large sign warning of a sharp bend to the left and this would be reflected in the headlights on a dark night. Ted's claim to have turned down the road by mistake is clearly shaky, at best.

Ted claimed that once he realised he had turned into Dike Road by mistake, he had no choice but to go on as there was nowhere to turn around, but this was simply not true. There were several driveways along Dike Road and Ted could have backed into any one of them to turn around if he so wished. Ted also claimed he was driving down the road at about 7 or 8 miles per hour, looking for somewhere to turn when the bridge suddenly appeared out of nowhere. But that too, is doubtful. When driving down Dike Road the bridge actually comes into view a good two to three hundred feet before you actually reach it, even in car headlights in the darkness. This point was examined in detail during the investigation and it was found that the car was almost certainly travelling at around 20mph, not the 7 or 8 that Ted had claimed.

However it happened and at whatever speed, Ted drove onto the narrow wooden bridge and the black Oldsmobile toppled off the unprotected edge on the right-hand side and into the water, with the two occupants still inside. Ted managed to get out of the submerged vehicle and claimed he made numerous attempts to rescue Mary Jo. He then said he rested on the bank for about 15 to 20 minutes before going back to the Lawrence Cottage, on foot, for help. He said that he rushed back as quickly as he could and that everywhere was in total darkness. He claimed he saw no lights and had no opportunity to raise the alarm on the way but this, again is not true.

Ted said he saw no lights on his walk back to the cottage, but there were plenty. Just 100 feet from Dike Bridge was the Malm house with a light on, but he passed it by. He also passed four other cottages, each with lights on at that time and each with a phone from which he could have raised the alarm, but he passed those by, too. He even passed the unmanned volunteer rescue station with a glowing red light on the top and an unlocked door leading into a room with a phone from which people could call the emergency services, but he chose to ignore that as well.

Ted also lied about how he knew what time it was when he arrived back at the cottage. In his testimony he stated that when he got back to the cottage, he saw Ray LaRosa outside and he asked him to go in and fetch Joe Gargin. Ted said he did not go into the house himself but, instead, got into a rented car that was parked outside to wait for Gargin to appear. He said he knew that it was 12.20am because he distinctly remembers looking at the clock on the car dashboard as he climbed in, but this was another blatant lie. The rented car was a Valiant 100, and that particular model had no clock in the dashboard.

Whatever time it was, Ted claimed that he related his story to Gargin and Markham, who had just joined them from the house, and the three of them drove back to Dike Bridge. He claimed that when they got there, Gargin and Markham made several attempts to rescue Mary Jo from the car themselves but were unable to do so, but he made no mention of this in his original statement to the police. He said that Gargin and Markham then drove him to the ferry landing so he could cross over to Edgertown and report the accident to the police but when they got there, the ferry was closed. The fact is that any one of them could easily have reported the accident by phone from the Chappaquiddick side of the channel, but none of them did.

Another interesting point here is that although the ferry usually closed around midnight, on the night in question, it stayed open much later. Ferry operator, Jared Grant said he kept the ferry open until 1.20am that night as he knew the Senator was hosting a party and he thought he and his guests might want to use it. He did not see Ted or any of his associates in that time, but he did see several boats running back and forth between Chappaquiddick and Edgertown, and that was unusual at that time of night. So how did Ted get across?

Ted claimed that on finding that the ferry was closed, which it could not have been, he swam the 500ft channel to Edgertown. But this, too is in question. Ted was a good swimmer but the water was icy-cold and the current very strong, so he would have had great difficulty swimming across, which he said he did. He was also supposed to be in shock and suffering from concussion and a bad back and this would have further hampered any attempt to swim the channel. This begs the question, could he have crossed by boat? We have already seen how Jared Grant said he saw boats running back and forth that night and a Mr Balloue from Rhode Island said he saw three men crossing the channel in a boat at around 2am. To add weight to this argument, a local resident said that his boat had been used in the night and tied up in a different place the next morning.

We can only speculate as to why Ted should lie about how he got back to Edgertown but by his own account, he wound up back in his hotel room and by 7.30am, he was in the lobby of the hotel chatting casually with other guests. He was dressed in a sports shirt and slacks and appeared calm and relaxed, some even said, jovial. There was absolutely nothing in his behaviour that might suggest he had just been involved in a serious accident and he was in no way stressed, or even tired.

As we have seen, Ted went on to say that at around 8am he was joined at the hotel by Gargin and Markham and that they had a, "heated conversation." Gargin and Markham were astonished and appalled that Ted had not yet called the police, but still they did not do so. Instead, they took the ferry back to Chappaquiddick and only then, when they reached the other side and heard that the car had been discovered, did they finally go the police station in Edgertown. It was now 10am, a full nine hours since the accident had happened. In his statement, Ted covers this part of the story by saying.

"I remember walking around for a period and then going back to my hotel room. When I fully realised what had happened this morning, I immediately went to the police."

It is up to the reader to decide whether the word, immediately adequately describes a nine hour delay?

Cause of Death?

Back at Chappaquiddick, medical examiner, Dr Donald Mills declared that Mary Jo had died from drowning, but even this was disputed at the time. John Farrar, the diver who recovered Mary Jo's body from the car asserted that she had not died from drowning but from suffocation.

"She didn't drown," he stated. "She died of suffocation in her own air void. It took her at least three or four hours to die. I could have had her out of that car in twenty five minutes after I got the call. But he (Ted) did not call."

If what Farrar says is true, and we have no reason to suppose otherwise, then the implications are that Mary Jo Kopechne may have died terrified and alone, waiting in the cold and total darkness for a rescue that never came?

Farrar is not the only witness whose testimony does not support Dr Mills' findings. Undertaker, Eugene Frieh was also at the scene when the body was recovered and he disputed Mills' claim that with just the slightest pressure on the chest, water oozed out from the nose and mouth. Frieh was standing right next to Dr Mills when he made those observations and he said he did not see any significant outpouring of water. Frieh said, "It produced some water flow, water and foam; mostly foam. Very little water was expelled from the lungs."

Some medical professionals have disputed Frieh's claims and have supported Dr Mills in concluding that the amount of water emanating from the nose and mouth did indicate death by drowning, despite Frieh's comments on the foam. Pathologist, Dr Werner Spitz stated that the water and foam were both consistent with a death from drowning and he suggested that this foam may explain the slight traces of blood that were found on the back of Mary Jo's blouse. These stains were found when the clothing was examined later and their presence has been the subject of much debate. Dr Spitz said they were the result of blood-soaked foam running down Mary Jo's face and into the water but this theory has never been proven and some experts consider it extremely unlikely. It has even been suggested that these stains may not have been blood at all but may have been grass stains?

In any event, Dr Mills declared that there would be no autopsy and Mary Jo's body was quickly removed from Chappaquiddick and out of the jurisdiction of Massachusetts, and the reason for this has never been adequately explained. When he received the medical report at 10am on the Sunday morning, DA for the southern district of Massachusetts, Edmund Dinis immediately ordered an autopsy, but he was told that the body had already been flown out. In fact, the body was not flown out until 12.30pm that day so at the time of the request it was still available. It is standard practice for autopsies to be performed on victims of auto accidents, especially when the victim is a young woman of child-bearing age. Former medical examiner, John Edland said.

"It's a real farce to bring the body of a dead girl out of a car after nine hours and have someone make a pronouncement that it is a routine drowning."

An autopsy would have determined the exact time and cause of death and would have been able to determine whether any sexual activity had taken place that evening. We do know that Mary Jo had consumed very little alcohol as she had a low blood-alcohol level of 0.9%, but we know nothing of her intentions on leaving the party or her movements in the short time between leaving the party and her death. An autopsy would also have settled the question of whether Mary Jo had been pregnant at the time, as some had claimed. If Ted's story had been true, he would have had everything to gain and nothing to lose by agreeing to an autopsy. As it was, these and other questions would remain unanswered.

We will never know for certain what happened that night as there will never be a trial and many of the key witnesses are now dead so we are left with the question, why did Ted lie about it? If Sherriff Look's statement is correct (and we have no reason to suppose it is not), there is a gap of an hour between the time Ted claimed they left the party and the time they were seen by Look, and many have wondered what might have happened in that hour. Many believe that what really happened that night was that Ted and Mary Jo left the party to be alone together and that they were seen in the car by Sherriff Look. This startled Senator Kennedy, who did not want to be seen in a compromising position, alone with a young, single woman in the middle of the night and he panicked. He drove off at high speed to avoid Sherriff Look and he turned into Dike Road in order to escape. When he reached the bridge he was travelling too fast, lost control of the car and it plunged over the side. This theory has never been proven and has always been vehemently denied by Ted Kennedy, but it would help explain some of the discrepancies in timings and why Mary Jo left her purse and hotel keys at the house.

At a court hearing on Friday, July 25th Ted pleaded guilty to a charge of leaving the scene of a crash after causing injury. Ted's lawyers requested that any jail sentence should be suspended, citing Ted's good character and prior reputation and on the grounds that he had no prior record or convictions. This, despite him having convictions for speeding, reckless driving, running red lights and even allegations of drunk driving. Judge James Boyce accepted the plea and sentenced Ted to two months incarceration, the minimum allowed for such an offence, which was suspended. Ted Kennedy walked out a free man and later addressed the nation on TV, asking for forgiveness and seeking advice from his voters on whether or not he should resign from the Senate, which he did not.

From the very beginning, there were those who did not believe Ted's story and there were calls to have the case re-examined. In August, the District Attorney for the Southern District of Massachusetts, Edmund Dinis petitioned to have the body of Mary Jo Kopechne exhumed so that a full post-mortem could be carried out but his request was denied by the authorities and opposed by Mary Jo's parents who, it was claimed, had been paid off by the Kennedys. The Kopechnes said that they had objected to the exhumation on religious grounds as they felt it would be an affront to God to have their daughter's body exhumed for no good reason and that she should be left to rest in peace. They were persuaded into this course of action by his Eminence,

Richard Cardinal Cushing, one of the highest ranking churchmen in the country and a very close friend of the Kennedys.

The inquest into the death of Mary Jo Kopechne took place in Edgertown in January 1970 and was presided over by Judge, James A Boyle. At the request of the Kennedy lawyers it was conducted in secret, which was most unusual, and the 763 page transcript of the proceedings was not released until four months later. The inquest lasted four days and at the end of it, Judge Boyle accepted Ted's story that he had turned into Dike Road by mistake. Judge Boyle stated that,
"There is probable cause to believe that Edward Moore Kennedy operated his motor vehicle negligently and that such operation appears to have contributed to the death of Mary Jo Kopechne."
Despite this damning conclusion, District Attorney, Edmund Dinis chose not to prosecute Ted for manslaughter, which he easily could have done.

The Kopechne family did not bring any action against Senator Kennedy and seemed happy to let the matter rest. They said that their reason for not taking such action was that they did not want people to think that they were looking for blood money, but they did receive money from the Kennedys. It later emerged that they had received over $90,000 from Kennedy's insurers and a further $50,000 from Ted personally. There was even speculation that they may have received considerably more.

That should have been the end of the matter, but there were still many who could not accept Ted's version of events and Chappaquiddick had already become the story that just would not go away. The Kennedy machine would spend years trying to bury the incident deep in the past but before they could begin to do so, there would be one more attempt at establishing the truth.

In March, 1970, Leslie Leland, the Foreman of the Grand Jury for Dike's County, Massachusetts sent a letter to the Chief Justice of the Supreme Court requesting a special session of the Grand Jury to examine the case. The Chief Justice at first denied having received the letter, but Leland produced a document of receipt with the Chief Justice's signature on it and the session was duly granted. It was scheduled for April 6th 1970.

When the day arrived, Judge Wilfred Paquet told the Grand Jury that they could summon any witnesses they thought might prove useful but they were not permitted to view the transcript notes of the inquest, nor could they question any of the inquest witnesses. District Attorney Dinis told the Grand Jury that he had seen the notes from the inquest and that there was just not enough evidence to indict Senator Kennedy on potential charges of manslaughter, perjury or driving to endanger life. In the end, the Grand Jury called four witnesses who testified for a total of just 20 minutes, and no indictments were issued. The Chicago Tribune reported that.

"This remarkable ruling deprived the Grand Jury of access to the record and amounted to a directive to the District Attorney to pledge that there would be no prosecution of Senator Kennedy. The Senator has been given special benefits and kid-glove treatment from every court before which he has been represented."

So, it was all over at last and Senator Edward Moore Kennedy was able to put the whole thing behind him and get on with his life. But it was never going to be quite so simple. The incident at Chappaquiddick put paid to Ted's political ambitions and he has been vilified in the press and the media since the day it happened. There are many who still refuse to believe his story and there have been numerous alternative scenarios put forward as to what might have happened.

Many believe that Ted was not driving the car when it went off the bridge but that Mary Jo Kopechne was in the driving seat. A BBC documentary, broadcast in 1994 speculated that Ted and Mary Jo had left the party to be alone together and that when they saw Look's police car, Ted panicked as he did not want to be seen in a compromising position. It says he jumped out of the car and hid in the bushes, leaving Mary Jo to drive off on her own and arranging to meet up with her later. The story goes that, being only 5'2" tall, the Oldsmobile was too big for Mary Jo and as she was unfamiliar with the road, she did not see the bridge and drove off the edge into the water. Ted had no knowledge of this until told by Gargin and Markham at the hotel later that morning. This would explain Ted's apparent lack of concern when he was seen in the hotel lobby that morning and would account for some of the contradictory evidence found at the crash-site.

Another theory put forward by researcher, Richard Sprague claims that Mary Jo was murdered and that Ted was framed. Sprague speculates that Ted and Mary Jo were in the car alone when they were ambushed. Ted was dragged from the car and knocked out while Mary Jo was plied with alcohol before being placed back in the car. The car windows were then smashed and the car pushed over the bridge. Mary Jo survived and regained consciousness but she was trapped in the car and died from asphyxiation whilst trying to breath in an air pocket. The unconscious Ted Kennedy was taken to his hotel room in Edgertown while the attackers called Gargin at the cottage to tell him what they had done. Ted and Mary Jo had been seen leaving the party together and Ted would surely be implicated in her death, so they had to make up the story of the accident and the confused state of mind to try and cover his tracks. The intention was not to kill Ted, but to ruin his political career and to prevent another Kennedy from entering the Whitehouse.

There is some evidence to support this version of events, but there are problems with it, too. The damage to the car might support this theory, as might the head injury sustained by Ted. In addition, Mary Jo was said not to drink alcohol and although traces were found in her body, these were very slight and insignificant. It is claimed that subversive Government forces were at play here and that Ted's children were threatened if he did not co-operate. This has never been proven but in a Watergate recording made in 1973, Presidential Counsel, John Dean can be heard saying to Nixon, "If Teddy Kennedy knew the bear-trap he was walking into at Chappaquiddick…." It is not known how the sentence ends but it is a rather revealing statement, all the same.

Ted has had his defenders, too. Helga Wagner, Ted's girlfriend at the time and who claimed to have been the love of his life, has always protested Ted's innocence. She says they should have taken Ted straight to hospital as the victim that he was and that he should never have been badgered or brow-beaten into making a statement so soon after a serious head injury. She agrees that the delay in reporting the incident was wrong but says it was understandable, given his confused state of mind at the time; but she would say that, wouldn't she? As for Ted being interested in the straight-laced Mary Jo Kopechne, she says this is highly unlikely, stating.

"She just wasn't Ted's kind of babe. She was a long way from being a bimbo."

Before the incident at Chappaquiddick, Ted was on a clear path to the Whitehouse and a 1968 poll showed that 79% of Americans thought he would be the Democratic nominee in 1972. But Chappaquiddick changed all that. Ted won re-election to the Senate in 1970, but he began to doubt his ability to become President and to lose his appetite to try. His reluctance was, in part due to the danger he felt he was in and he reportedly commented.

"I know that I am going to get my ass shot off, and I don't want to."

Ted suffered in his personal life, too. Shortly after attending the funeral of Mary Jo Kopechne, Ted's wife, Joan suffered a miscarriage that she blamed on the stress of Chappaquiddick. In 1973 Ted's son, Edward Kennedy Junior was diagnosed with a rare form of bone cancer and his leg was amputated. He then underwent a long and difficult course of experimental drug treatment before a triumphant return to the ski slopes just two years later. Ted's other son, Patrick was suffering severe asthma attacks and Joan was several times admitted to facilities for alcoholism and was once arrested for drunk-driving following a traffic accident.

In the weeks and months following the Chappaquiddick incident, Ted must have reflected many times on a comment he himself made in his July '69 television address, when he wondered whether, "Some awful curse actually did hang over the Kennedys?"

In spite of all his troubles, Ted never gave up on his career and he worked harder than ever in the Senate. He campaigned vigilantly on Civil Rights and for national health insurance and he played a leading role in aiding the passage of the National Cancer Act in 1971. Ted developed a genuine and sincere empathy for the poor and the underprivileged and he was never afraid to tackle difficult and contentious issues head-on. In this respect, he was more than a match for his older brothers and throughout his long career, he had more success in the Senate than either of them.

In 1971, Ted made his first speech on the troubles in Northern Ireland, contentiously stating that Ulster had become Britain's Vietnam. He said that British troops should leave the Province and he called for a united Ireland, stating that if Ulster Unionists could not accept that, they should go back to Britain. He spoke openly against the war in Vietnam and opposed Nixon's policies in Pakistan and East Bengal. In 1974 Ted travelled to the Soviet Union where he called for a full nuclear test ban and he gave a ground-breaking speech at the Moscow State University. He visited Hiroshima and China and in 1985 he visited South Africa, where he spoke openly against apartheid and spent a night in the Soweto home of Bishop Desmond Tutu.

But for all his good work in the Senate and on the world stage, Ted was still Ted, and his personal misdemeanours would continue to plague him. He drank heavily and he chased women and he struggled with his weight, often appearing sluggish and slow. He would go off on binge-drinking weekends with his nephews and was often seen "on the town" with fellow Senator, Chris Dodd. All of this put a strain on Ted's marriage and he and Joan separated in

1977. They were divorced in 1982, with Joan reportedly receiving a $4m settlement.

Ted was to find happiness again when in 1991, he met divorced mother of two, Victoria Anne Reggie. They were very happy together and Ted was devoted to her two children, treating them as his own. The couple were married in July 1992 in a civil ceremony at Ted's home in McLean, Virginia. Victoria was good for Ted and she had a calming influence on him, helping him to kerb his drinking and focus more on his work in the Senate.

Having had his hopes for the presidency dashed in '72, Ted considered running again in '76. He was again thought by many to be the hot favourite for the Democratic nomination but the Chappaquiddick incident raised its ugly head once more and Ted was forced to withdraw from the race. In 1974 he announced he would not run in the 1976 election and that his decision was firm and final. That election was won by fellow-Democrat, Jimmy Carter and Ted suddenly found that he was no longer the most influential Democrat in Washington.

The Carter years were a difficult time for Ted as the two of them did not see eye to eye and in late 1979, Ted finally announced that he would run against Jimmy Carter in 1980. Carter had been unpopular and Ted started out well but Carter slowly gained on him and began to take the lead. Add to this the fact that Chappaquiddick came up yet again, and Ted was forced to concede defeat once more. Chappaquiddick had beaten him three times and he finally realised it would never go away. As it was, Carter lost the election to Republican, Ronald Regan and Ted found himself in a minority in the Senate for the first time in his life. He continued to battle on, however and after choosing not to run for President in '84 and again in '88 he had all but abandoned his hopes of ever reaching the Whitehouse.

In 1991 Ted was again in the spotlight, this time for his involvement in the very public and highly controversial Kennedy Smith rape case. In March of that year, Ted was in a bar in Florida with his son, Patrick and his nephew, William Kennedy Smith when they met two young women. All five went to a house owned by the Kennedys and William Kennedy Smith went for a walk along the beach with one of the women, Patricia Bowman. Bowman later accused Kennedy Smith of rape and after much deliberation by the police, he was eventually charged with the offence. Kennedy Smith strongly protested his innocence and was acquitted at his trial in December, but the whole affair cast a dark shadow over him and Ted was again branded an irresponsible profligate.

Ted seemed doomed to suffer in his personal life and in January 1995 his mother, Rose died at the age of 104. Ted had always been very close to his mother and this broke his heart. This was followed in July 1999 by the death of his nephew, John F Kennedy Junior in a plane crash. Once again, it was Ted who was left to pick up the pieces and to hold the shattered family together.

In May 2008, Ted suffered a seizure and was taken to Cape Cod Hospital where it was discovered that he had a brain tumour. On June 2nd he underwent brain surgery and it was thought to have been successful, although the after-treatment left him weak and lacking energy. But Ted had always been a fighter, and he refused to lie down. In January 2009 he attended Barack Obama's inauguration ceremony and in March of that year he was granted an honorary knighthood by the British Government for his involvement in the Northern Ireland peace process.

Ted fought bravely on following his operation in 2008, but it was a battle he could never win. He succumbed to brain cancer on August 25th 2009. He was 77 years old.

Aftermath

There can be no doubt that Chappaquiddick ruined Ted's chances of ever becoming President of the United States, but it did not prevent him from being a great Senator. He was re-elected to the Senate no less than 7 times and he became one of the longest-serving Senators in American history. His biographer, Adam Clymer said of him.
"Ted deserves recognition not just as a leading Senator of his time, but as one of the greats in history."

Ted was described as a warm, vivacious person who it was hard not to love, but he had more than his fair share of critics, too. Many would never forgive him for what happened at Chappaquiddick and he was often berated for his weak and flawed character. "If his name was Edward Moore instead of Edward Moore Kennedy," Ed McCormack once said, "he would be a joke."

And what about Mary Jo Kopechne? We must not forget that whatever happened at Chappaquiddick, an innocent young lady died and many feel that there has been no justice. Whatever Ted's involvement in the events of that night, he remains largely responsible for her death. Ted no doubt felt remorse for the death of Mary Jo Kopechne and in the end, the affair cost him his career and his reputation. But it cost Mary Jo her life.

9 JFK JUNIOR

Like many children of great people, John F Kennedy Junior spent his whole life trying to find his own identity and to escape the fact that he was, like it or not, the son of perhaps the most famous President in American history. John F Kennedy Junior never really knew his father and he said he had no recollection of that famous salute he had made on his third birthday, as he stood before the coffin of the slain President on the day of his father's funeral. He had no real memory of those happy days when he had played on the Whitehouse lawn with his sister, Caroline and only the faintest recollection of his father secretly feeding him gum as he hid under the desk in the Oval Office. But his problem was that many people did remember and they would never let him forget that he was the son of JFK and, as such, was a precious link to the days when the Kennedys ruled in Camelot.

John F Kennedy Junior was born in the Grangetown University Hospital on November 25th 1960, just 17 days after his father had been elected President of the United States. John spent the first three years of his life in the Whitehouse but when his father was murdered in November 1963 his mother, Jackie moved herself and the children into a 15 room apartment overlooking Central Park in New York. Jackie's life had been shattered by the death of her husband but she was determined that from that moment on, she would do all she could for her children. "They're all I have left," she would say, and she swore to protect them at any cost.

Jackie feared for her children following the murder of JFK and seeing nothing but tragedy if she remained tied to the

Kennedy clan, she distanced herself from the family. She had always been different from the other Kennedy wives and she wanted her children to be different, too. She felt isolated and alone and even considered moving to Europe to escape the unhappy memories and the intense, obtrusive media attention. But if Jackie was falling, it was Bobby who was there to catch her. The two had always been very close and the death of Jack had brought them even closer. They were deeply united in their grief for Jack and Bobby became a prominent figure in Jackie's life. It soon became obvious that the two of them were more than just friends, comforting each other in their time of need and the press and the media had a field day with it. They were becoming headline news for all the wrong reasons and were forced to cool things down for a while, but Bobby remained very close to Jackie and became a kind of surrogate father to her children. He was fiercely protective of them and was always there for them any time of the day or night, much to the annoyance of Ethel, who had always been somewhat jealous of Jackie.

Jackie had already made up her mind that she would bring up her two children in her own way and on her own terms, away from the Kennedy influence and the wayward behaviour of the other Kennedy children. Her children would not be Kennedys. They would be different and they would grow up to be good, honest, respectful people. This would start with their schooling and she made a conscious decision to send young John to the Collegiate School in New York, specifically because they had students from a wide variety of backgrounds. John later studied at the Phillips Academy before enrolling at the Brown University where, wishing to learn more about his father and his times, he gained a Bachelor's Degree in History in 1983.

John Junior was not a good scholar. He was rather unfocussed as a child and often struggled to keep up with his fellow students. He did, however, try to improve himself in any way he could and when he left Brown he travelled to India, where he studied at the University of New Delhi and met Mother Teresa. He then spent some time in Africa, where he went deep into a diamond mine to gain an insight into the lives of the people working there and to help him understand the divides that existed among different people in different parts of the world. He saw for himself the shameful living conditions of the poor coloured workers and the harshness of the apartheid regime and the experience had a lasting effect on him. He also spent some time in Guatemala, working for the Peace Corp set up by his father.

In his student days, John had been a typical wayward teenager. He experimented with drink and drugs and chased the girls as vigorously and enthusiastically as any of his raunchy friends. He let his hair grow and had a good time but as he grew older, he began to settle down and to look to his future. He had always had a keen interest in acting and at one point even considered this a possible career, but his mother strongly disapproved of the idea. Jackie had a very low opinion of actors and show-biz types following her own experiences with people like Frank Sinatra and Marilyn Monroe, and she did not want her son to be involved in that scene. John was never afraid to do his own thing in his own way but he did respect his mother's views and wishes, so he eventually abandoned that particular career aspiration. He then took a job with the New York Office of Business Development, but he soon left the post because his privileged and sheltered upbringing proved a disadvantage in dealing with real-life issues and that limited his progress there.

But John Junior was anything but a quitter. In 1989, he earned a degree from the New York University Law School and it was now that the world had its first real glimpse of John's endearing and often self-deprecating sense of humour. He failed his Bar Exam twice, finally passing on his third attempt in July 1990 and he was goaded in the press over it. He was, by now, a famous and well-known celebrity and the tabloids had a field day with headlines like, "Hunk Flunks" splashed all over the front pages. But at least John saw the funnier side, too. When asked about this in an impromptu interview in the street he said, with a wry smile.

"Obviously, I'm disappointed to have failed again. But, God willing, I'll be back there in July and I'll pass it then, or I'll pass it the next time, or I'll pass it when I'm 95."

On another occasion, he was walking down the street with a friend when a passer-by asked,

"Say, aren't you John Kennedy?"

"Yes," replied John.

"Well," said the stranger, "I think maybe you should be home studying?"

"You're so right, Pal," quipped John, as he hurried by.

John did, finally, pass his Bar Exam then he worked for four years as a prosecutor in the Manhattan District Attorney's office before turning his back on Law once again. He worked very briefly as a television presenter, but he still struggled to find his own identity and to choose his own way in life. He had become America's most eligible bachelor and had been voted "The sexiest man alive" by People Magazine, but he hated the fame and celebrity. He never really liked the glare of publicity, except when he could use it to promote good causes, and he only ever gave one official print interview in his life. He desperately wanted to be his own man and to make his own way in the world on his own merits, not as the son of JFK. An old school friend, Faith Stevelman once said. "He wants to be perceived as his own man. He's not John F Kennedy Junior, he is just himself."

"The press make him out to be a narcissistic celebrity brat," she added, "but he's not. People want to see him that way because of his father and because of his name, but he has a life that's much more than that. He likes being in the world."

But John did have his wayward side as well. He was always a daring risk-taker and he was notorious for his matter-of-fact attitude to life and poor punctuality.

"You never knew where you were with John," friends would often say. He had a tendency to ignore parking tickets and seemed to think that Manhattan traffic laws simply did not apply to him. On becoming Assistant DA, he had to pay $2,300 in outstanding parking penalties in order to have a clean record to enter. This is not to say he was arrogant or egotistical. He was simply a product of his privileged and sheltered upbringing and this gave him an air of detachment and recklessness that would be quite alien to most of us. He enjoyed life and he had a wide and varied circle of friends and of course, lots of girlfriends, too.

John's love life was forever in the media spotlight and the paparazzi followed him everywhere. He was America's most eligible bachelor and his every move was photographed and reported in all the papers and magazines. He had lots of girlfriends, some more serious than others and he enjoyed the New York night-life and the playboy lifestyle he had been living. He dated many of the rich and famous names on the New York scene, including high profile stars like Madonna. They shared the same personal trainer and the star had made John a target and went all-out to get him. She later admitted that she went after John because of his father's relationship with Marilyn Monroe, as she was obsessed with Marilyn and wanted to mirror her life as closely as possible by dating a Kennedy. Jackie was in two minds about the relationship as she admired Madonna as a performer but was not too happy about her son being romantically involved with her. She need not have worried, however, as the affair was short-lived and they soon broke up to go their own separate ways.

Another of John's celebrity girlfriends was Darryl Hannah and it was during his time with her that John experienced one of the most devastating and shattering episodes of his life. In early 1994 John's mother, Jackie was diagnosed with Non-Hodgkins Lymphoma, which proved to be a very aggressive form of cancer and spread very quickly. She battled the illness with the grace and composure one would have expected of her but her fight was, in the end, a futile one. Jackie Kennedy Onassis died peacefully in her sleep with her family and close friends around her, on May 19th 1994.

John was heartbroken. He and his mother had been very close and she had always had a big influence on how he lived his life but now she was gone, that would all change. He felt the grief and anguish of losing his treasured mother but at the same time, he felt a new sense of freedom that he had never known before. He had often done things to please and placate his mother but now, for the first time in his life, he felt free to do exactly as he wanted.

Friends wondered how John would cope with the loss of his mother and they were afraid he might spin off the rails in his struggle to cope, but he soon settled down and began to mature and to mellow. He began dating Calvin Klein executive, Carolyn Bessette and the two of them moved in together in John's New York apartment. They were good for each other and were very happy and the couple married in a secret ceremony on Cumberland Island, Georgia on September 21st 1996. But Carolyn had not fully appreciated the pressures of being a Kennedy wife and the constant, unrelenting media attention would put an enormous strain on her and on their marriage.

It was around this time too that John at last began to find his own direction professionally. Everyone had expected him to enter politics and that would always be an option later, but he wanted to do other things first. He was asked about this in a TV interview and replied that he had no immediate plans to enter politics but, never say never. John did deliver a key speech on behalf of his uncle, Ted at the Democratic National Convention in 1988 and it was very well-received. But, despite all the praise and admiration and the cries of, "He's a natural," he had little else to do with politics before his untimely death. However, many of John's friends were convinced that he did have every intention of entering politics, and very soon. His close friend, William Noonan says in his book, *Forever Young; My Friendship with John F Kennedy Junior* that John was going to run for the New York Senate seat won by Hillary Clinton in 2000. He says that if John had lived, Clinton never would have run and John would have been elected. He says that John was really quite ambitious and that he would have gone all the way to the top.

But John's immediate career choice was publishing. He knew from experience the power and influence of the media and in 1995, he joined with PR magnate, Michael J Berman in starting up *George,* a new and exciting monthly magazine. The idea was to marry-up the usual topics of celebrity gossip and news with political and social content to target a young, politically-minded and socially aware audience. At first, *George* did very well, at one point becoming the best-selling political magazine in the country and it filled an obvious gap in the market at that time. John was not afraid to tackle controversial and contentious subjects head on and he even published an interview with director, Oliver Stone on his film about JFK's assassination. John had found his niche and was very happy with his new-found career and he was enjoying the freedom that the loss of his mother's influence had given him. It was around this time, too that he began to take flying lessons. This had long been an ambition of his and he took to the skies as often as he could. His mother had always tried to dissuade him from flying as she had seen far too many people die in plane crashes, but she was no longer there to keep him in check and he went ahead and trained as a pilot, with disastrous consequences later.

Everything had been going well for John Junior but by the mid 1990's, he began to experience problems. His magazine, *George* was in financial difficulty and he allegedly told a friend in 1999 that he might have to pull the plug on the whole enterprise (although this was disputed by others). He was under pressure from his wife, too. She was happy to be with John but she was struggling with the pressures of being married to a Kennedy and in the public eye all of the time. She said she could not even go for a pizza or take the dog for a walk without having cameras and microphones shoved in her face and she was beginning to crack under the strain of it all. She had become depressed and had tried to talk to John about it but he just dismissed it and told her not to worry. John's personal assistant, Rosemarie Terenzio said John really felt for Carolyn and knew just what she was going through, but he was just frustrated because he couldn't protect her from it. The relationship became ever-more strained through the summer of 1999 and on July 13th John moved out of the apartment and checked into the Stanhope Hotel in New York, following a heated argument with Carolyn.

John's sister, Caroline even said that John was depressed following an argument with her over the inheritance of their mother's home in Martha's Vineyard. John was buying out Caroline's share and he was said to have been disappointed in her actions over the affair.

Things were getting out of hand and John decided they needed to get away for a while to spend some quality time together and in mid-July, he saw the ideal opportunity. His cousin, Rory had decided it was time to marry and John and Carolyn had been invited to the wedding at Hyannis Port on Saturday, July 17th. John thought the break would do them both good and he was looking forward to spending a weekend with the family, but Carolyn may not have been so keen. According to Rosemarie Terenzio (in her book, *Fairy Tale Interrupted*), Carolyn had been depressed and did not want to go on the trip. Terenzio says that she was the one who had persuaded Carolyn to get on the plane on that fateful Friday and that had she not done so, Carolyn would not have gone. John's friend, Bill Noonan even says that they were not really going for the wedding at all. Noonan says that John was going to Hyannis Port to celebrate Noonan's 5th wedding anniversary and that, although they would attend Rory's wedding as well, this was not the real reason for the trip.

Whatever the reason, John's plane took off into the blue on Friday, July 16th 1999 with two passengers; his wife, Carolyn and her younger sister, Lauren Bessette. They would never make it to Hyannis Port.

The Plane Crash

Like any Kennedy death, the events of that fateful Friday evening have been shrouded in mystery and controversy but the official version of what happened is, more or less, as follows.

John F Kennedy Junior, an experienced pilot with over 300 flying hours decided he would fly himself and his wife to Hyannis Port on the evening of Friday, July 16th to attend the wedding of his cousin, Rory the following day. His wife's sister, Lauren Bessette would also come along and they would drop her off at Martha's Vineyard on the way. John had his own plane, a Piper Saratoga, that he would use for the flight and he asked the airport support team to have it ready for the flight that day. He had only recently acquired the aircraft, having traded-in his much smaller, and less powerful Cessna to buy the Saratoga just a few months earlier. He was not yet fully familiar with this new aircraft and that would prove to be a very important factor in the events that followed.

On Friday afternoon, John worked in his office as usual and was later joined there by his wife's sister, Lauren Bessette. They were to drive to the airport, where they would meet with Carolyn for the trip. At around 4pm John called his friend, Billy Noonan to say he was running late (John was always late) but he seemed in no particular hurry. He carried on working and even took the time to write an email to a friend before checking the weather on-line at 6.32pm. The report said, 6 to 8 miles visibility, hazy, marginal for VFR. VFR stands for *Visual Flight Rules*, which means pilots who are not qualified to fly on instruments alone are not allowed to fly when visibility is poor. To fly VFR the pilot must be able to see the ground in order to navigate and fly safely by looking down at identifiable landmarks, so to fly at night or in poor visibility, they must be trained and qualified to fly IFR (*Instrument Flight Rules*), which JFK Jr was not.

John knew that flying conditions that day were marginal for VFR and that it was already getting quite late, but he appeared calm and relaxed and was in no hurry. In fact, he and Lauren hit heavy traffic on the way to the airport and did not arrive until around 8pm and still, they seemed in no rush. They met with Carolyn at the airport, where they chatted over a coffee before finally boarding the plane for the relatively short flight to Martha's Vineyard.

It is now that we see the first of a series of bizarre and unexplainable events that have given conspiracy theorists so much ammunition over the ensuing years. Firstly, it is claimed that John did not file a flight-plan for this trip. There was no rule to say he had to do this but it was considered good-practice and sensible to do so, and he had usually done so in the past. Given that he was flying in what he knew to be poor conditions, one would have thought he would have filed a flight-plan on this occasion so that his plane could be clearly identified and tracked on radar all the way. It would still be tracked without a flight-plan (as we shall see) but in the absence of such a plan, the radar operators would not know which "blip" on their screen was John's plane. If a pilot files a flight-plan, the air traffic controllers can give the radar plot a reference number and track it through a system known as *Flight Following*. Richard Bunker, a very experienced flyer and aeronautical inspector, said on the subject.

"John Kennedy did not file a flight-plan so would not have benefited from Flight-Following, but I have always used Flight-Following. There is nothing worse than flying, especially on the Cape and the islands at night and in those conditions. I've done it, and I wouldn't do it VFR for a bet!"

Another experienced pilot, Michael Danziger has also said that John should have filed a flight-plan that night and finds it hard to believe that he didn't.

"I can't remember a time in over 2,000 hours of flying when I have taken off and not used ATC FF (Air Traffic Control, Flight Following)," he said. "The easiest and safest way is to fly overland so you can see the lights. Out over the sea, darkness blocks-out the horizon and you are in a void. You can't tell up from down and it's like flying in the abyss. You just don't know which way is up and looking out the window, you see nothing."

Records show that sunset on that particular evening was at 8.27pm and by that time, twilight was falling rapidly. "Once the sun is down," said Kyle Bailey, a fellow Essex County pilot, "It gets dark very quickly. It was dusky and hazy that night and on seeing this, I chose not to fly that evening."

Another point of note is that according to official records, John did not take a flight instructor along with him. Although he was a qualified pilot, John was still in the early stages of his flying career and he tended to take a flight instructor with him on most of his flights. He was still restricted to Visual Flight Rules (VFR) and he must have known it would be dark well before he reached his destination, so it seems strange he did not take an instructor along on this occasion. This becomes even more inexplicable when we take into account the flying conditions and the fact that he was flying a relatively strange aircraft. He had flown just 36 hours in his new plane and only 3 of those hours without a flight instructor on-board. Also, the Saratoga was a more powerful aircraft than the Cessna and had certain handling characteristics and peculiarities with which John would have been unfamiliar.

At 8.38pm, with his two passengers and their luggage on board, John acknowledged clearance from the tower controllers and began to prepare for take-off.
"Right down-wind, departure 22."
According to the official account, this was the last anyone ever heard from JFK Junior. With less than one hour's night-time flying experience in his new plane (and that, with an instructor on-board), JFK Junior disappeared into the darkening sky for the 30 mile flight to Martha's Vineyard.

Eye-witness accounts say that the take-off was quite normal but that visibility was poor due to an evening mist that had rolled in over the coast. John then began a steady climb to his cruising altitude of 5,500ft then levelled-off to follow the southern coast of Connecticut. He could then have taken the far safer option of following the coast to maintain visual contact with the ground but at 9.26pm, off westerly Rhode Island, he turned out to sea towards Martha's Vineyard. The flight was in no way unusual up to this point and John's plane was plotted cruising at 180mhp through the night sky towards his destination. There is no evidence that they were experiencing any problems with the aircraft or with the weather and they were in no real hurry. So why did John abandon the safe, easy option and take the more hazardous route over the sea in darkness, just to shave a few minutes off the flight time? The official record offers no explanation for this.

The official version of events then goes on to say that at 9.40pm, Kennedy's plane was detected about 13 miles west of Martha's Vineyard on its final approach at 2,500ft and descending. The trajectory and rate of descent seemed quite normal until, without warning, the plot disappeared from the radar, indicating that the plane had fallen out of the sky. The official report says that there had been no attempt by the pilot to contact Hyannis Port by radio and that at this point in time, they had no idea who the occupants of the aircraft were or what had happened to it. The statement that there had been no radio contact is a contentious one, and we will return to that point later.

There then followed a strange inertia amongst airport and Coastguard officials that has never been satisfactorily explained. John was notoriously unreliable and was always running late, but friends and family began to worry when he failed to arrive at Martha's Vineyard. Late in the evening, a friend of Lauren Bessette rang the airport at Martha's Vineyard and asked them to trace the plane, but that call seemed to fall on deaf ears. The airport had called the Coastguard at around 10pm to tell them they had had a radar plot drop-out, but the Coastguard failed to react.

Family and friends were waiting for John and his passengers and they were growing ever-more concerned with every passing hour. At around midnight, a friend of Lauren's contacted Carole Radziwill, close friend of Carolyn Bessette and cousin of JFK Junior to ask if she had any news and Carole said she would enquire and get back to her. Carole telephoned all the local airports to ask if they had seen or heard from John's plane then, finding out nothing, she telephoned the Coastguard at 2.15am on Saturday to report it missing. She then called Lauren and Carolyn's mother to give them the news.

A search was eventually begun and at 3am an emergency beacon signal was detected off Long Island, but this signal was lost at around 6am and proved to be a false alarm (another incident to which we will return later). The search and rescue operation continued through the early hours of Saturday morning but was somewhat sporadic and disorganised. It was not until mid-morning that a more extensive operation was launched and an all-out effort made to try and locate the crash-site; and this, only at the intervention of President Clinton following a call from Senator Ted Kennedy.

The Kennedy family postponed Rory's wedding and on the Saturday afternoon, they held an outdoor Mass at their home in Hyannis Port. They were still hopeful that John and the Bessettes would be found alive and prayed for their safe return. Meanwhile, the search continued and by 7pm on the Saturday, they had narrowed their investigations to an area SW of Martha's Vineyard, following the discovery of some wreckage and debris on the beach in the afternoon. This turned out to be an airplane tyre, a few pieces of carpet and a suitcase bearing the name of Lauren Bessette. People began to fear the worst and by Saturday evening, the NOAA (National Oceanic and Atmospheric Association) survey ship, *Rude* joined the operation to search the sea-bed with side-scan sonar. By now, the Coastguard were no longer looking for survivors but for wreckage and at 9.35pm on Sunday, Rear Admiral Richard Larrabee announced that the operation had switched from one of search and rescue to one of recovery.

By Monday, July 19th the search was in its third day and the crash-site had still not been found. The *Rude* worked around the clock, dragging its side-scan sonar whilst technicians watched their screens for signs of wreckage in about 180ft of water. The sea-bed was very rocky and it was proving difficult to distinguish between man-made objects and natural rock formations as they combed the area in long, sweeping runs up and down the murky waters off Martha's Vineyard. Hour after hour the technicians watched, bleary-eyed as the fuzzy images flashed by on their screens then early on Tuesday morning, they eventually found a plot that they thought looked promising. They anchored over the site and, having been joined in the search by the well-equipped salvage vessel, *USS Grasp* they lowered cameras into the water for a closer look.

There could be no mistake. They peered into the gloom and could clearly see the white underbelly, red top and gold band down the middle of N9253N, JFK Junior's Piper Saratoga. The plane had fragmented on hitting the water and was completely destroyed. The cabin had been ripped open and the wings torn off and wreckage was scattered over a wide area. It was hard to make things out at first but on looking closer, they could see the broken body of JFK Junior, still strapped firmly into his seat. The bodies of the two passengers were found later.

The recovery team dredged the sea-bed for more wreckage and the pieces were taken to Otis Coastguard Airbase for examination by air crash investigators. They determined that the aircraft had hit the water at tremendous speed and the fragmentation that occurred on impact was extensive.

"And, of course," said Richard Bunker, "when you get fragmentation of the aircraft, you get fragmentation of the bodies, too. It's not pretty."

The wreckage had been scattered over a wide area and much of the aircraft was not recovered at all. The control panel, a couple of seats and numerous pieces of shattered and broken metal were all that remained of John Kenney Junior's Piper Saratoga when it was re-assembled for examination and analysis.

The autopsies on the bodies were brief, lasting less than 4 hours and found no evidence of drugs or alcohol in any of the crash victims. After much discussion within the family, it was decided that all three bodies would be cremated and the ashes scattered at sea, close to the crash site and on Thursday 22nd July, fourteen family members and friends boarded the USS Brisco for the ceremony. The press and media gathered on the shore as the ship and its passengers sailed out into open water for a private ceremony at the site where John and the Bessettes had died. They scattered flowers originally meant for Rory's wedding then said prayers for the deceased. The families later held memorial services; one for John at the St Thomas More Church in New York and another for Carolyn and Lauren, at a church in Greenwich, Connecticut.

Official Report Findings

It was almost a full year before the official report on the cause of the crash was published by the NTSB (National Transportation Safety Board). They concluded that the crash had been a tragic accident, the pilot having lost control due to a phenomenon known as *Spatial Disorientation*; a confusion of the senses arising from a disparity of information to the brain from the eyes and the inner ear. The report found no evidence of mechanical or electrical failure, no instrument malfunction and no shortage of fuel. The cause of the crash was found to be, "Pilot Error."

The investigators pieced together the available evidence and came up with a sequence of events which goes (briefly) as follows;

JFK Junior took-off from Essex County Airport with two passengers on board at 8.38pm on Friday, July 16th 1999, following an inexplicable delay of almost an hour at the airport.

He did not file a flight plan. He made no further contact with Air Traffic Control and he did not take a flight instructor along.

Darkness was falling but the weather was reasonably fine with at least 8 miles visibility, although the report did say that this was marginal for Visual Flight Rules.

JFK Junior did not follow the coast but flew out over the sea and at 9.40pm, he began his final approach to Martha's Vineyard airport to drop-off John's sister-in-law, Lauren Bessette before flying on to Hyannis Port.

At 13 miles out, John made a left turn and climbed back up slightly to 2,600ft. The report says that he had no visual reference points, so must have been flying on instruments.

He began to descend very quickly and, feeling the sudden increase in speed, he pulled back on the stick to climb back up, not realising he was still in a left turn.

"He would have known that the aircraft was doing something he didn't like," said Richard Bunker, "so he would have tried to correct it." His instincts told him to turn in the opposite direction so, still falling, John then instigated a turn to the right.

Turning sharp right and descending fast, the aircraft went into what is called a *graveyard spiral* and with its nose down at a steep angle and turning hard to the right, the aircraft crashed into the sea at high speed.

The report then goes on to criticize John even further by stating that a qualified instructor had offered to fly with him that day but he had declined the offer, stating he wanted to do it alone.

So much for the official version of events. This scenario does seem quite credible and people are killed in light aircraft crashes all the time, so most people accepted the report on face value.

<u>The Hidden Truth?</u>

The official verdict was that JFK Junior died in a tragic accident and had no one to blame but himself. There was no lone assassin, no Palestinian gunman waiting in the pantry and no mobster hit-man hiding in the shadows. But on closer examination, the official version of what happened to John Kennedy Junior shows a great many inconsistencies and leaves a lot of unanswered questions. However one views and interprets the evidence in this case, there would appear to be three alternatives as to what might have happened to John and his passengers that night. Was it a tragic accident, as described by the official report, was it suicide or were they murdered?

We have already seen the evidence in support of this being an accident, so let us now consider the possibility that John killed himself and his passengers by deliberately crashing his plane into the sea, as some people have suggested. When investigating a suicide, the obvious question to ask is, why? What was the state of mind of the victim at the time and why would they resort to such extreme measures?

John F Kennedy Junior was not in a suicidal frame of mind on July 16th 1999; far from it. He and Carolyn had been going through a rough patch in the summer of that year, but this was in no way serious enough to make John want to kill himself. If we apply that logic, we would see millions of suicides every day. John was concerned about Carolyn and wanted to help her cope with the pressures of being a Kennedy wife. They were making a go of things and John had told close friend, Keith Stein shortly before the flight that he was happy and that he was even looking forward to fatherhood. He said this in a way that made Stein think it may even have been imminent, so it is possible that Carolyn may have been pregnant at the time of the crash? We can also rule out the failing health of *George* Magazine as a cause of John's depression. The magazine was experiencing financial difficulty and John had commented to friends that he may have to close, but he was still fighting to save it when he died. On that very morning, he had held a meeting with staff and told them he would not let the magazine go under as long as he was alive. He was said to be positive and upbeat at the meeting and seemed full of hope for the future.

We must also ask ourselves, would a responsible man like JFK Junior, if he did decide to end it all, take other, innocent people with him? John was reckless and sometimes careless with his own life and safety, but he would never put other people's lives at risk; especially not those of people he loved. If he did want to end it all by crashing his plane, he would surely have chosen a time when he was flying alone, which he occasionally did. He was also actively developing his flying skills and having bought a new and more powerful aircraft, was clocking up flying hours to gain his IFR (Instrument Flying Rules) licence. Add to this the fact that many close friends were certain that he had planned to enter politics in the near future and we have to conclude that suicide is not an option we should consider in this case.

So, that leaves only murder. Could John and his passengers have been murdered by a person or persons unknown? This may sound outlandish and hard to believe but it is a distinct possibility so it should be explored. One way we can do that is to go back over the events of that night to examine some of the conflicting evidence and consider alternative scenarios, which we will do shortly.

The first thing that John did in preparation for his flight was to check the weather, which he did late in the afternoon. The report came back to say, "Hazy, 8 to 10 miles visibility, marginal for VFR." This is considered by some to be somewhat contradictory. Aviation experts say that 8 to 10 miles visibility is well within limits for VFR flying and could, in no way, be described as marginal. In addition, witnesses on the ground say there was very little haze that night and that the moon was clearly visible in the sky, indicating there was no (or very little) cloud. One witness even said he could see airplanes out over the sea approaching Martha's Vineyard and that the night was clear. This is also backed up by radar images from the area that show no cloud cover or fog over Martha's Vineyard. Early on Saturday morning, within a very short time of the crash, CNN, acting on information received, stated that weather could be ruled out as a contributory factor. As we shall see, this story was soon to change quite significantly.

The official report states quite categorically that JFK Jr did not file a flight plan and made no further contact with Air Traffic Control after acknowledging clearance for take-off, thus having no specific ID reference on radar. This is a very hard pill to swallow. Friends and fellow fliers all say that John always filed a flight plan. All of John's flying instructors describe him as a talented and responsible pilot. He would always follow the rules and was a very competent and safe flyer. We should view this with some degree of caution as we do know that he often did take risks, but he was not stupid. He would do nothing that would endanger life and, as it is good practice (though not compulsory) to file a flight plan for every trip, we should consider it a strong probability that he did so on this occasion.

If JFK Junior had filed no flight plan he would still be seen on radar, but controllers would have no information about how many people were in the plane, where they were flying from or where they were going and this would, of course, hinder any search and rescue operation should the plane experience difficulties. By filing a flight plan, controllers would assign a tracking number based on the registration number of the aircraft and if it got into trouble, they would carry out an N-TAP investigation to track and find it (N-TAP is based on the "N" registration number of the aircraft in question, in this case N9253N). This would then lead the Coastguard directly to the last known reference point of the aircraft and tell them exactly what they were looking for. Not only does it make good sense to file a fight plan, it seems incredibly foolish not to do so.

The official version of events that night goes on to say that after acknowledging permission to take-off at Essex County, John had no further radio contact with controllers. Again, one has to understand just how unlikely this is to see why it is so hard to accept. Anyone who has flown a light aircraft will know that when doing so, it is necessary to talk to controllers all the time, especially in areas of heavy traffic. This is one of the real sticking points in this story. Aviation experts and experienced fliers all say they find it very hard to believe that John would have had no further contact with controllers after take-off. What is more, it is standard practice when approaching Martha's Vineyard at night to contact the tower to advise them of your approach and intention to land. John had made this trip many times in all conditions and would have known this well enough. He was, by now, a relatively experienced pilot and talking to controllers, especially on approach to Martha's Vineyard, would have been pretty much unavoidable. But he did talk to them, and this is on record.

Within a very short time of the crash, both UPI (United Press International) and WCVB-TV News were reporting the incident and saying that John had, in fact, radioed the tower at Martha's Vineyard on approach. The UPI press release states categorically that according to information received from Martha's Vineyard ATC, John Kennedy did talk to the tower on approach. The report states that.

"At 9.39pm Friday, Kennedy radioed the airport and said he was 13 miles out and 10 miles from the coast." ABC News then goes on to say.

"In his final approach message, Kennedy told controllers at the airport that he planned to drop off his wife's sister then take off again between 11pm and 11.30pm for Hyannis Port. Moments later, radar equipment operated by the Federal Aviation Administration showed the plane went into a dive and dropped 1,200ft in just 12 seconds."

These reports are said to be based on information received from the authorities at Martha's Vineyard shortly after the crash and long before any wreckage had been recovered. Coastguard Communications Officer, Petty Officer Todd Burgun, when asked to clarify or confirm the report that JFK Junior had contacted the tower, said.

"All I really know at this time is that it was at 9.39pm and it was with the FAA (Martha's Vineyard Flight Controllers) and it was on the final approach to Martha's Vineyard."

Todd Burgun was a very experienced Coastguard official and had personally participated in hundreds of air-sea rescues, so he would know what would be standard procedure on approach to Martha's Vineyard and how quickly a search would be initiated if a radar plot were to inexplicably disappear. He was also an official spokesman and communications officer and any statement made by him would be the "official word." The curious thing here is that shortly after making this statement, Burgun was removed from the picture and by mid-day on Saturday, the press were advised that in future, all questions should be directed at the Pentagon. The Pentagon! This was unheard of; a civil air search operation taken from the control of the Coastguard and handed over to the military. At 1.35pm on Saturday, the story began to take a more sinister turn when Lt Colonel Steve Rourke of the US Air Force, when asked about radio contact, said.

"I only know for certain that they did not talk to the tower at Martha's Vineyard."

"So they never made contact with the Tower at Martha's Vineyard?" asked a reporter.

"That's my understanding," replied a sheepish Col. Rourke.

And there you have it. A complete turnaround once the military had taken control. But the press and the media refused to accept this and they doggedly pursued the matter for the rest of the day. Why the change in story? Why had the military taken control? Something just didn't smell right.

The questions about a flight plan and of radio contact are important as they have a significant bearing on what information would have been available to Air Traffic Control and the Coast Guard and how they dealt with it. The point is that if John had filed a flight plan and if he had radioed the tower on approach, they would have had a clear identification on him and, therefore, would have known the exact location of the crash site; which, actually, they did. All the evidence (and logic) would suggest that JFK Junior did file a flight plan and that he did contact the tower at Martha's Vineyard at 9.39pm. This is the exact time given for the radio contact in the early press release and it ties in with radar information later made public by the FAA, but it took the authorities over 5 hours to react and launch a search. Why?

Even if they had no formal ID for the aircraft, they would have seen a radar plot drop out and would have known something was wrong, and they would have investigated this. But John did radio in and they did have a plot for him on the radar, so why the delay in responding? When a pilot contacts ATC, the aircraft information is entered into the system and if that plot falls below 100ft an automatic alarm is activated to alert the controllers that there has been a problem and this then triggers an immediate search. If John did contact the tower, this must have happened at Martha's Vineyard Air Traffic Control centre. They would have had a known radar plot and would know exactly where the plane went down.

The failure to act on known information became a nagging thorn in the side of the family, and of the press. The claim by the authorities was that they had not been notified that the plane was missing until well after 2.30am on Saturday, but that is not true. Family and friends tried numerous times to get a response from the Coastguard and the FAA, but met with little success. John was known to be unreliable and was often late but when the plane failed to arrive at Martha's Vineyard, family and friends became concerned. They were supposed to arrive at Martha's Vineyard well before 10pm and shortly after that time, a friend of Lauren's contacted the airport and asked them to trace the plane, but that call seemed to go unheeded. There were other calls, including one from John's uncle, Ted but still, there was little response. Finally, after checking with every airport in the area John's cousin, Carole Radziwill rang the Coastguard direct at 2.15am to tell them herself that the plane was missing; thus by-passing the FAA, who seemed to be ignoring every request for a search.

This was a last-ditch attempt to get a response and the family had been trying to raise the alarm since 10pm on Friday. The Coastguard would always dispute this, saying they were not notified until 3am on Sunday, but this is clearly not the case. In a press conference early on Saturday morning, Linda Killian of People Magazine asked.
"I just wonder if there's any information about why, when the plane was expected in about 9.30, if there's any idea why you were not notified until 3am in the morning?"
The question was not answered.

The Coastguard did act on Carole's 2.15am call; they called the FAA. The FAA had no choice but to act this time so they, in turn contacted the Air Force. The Air Force then contacted the Coastguard and told them that the Air Force was now in charge and that the military would be controlling things from now on. The Air Force then sent the Coastguard on a wild goose-chase search of a massive area, miles away from the area where the plane went down. Then, to add to the confusion, an emergency locator beacon signal was detected off the coast of Long Island and it was thought this might be the beacon from John's plane. All aircraft carry such a device, which is triggered in the event of a crash and sends out a signal to help the rescue teams locate the crash-site. As it happened, this proved to be a false alarm and the search of that area was called-off at around 6am. The beacon was never found and no explanation was ever given for the presence of such a signal.

Enough was enough and at 6.30am, frustration getting the better of him, Senator Edward Kennedy called President Clinton's aid at the Whitehouse and insisted he wake Clinton up as he wanted to talk to him right away. Clinton came on the phone and Ted told him the sad story and asked him to intervene and call a proper, full-scale search for the missing plane. Clinton then called the Air Force and they sent out a further 2 planes and 2 helicopters to conduct another wild goose-chase search that went on for a further 5 hours.

This was quite inexplicable. Why was it taking so long to home-in on the correct location of the crash? The plane was known to be flying to Martha's Vineyard and was known to be around 13 miles to the west on its final approach, so what was the problem? They had the exact location from the radar information and even if they didn't, they must have had some idea where the crash-site might be. The New York Times actually stated that the radar information had been made available to the Air Force before 5am, but still they continued their aimless search in entirely the wrong place. The radar information clearly showed that the aircraft had gone down on the western approach to Martha's Vineyard but in a press conference on Saturday morning, Air Force spokesman Colonel Rourke was still being evasive. When asked by an ABC reporter if, now that they knew the aircraft had come down 13 miles west of Martha's Vineyard, they would be focussing their search in that area, he replied.

"We'll continue on the same track that we're on, which is to search the entire area. We have nothing that pinpoints one area or another, so we will have to continue to search the entire area."

The reporter then asked, "Have you heard no report at all about 13 miles off Martha's Vineyard? The radar indicated that at some point the plane may have gone into a dive?"

"The radar position is just a last possible position," replied Col. Rourke, "and it can't even be confirmed that it's the aircraft we're looking for."

This information on the radar position was widely known amongst press and reporters by then so it must have been known to Rourke. And unless other aircraft had been reported missing in the area (which they had not), what else could it be?

The press were being fed confused and conflicting information about where the search operation had been looking for John's plane and why. Early reports stated that John had radioed the tower on approach to Martha's Vineyard and although we cannot know for sure, he was probably following a flight-plan he had already filed earlier in the day. The early reports said there was no sign of stress or anxiety in John's voice when he made this radio contact and that his approach seemed quite normal. And yet, no search was launched until Saturday morning and once the Air Force took control, the story began to change. The press knew they were being fed duff information and were quite rightly asking, why?

Having searched 1,000 square miles of empty Ocean, the search and rescue operation finally moved to the area around Martha's Vineyard on the Saturday afternoon. It had been 15 hours since the plane had gone missing but the Coastguard were, only now, doing what the family and press had been asking them to do all along.

As we have seen, around mid-afternoon on the Saturday, the first indications of the extent of the disaster began to appear when wreckage began to wash ashore around Martha's Vineyard. People began to fear the worst and these fears were only heightened when the luggage washed ashore was found to bear the name of Lauren Bessette. The Kennedy family announced that they were still hopeful that John and the Bessettes might still be found alive, but that hope must have been fading fast. Other personal items were also found, including John's blue duffle-bag, an important piece of evidence which we will now consider in more detail.

At this point, the search and rescue operation would appear to have been exactly as described in the official version of events. Wreckage was found, then the aircraft and the bodies of the occupants recovered and the pieces brought ashore. But the next question raised by the doubters was, did they really recover all of the bodies and how many people were on board? Well, the place to find answers to those questions would be in John's Flight Log, which friends said he always kept in a blue duffle-bag; the same blue duffle-bag recovered on the beach at Martha's Vineyard. The problem here is that although the official report states that the bag was recovered undamaged and intact, the Flight Log is not mentioned. The report suggests it was not in the bag and it has never been found. Every pilot has a log book in which they record the details of every flight they take and it is a legal requirement to do so. John certainly did have such a log and would have kept it with him every time he flew. So where was it?

This is important because the Flight Log is a vital piece of evidence in any air disaster and is considered key to any investigation. It tells the rescue people how many people were on the plane and who they were, essential information if they are to know how many people they are looking for. It is also important for other reasons, such as telling insurance companies who may have been the victims in any crash and to help coroners confirm the details and circumstances of any deaths. This is no small point and John was a meticulous pilot. He always filed his paperwork and completed any necessary documentation in full and in good time. Friends say he would surely have completed his Flight Log and if it could be found, it would show beyond doubt who was on the plane.

The Flight Instructor?

This brings us back to the question of whether or not John took a flight instructor along on that Friday. The official version of events says that he did not and no one can prove otherwise, but there is strong circumstantial evidence to suggest that he may have. We must bear in mind that JFK Junior almost always took a flight instructor along when flying. This is not to say that he did so every time and he may not have done so on this occasion, but we should consider the evidence before making any judgement on the issue.

When Carole Radziwill called the Coastguard at 2.15am she told them that the missing plane had four people on board; JFK Jr, Carolyn and Lauren Bessette and a flight instructor. She could not have known this for certain, of course, as she was not present when John and his passengers boarded the plane, but she obviously presumed there would have been a flight instructor on board. In fact, there were no eye-witnesses to who boarded the plane that night, so we can never know for sure. But JFK Junior was a good and cautious pilot and, having passed the written exam for IFR (Instrument Flight Rules) flying, he was now clocking-up hours to full qualification, and he would have needed a flight instructor along to do this. Could this have been the reason for the unexplained delay at Essex County Airport? The sun was going down fast and dusk was falling, yet John and his passengers chatted for over half an hour for no apparent reason. Why did they not get away as soon as they were all together, unless they were waiting for a flight instructor? This may also explain the casual, no-hurry attitude that John seemed to display at the time. If he was to have a flight instructor on board, the time did not really matter. It would also be better to clock-up instrument flying hours in darkness, so that may have been another good reason to take his time?

And then there was the new plane to consider. John had only had this plane for a couple of months and had only flown 3 hours in it without a flight instructor, and those were in daylight. If his usual habit was to have an instructor on-board, it is only logical he would do so now. The Piper

Saratoga had a fairly complex Auto-Pilot system, far more advanced than anything he had used before and this was found to be in the OFF position. This system could control ascent and descent but John was probably not yet fully familiar with the system and its capabilities, so he was flying manually. This would be no problem, even in the dark, with an instructor sitting next to him to offer advice and to take over if he got into difficulty.

One final point on this subject is a conversation that took place between JFK Junior and Richard Blow, his partner in the *George* Magazine enterprise, on the day of the flight. John had broken his leg and had had the plaster cast removed only the day before and when the two had lunch together on the Friday of the flight, Blow expressed concern over this. He told John he was worried about him flying with a newly-mended leg, but John explained that you don't need use of your feet to fly a Piper Saratoga. You do need to use them to steer the aircraft on the ground, but John told him not to worry because he was taking and instructor along.

So if there was an instructor on board, why did they not find his body? We have already seen that the Saratoga fragmented on impact and as a result, not all of the aircraft was found. There have been reports that one of the seats was missing and if this was the case, it could explain why the instructor's body was never found. John's body was still strapped into the front seat and this could have been the case with the instructor if, in fact, there was one on board. He could have been thrown, still in his seat, far away from the point of impact and never found. This would still leave one wondering why, if there was an instructor on board, he was not missed by his own family and friends and there are those who have theories on that, too. With no Flight Log we will never really know, but we will return to this point in just a moment.

The Fuel Selector Valve (FSV)

The issue of the Fuel Selector Valve is one of the most puzzling aspects in this case and is certainly one of the most difficult to explain. Buried deep in the official report into the cause of the crash, there is a seemingly casual comment stating that, "the Fuel Selector Valve was in the OFF position." This apparently insignificant observation is, in fact, enormously important in this case and it cannot be satisfactorily explained. In order to fully understand and appreciate the weight and significance of this statement, we must first understand what a Fuel Selector Valve is and how it is used.

The Fuel Selector Valve (FSV) is essentially a safety device that controls the flow of fuel to the engine when the engine is running and it cannot be turned off accidentally as it has a fail-safe mechanism to prevent the pilot from doing so. In a Piper Saratoga, the fuel is stored in the wings and the FSV is used to switch between one tank and the other in order to maintain balance and stability when the aircraft is in flight. The pilot will switch the valve to the left or right to select the tank he wants and he will monitor this throughout the flight. In normal flying conditions he would never turn this valve to the OFF position. To do this would cut the fuel supply and the engine would stop running. There are, however, times when he might potentially want to cut the fuel from the engine in case of an emergency, such as an engine fire or a fuel leak that might pose a risk of fire, but in normal flight it should stay in the ON position. In any case, to turn off the valve would still allow the pilot ample time to take appropriate action and to radio for assistance as an aircraft like the Saratoga can easily glide for several miles, under full control, after the engine has been cut. A stall in an aircraft is not the same as a stall in a car. If the engine in a car cuts-out, the car will stall and will stop almost immediately. If an aircraft engine cuts-out, the aircraft will continue to glide and gradually descend for some time as the speed begins to drop. An aircraft only stalls when the speed of the aircraft drops so low that the airflow over the control surfaces is reduced to such a rate that the aircraft can no longer maintain controlled flight. In such an instance, the aircraft would then lose its aerodynamic qualities and will fall from the sky.

So why was the FSV in John's plane in the OFF position? The report states that there had been no mechanical or engine failure and there was plenty of fuel left in both tanks. There was no evidence of fire and if John had experienced such a problem, he would certainly have communicated this to the ground. This doesn't fit the suicide theory either. Cutting the fuel to the engine would still allow the plane to glide several miles before coming down, as we have just seen. And yet, buried deep on page 333 of the 400 page investigation report is a diagram, based on radar information, showing quite clearly that John's plane fell, suddenly and very quickly out of the sky. If the engine had been cut, this would have shown a gradual, controlled descent. John could have just pushed the stick forward and deliberately plunged his plane into the sea, killing himself and his two passengers but if so, why take the trouble to turn off the FSV first? It makes no sense and the position of the FSV has never been satisfactorily explained.

Murder Theories

Once again, we are talking here about a Kennedy and from the start, there were those who would cry, conspiracy. These people have put forward numerous theories for what might have happened to John's plane that night and we will consider the two most popular theories here.

The first revolves around the issue of the flight instructor. This theory goes that there was, in fact a flight instructor on board (for all the reasons we have discussed earlier) but that he had been planted, by person or persons unknown, to kill JFK Junior on a given command. The reader may recognise this scenario? We are talking again of a Manchurian Candidate, a person hypnotised and brainwashed to carry out an act of murder in response to a previously arranged trigger or command, as may have happened in the assassination of Robert Kennedy. These things do happen and this method has been used by various military and intelligence agencies for many years. There have been political assassinations that are known to have been carried out in this way but if JFK Junior was a victim of such a plot, we must ask who could do such a thing and why?

This theory takes its routes from the outspoken and sometimes controversial nature of JFK Junior's *George* magazine. John had always shown a willingness to seek-out and print the truth and he once published an article about his father's assassination. This bravado attitude in John was one of the reasons why people thought he would one day go into politics and some even thought that if he ever became President, he would re-open the case on his father's murder and track down those really responsible. This may well have given people cause to want John killed, but many believe that the real reason behind his death had less to do with the

Mafia or the CIA and more to do with the Israeli Secret Service and the murder of Israeli Prime Minister, Yitzhak Rabin.

Yitzhak Rabin was murdered on November 4th 1995, at the end of a rally at the Kings of Israel Square in Tel Aviv. He was shot by a Jewish Israeli student named, Yigal Amir and just as with the killers of Jack and Bobby Kennedy, Amir was said to have been acting alone. But again as with Jack and Bobby, there were those who would dispute that.

In a 13 page article published in *George* magazine, the only mainstream publication in the US to cover the story, John claimed that Rabin had been murdered in a conspiracy. The article claimed that Amir was goaded into killing Rabin by an undercover agent of *Shin Bet*, the Israeli security agency. To publish this was a very bold and dangerous move and the article caused quite a stir in the Israeli Government and security agencies, but John was determined to find the truth. Catherine Crier of Fox TV's, "The Crier Report" alleged that John was about to meet high-ranking Mossad officials at the time of his death to get the full story on the Rabin assassination. Also, German newspaper, Frankfurter Allgemeine Zeitung reported that JFK Junior had met with deputy chief of Mossad, Amiram Levine to get more information, just two days before the crash. John obviously felt he was onto something, and friends had warned him to be careful.

The theory goes that in order to silence John, Israeli Intelligence (or some other similar body) planted a Manchurian Candidate on John's plane to crash it into the sea and kill him. This would, of course kill the assassin as well, but a good subject could easily be hypnotised to do such a thing. In this scenario, this is how we could account for the missing flight instructor. It is alleged that there was a flight instructor on board and that he was, in fact, a Manchurian Candidate. He would be programmed to plunge the aircraft into the sea at high speed, first turning off the FSV to cut the engine and ensure that no one could regain control and recover the aircraft from the dive. This would also account for the missing Flight Log and why the blue duffle-bag was found empty. The theory is that this is also why the search was delayed and sent off looking in the wrong area. This would give the authorities time to recover the body of the Manchurian Candidate in secret and away from prying eyes.

This theory claims further support from the fate of Egyptian Airlines flight 990. Fifteen weeks after the crash of JFK Junior, Egypt Air 990 crashed into the sea just 50 miles from the spot where John's plane went down. They could find no apparent reason for the crash and it was suggested it may have been down to pilot error and there was one very significant and startling similarity with John's case. On examining the wreckage, the investigators found that the FSV on the aircraft was in the OFF position. Again, they could find no logical reason for this, but many spotted the link with the findings in the Kennedy case. There may have been a very simple and innocent reason for the valve being in the OFF position in both cases, but it is hard to see what this could have been.

The second, alternative theory is that the plane may have exploded in mid-air, and this scenario could also be linked to the reasons given for the above version of events. An explosion on board may seem a far-fetched and fanciful idea but once again, there is fairly strong evidence to support this theory and we should, at least, consider it.

On July 21st 1999, The New York Daily News reported that Victor Pribanic, an attorney from Pittsburgh may have heard just such an explosion in the area at the time of the crash. Pribanic says he was fishing for bass off Squibnocket Point on the Southern tip of Martha's Vineyard that Friday night when a noise broke the eerie silence. Pribanic says.

"I heard an explosion over my right shoulder. There was no shock wave but it was a loud bang."

Pribanic had fished off that coast for over 20 years so he knew the area well and he pinpointed the source of the noise to be about 4 miles offshore, out near Nomans Island. He said that just before hearing the noise he noticed a small aircraft flying low over the water towards the island, but he didn't know whether this was Kennedy's aircraft. Pribanic said the sky was clear (though a bit hazy) and he could see the moon, so it seems logical that JFK Junior would easily have been able to see the lights of Martha's Vineyard on his approach.

When he heard the news of the crash the next day, Pribanic immediately called Martha's Vineyard Airport and they put him in touch with West Tisbury Police, who passed the information on to the National Transportation Safety Board. There were also rumours that a Martha's Vineyard Gazette reporter had claimed he had seen a bright flash and the plane fall into the sea, but this reporter has not been identified and has never been traced.

There may or may not have been a bomb on board, but the question does deserve a closer look. Some claim that an FBI report into the crash said that a bomb had been planted in the tail section of the plane and that the type of explosives used were those used by certain foreign intelligence agencies. Some also believe that a bomb could have been rigged in an oxygen cylinder or a fire extinguisher and triggered by altitude sensors. All of this is quite possible but in the absence of hard evidence, it may take quite a leap of faith to believe it. There can be no denying that the search and recovery operation was inexplicably delayed and was shrouded in secrecy, and there would appear to be no logical reason for that. Also, although the report does say that the aircraft fragmented on impact, one has to see pictures of the wreckage to see the extent of this damage. A light aircraft would surely break up on hitting the water at high speed but the wreckage of John's plane is completely unrecognisable. It is shattered into thousands of tiny fragments and to an untrained eye, it could easily look like the result of a violent explosion.

Accident, suicide, Manchurian Candidate or bomb: it is again for the reader to consider and decide for themselves. The circumstances surrounding the death of JFK Junior and Carolyn and Lauren Bessette are somewhat strange and they do leave a lot of unanswered question. The official report does seem to make some outlandish claims and there are a great many inconsistencies that are very difficult to ignore or deny. For example;

JFK Jr was not an irresponsible, inexperienced pilot. He took his flying very seriously and all of his instructors had nothing but the highest praise for his flying abilities.

John was not suicidal at the time of his death. He had been going through a rough patch but was working on it and was, in fact, quite upbeat and optimistic about the future and may have been considering entering politics. He may even have been about to become a father.

John checked the weather before leaving his office and the report said 8 to 10 miles visibility, which is marginal for VFR. Witnesses on the ground said they could see the moon, suggesting the sky was really quite clear but it seems unlikely that John would risk his life, and those of his passengers, by flying VFR in such conditions.

John knew the light was fading and that dusk was beginning to fall, but he seemed in no hurry to get off as he drank coffee and chatted at the airport.

The evidence would suggest that despite claims to the contrary in the official report, John did maintain radio contact with the tower at Martha's Vineyard.

Radar records did show the exact spot where the plane disappeared, so the search should have focussed on the right area from the start.

Despite calls from the family as early as 10 or 11pm on the Friday, the authorities say they knew nothing of their concerns until 2.30am on Saturday.

It took an inordinately long time for the authorities to launch a serious, full-scale search and only then, on the intervention of President Clinton.

John almost always took a flight instructor with him when flying and would have done so for a difficult flight in which he was carrying passengers. He knew he would be flying in the dark that night and he was clocking-up hours for his IFR licence, which he could not do without an instructor. It seems only logical that he would have had an instructor along on this occasion but the report says he did not, and no body was found. Having an instructor along may also account for why John turned and flew out over the sea rather than take the safer option of following the lights along the coast and may account for the delay before take-off?

The Fuel Selector Valve (FSV) was found to be in the OFF position. No one has yet been able to offer a logical explanation for this.

The Final Farewell

In his recently released diaries, Robert Kennedy Junior said that there had been family feuding between the Kennedys and the Bessettes over the funerals even before the bodies were found. He says that the Kennedys wanted to bury them all in the Kennedy plot in Holyhood Cemetery, but Carolyn's mother was against the idea. She says she was bullied by the Kennedys and was told in no uncertain terms that they were going to bury John in Brookline and that she could do whatever she pleased. John's sister, Caroline sent her husband, Ed Schlossberg along to sort things out and Mrs Bessette said he was obnoxious and overbearing and that she was bullied by him the whole time. Schlossberg hated the Bessettes and did all he could to make life uncomfortable for them. They said he behaved like a tyrant towards them and he even tried to prevent RFK Junior from delivering a eulogy for John and Carolyn, saying that Kennedys do not deliver eulogies for non-Kennedys. In the end, they agreed that all three bodies should be cremated and the ashes scattered at sea, which they were, on July 22nd 1999.

In his diary, Robert Kennedy Junior recalls that the sea had more Jellyfish in it than he had ever seen before. He writes. "When we let go of the ashes, the plume erupted and settled on the water and passed by in the green current like a ghost. We tossed flowers onto the ghosts and some of the girls tossed letters from a packet they had assembled from John and Carolyn's friends. It was a civil violation, but the Coastguard let it go." He then went on to say.

"The next day, Ted delivered a eulogy at the St Thomas More Church. At the reception later, the Senator led a choir in three songs and danced his silly Teddy dances and sang loudly and beautifully, and he made everyone love him."

10 EPILOGUE

There can be no disputing the fact that the Kennedys suffered more than their fair share of tragedy and grief and this has given rise to the legend of the "Kennedy Curse." Many believed that a curse of some kind hung over the Kennedys and family members often alluded to it themselves. Bobby and Rose are both on record as having commented on the possibility of such a curse and Ted made reference to it during his address to the nation following the accident at Chappaquiddick. But can we really believe such a notion?

The simple fact is that there was no curse. When we examine all of these tragedies, both individually and together, we see that they can all be attributed to the basic laws of cause and effect. They were all the direct or indirect result of how the Kennedys lived their lives, and almost all of them could have been avoided. For all their wealth and power, the Kennedys were a troubled and dysfunctional family with a distorted view of the world and their place in it, and this was the root cause of almost all of their self-inflicted suffering.

Joe Kennedy was a ruthless, ambitious tyrant with major flaws in his character and an ego the size of Manhattan and he moulded his sons in his own image. He raised his children to believe that they were better than anyone else and that the normal rules of life did not apply to them, and this gave them a dangerous and misplaced sense of invincibility. The Kennedys saw what they wanted and they took it, with no thought for others and no fear of consequence. They made a lot of very dangerous enemies and the warning signs were always there, but they considered themselves untouchable and these warnings went unheeded.

Some of these tragedies were, to some extent, unavoidable but most were a direct result of poor decisions made for the wrong reasons. Joe Junior did not have to volunteer for that one extra mission and Kick did not have to board a plane that she knew would be flying into a storm. Rosemary could have been spared the agony of experimental brain surgery and both Jack and Bobby played a dangerous game that could only end in disaster. Nor did it stop there. Ted did not have to drive his car that night at Chappaquiddick and JFK Junior, flight instructor on board or not, could have followed the coast to Martha's Vineyard instead of flying out over the sea.

The simple fact is that most of these events have their origins in an obsessive determination to be the best at everything and to impress others. Joe Kennedy had set the mark and everyone had to achieve it, whatever the cost. He was relentless in his pursuit of wealth and power and as he pushed his children on to achieve his own ambitions, he became blind to the price he was having to pay to achieve them.

This legacy of misfortune carried on and the trail of tragedy continued into the second, and even the third generations of the family. In 1973 Ted's son, Edward lost a leg to a rare form of cancer and in 1986 his other son, Patrick was treated for cocaine addiction. In 1991 Ted was involved in the rape trial of his nephew, William Kennedy-Smith and in 2011 Ted's daughter, Kara died of a heart attack, aged only 51.

Bobby's children fared little better. In 1973 Bobby's son, Joseph Patrick died in a car crash on Cape Cod and in 1984 another son, David died of a drugs overdose. In 1997 yet another of Bobby's sons, Michael was killed when he collided with a tree whilst playing touch football on skis. As if that were not enough, in 2012 Mary Richardson-Kennedy, the estranged wife of Robert Kennedy Junior was found dead in her bath, having allegedly committed suicide.

Some of these more recent events can be attributed to nothing more than unfortunate coincidence but in many, we can still see the same destructive forces at work. People turn to drugs when the pressures of life become too great to bear and suicide is often the last resort of a desperately unhappy soul. Anyone can be killed in a car crash, but what makes someone thwart danger by playing touch football on skis in an area strewn with trees? These later events have the hallmarks of a family trying hard to achieve and coping in very different ways with the pressures that brings and are evidence that this obsessively competitive culture lived on long after Joe Kennedy had died.

But not all of Joe's children suffered, and some of the girls went on to live full and rich lives. Patricia Kennedy married British actor, Peter Lawford and the couple were instrumental in introducing both Jack and Bobby to the glitz and glamour of Hollywood. It was Lawford who formed the links with Marilyn Monroe and Frank Sinatra and it was Lawford who would clean up the mess afterwards. Patricia divorced Lawford in 1966 and after a long and hard battle with alcoholism, went on to find a new life of her own. She became a patron of the arts and devoted much of her time to helping charities for the mentally disabled and for drug abuse. She died in September 2007, aged 82.

Eunice was always the more caring of the Kennedy clan, and she continued in that vein all of her life. When Rosemary was rendered disabled by the failed lobotomy, it was Eunice who stepped in to look after her. Eunice worked for some time as a social worker and she was committed to helping the cause of the mentally disabled. She went on to found the Special Olympics and in 1984 she was awarded the Presidential Medal of Freedom, the highest civilian award in the US. Eunice died on August 11th 2009, just two weeks before her brother, Ted. She was 88 years old.

Jean was the youngest of the Kennedy daughters and at the time of writing, she was the last surviving child of Joe and Rose Kennedy. Jean was always the quiet one and was more reserved than the other children. She enjoyed a relatively happy life but she did experience some of the Kennedy tragedy when her son, William Kennedy-Smith was tried for rape in 1991. He was acquitted, but these were difficult times for her and she determined that she would emerge from the ordeal a stronger and more positive woman. Jean was appointed US Ambassador to Ireland in 1993 and served in that post until 1998. She played a major role in the Northern Ireland peace process and she, too was awarded the Presidential Medal of Freedom in 2011.

It hadn't all been bad. We must not forget that for all their faults, the Kennedys did a lot of good work and contributed a great deal to good causes, both in the US and across the globe. Kick worked tirelessly for the Red Cross during the war and both Jack and Bobby achieved a great deal in their campaigns on Civil Rights and social reform. Ted achieved more in the Senate than either of them and they all championed the cause of the mentally disabled following the loss of their sister to the illness.

So, what next for the Kennedys? The dream of the Whitehouse had died with JFK Junior, but they eventually came to realise that there were other ways to make a mark in the world and to achieve greatness. Caroline had inherited her mother's love of the arts and she worked for a time at the Metropolitan Museum of Art, before studying for a law degree at Columbia College. She hovered on the fringes of politics before being appointed US Ambassador to Japan in 2013. She is an active campaigner on Civil Rights and has recently been involved in a campaign to ban dolphin hunting.

The later generation Kennedys have generally taken a different, more measured approach to life and they bring with them a new hope for the future. Robert Kennedy Junior is now a successful author and broadcaster and his sister, Rory is an acclaimed documentary film maker. Times have changed, and so have the Kennedys. Theirs has been a long and difficult journey, but they are at last learning from their mistakes and are moving on.

Who knows, with this positive change in attitude and a less aggressive approach, we may well see another Kennedy in the Whitehouse one day?

ILLUSTRATIONS

The Kennedy family on the beach at Hyannis Port, around 1936

The Kennedys at home in happier times

A young Jack Kennedy on board PT109

Kathleen (Kick) in her Red Cross uniform

Joe Junior, wearing his Navy Flyer's Wings

Joseph Kennedy with Joe Junior and Jack, 1939

Kathleen, Rose Kennedy and Rosemary at the Palace Ball, 1938

Poor quality, but rare, photograph of what is believed to be Joe Junior with Pat Wilson

Wedding photo of Kathleen and Billy Cavendish, with a smiling Joe Junior in the background

Joe Junior, Kathleen and Jack in London, 1939

President John F Kennedy, official portrait

Robert Kennedy, official portrait

President Kennedy with J Edgar Hoover and Bobby

Jack and Bobby consider options at the height of the Cuban Missile Crisis

Jack and Jackie with John Junior and Caroline, 1961

Jack enjoys an intimate moment with young Caroline, 1962

A happy Jack and Jackie ride through the streets of Dallas, November 22nd 1963

Map showing the route of the Motorcade through Dealey Plaza on November 22nd 1963

A blood-spattered Jackie looks on as Lyndon Johnson is sworn-in aboard Air Force One following the death of President Kennedy

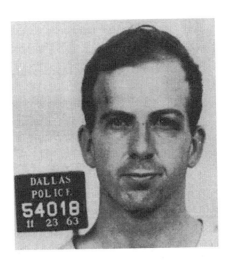

Lee Harvey Oswald, the alleged assassin of JFK (Dallas Police Mug-Shot)

Bobby, Jackie and Ted lead the procession of mourners at JFK's funeral

Ted Kennedy sporting a neck brace following the accident at Chappaquiddick

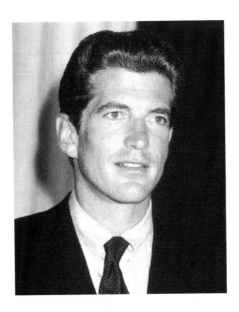

JFK Junior, shortly before his death

A Piper Saratoga light aircraft, similar to that in which JFK Junior and his passengers died

SOURCES AND FURTHER READING

<u>Books and e-books</u>

Rush to Judgement, *Mark Lane* (Bodley Head 1966)

The Lost Prince (The Young Joe Kennedy), *Hank Searls* (New York World Publishing 1969)

Oswald; Assassin or Fall Guy? *Joachim Joesten* (Merlin Press 1964)

The Dark Side of Lyndon Baines Johnson, *Joachim Joesten* (Iconoclassic Books 2013)

The Kennedy Conspiracy, *Anthony Summers* (Sphere 1989)

JFK; the Dead Witnesses, *Craig Roberts and John Armstrong* (Consolidated Press 1995)

Crossfire, *Jim Marrs* (Simon and Schuster 1993)

The Men on the Sixth Floor, *Glen W Sample and Mark Collom* (Sample Graphics 2011)

The Girl on the Stairs, *Barry W Ernest* (Pelican Publishing 2013)

John F Kennedy,: An Unfinished Life, *Robert Dallek* (Little, Brown and Co)

RFK; A Candid Biography, *David Heymann* ((Arrow Books 1999)

Who Killed Bobby? *Shane O'Sullivan* (Union Square Press 2008)

Death at Chappaquiddick, *Richard and Thomas Tedrow* (Pelican Publishing 2000)

Senatorial Privilege, The Chappaquiddick Cover-Up, *Leo Damore* (Dell Publishing 1989)

The Missing Kennedy, *Elizabeth Koehler-Pentacoff* (Bancroft Press 2015)

Rosemary; the Hidden Kennedy Daughter, *Kate Clifford Larson* (Houghton Mifflin Harcourt 2015)

Kathleen Kennedy; Her Life and Times, *Lynne McTaggart* (Doubleday 1983)

Bobby and J Edgar, *Burton Hersh* (Basic Books 2007)

The Enemy Within, *Robert F Kennedy* (Popular Library 1960)

Films and Documentaries

The Men Who Killed Kennedy (TV Documentary Series) *The History Channel 1988*

The Kennedys (The Kennedy Legacy) *Biography TV*

The Second Gun (The Assassination of Robert Kennedy), Dir Gerald Alcan *American Films Ltd*

Printed in Great Britain
by Amazon